International Humanitarian Law and the International Red Cross and Red Crescent Movement

This book provides a key reference on the role of the Commonwealth and its member states in relation to international humanitarian law (IHL). It provides insights in the implementation of IHL in Commonwealth states and, particularly, the challenges faced by small states. It examines the progressive development of IHL in the Commonwealth and provides an analysis of some of the landmark decisions emerging from the Special Court for Sierra Leone.

The book was developed collaboratively between the Commonwealth Secretariat and the International Red Cross and Red Crescent Movement. In this regard, it contains insights in the work of the Secretariat with regard to implementation of IHL and an assessment of legislation enacted by Commonwealth states as well as an accession chart to IHL instruments. It expounds on the work of the Movement, including the role of National Societies, the International Humanitarian Fact-Finding Commission, and the development of international disaster response law, rules and regulation.

This book was based on a special issue of *Commonwealth Law Bulletin*.

Aldo Zammit Borda is Legal Editor at the Legal and Constitutional Affairs Division, Commonwealth Secretariat.

International Humanitarian Law and the International Red Cross and Red Crescent Movement

Edited by Aldo Zammit Borda

Routledge
Taylor & Francis Group
LONDON AND NEW YORK

First published 2010
by Routledge
2 Park Square, Milton Park, Abingdon, Oxon, OX14 4RN

Simultaneously published in the USA and Canada
by Routledge
711 Third Avenue, New York, NY 10017

Routledge is an imprint of the Taylor & Francis Group, an informa business

First issued in paperback 2012

This book is a reproduction of Commonwealth Law Bulletin, volume 34, issue 4. The Publisher requests to those authors who may be citing this book to state, also, the bibliographical details of the special issue on which the book was based

Typeset in Gill Sans by Value Chain, India

British Library Cataloguing in Publication Data
A catalogue record for this book is available from the British Library

ISBN13: 978-0-415-56571-4 (hbk)
ISBN13: 978-0-415-81486-7 (pbk)

Contents

Notes on Contributors

Aldo Zammit Borda is Legal Editor at the Legal and Constitutional Affairs Division of the Commonwealth Secretariat. He holds an LLD from the University of Malta and an MEconSc from the University College Dublin.

Ruona Iguyovwe served as a consultant with the Criminal Law Section, Legal and Constitutional Affairs Division, Commonwealth Secretariat.

Melissa Khemani worked as a Legal Researcher in the Criminal Law Section, Legal and Constitutional Affairs Division of the Commonwealth Secretariat from 2006 to 2008. Prior to joining the Commonwealth Secretariat, she held positions with the Canadian International Development Agency, the Organisation for Economic Cooperation and Development (OECD) and the International Crisis Group, where she worked on various international development, conflict prevention and international criminal justice projects. Melissa is currently completing her LLM in International Legal Studies at Georgetown University Law Center in Washington, DC. She also holds a BA in Political Science from McGill University and a LLB from the University of London, King's College.

Joshua Brien is a Legal Adviser in the Economic and Legal Section of the Special Advisory Services Division of the Commonwealth Secretariat. Joshua is a public international law specialist. He has extensive experience in the conduct of maritime boundary negotiations and has participated in international law cases involving Australia brought before the International Tribunal for the Law of the Sea, International Centre for Settlement of Investment Disputes, and the International Court of Justice. He provides legal and policy advice to Commonwealth member countries on matters concerning public international law, maritime boundaries and natural resources. Prior to joining the Secretariat, Joshua served as a senior lawyer in the Office of International Law in the Australian Attorney-General's Department from 1999 to 2005.

Leonard Blazeby worked as a Barrister and Solicitor in Australia for over ten years before joining the International Committee of the Red Cross in 2000. He was the Regional Legal Adviser based in Pretoria, South Africa from 2000 until 2005 and was the Deputy Head of Delegation from 2003. He was then Communications Coordinator for the ICRC regional delegation in Nairobi, Kenya before taking up his current position as Common Law legal adviser in Geneva in January 2008.

Michael Meyer is Head of International Law, British Red Cross. The views expressed are those of the author and do not necessarily represent those of the British Red Cross Society.

Charles Garraway is a Commissioner of the International Humanitarian Fact-Finding Commission. For further information on the Commission, please see the website: www.ihffc.org.

Susan C. Breau is a Reader in International Law at the School of Law, University of Surrey, Guildford, Surrey.

Ming Leung Wai is the Attorney General of Samoa.

Dr Helen Durham is a Senior Research Fellow and Program Director for Research and Development at the Asia Pacific Centre for Military Law, Melbourne Law School. She has a Law Degree with Honours and an Arts degree as well as a Doctorate of Juridical Science from the University of Melbourne. She welcomes all feedback.

Victoria Bannon is the Coordinator of the International Disaster Response Laws, Rules and Principles Asia Pacific Programme for the International Federation of Red Cross and Red Crescent Societies, based in Kuala Lumpur, Malaysia. Victoria has a Bachelor of Arts degree (BA), a Bachelor of Laws degree with Honours (LLB Hons) from the University of Adelaide (Australia), and a Master of Laws (LLM) from the University of Melbourne (Australia), specialising in international humanitarian and disaster law. The views of the author do not necessarily reflect those of the International Federation.

Foreword

Foreword

International humanitarian law is designed to protect the victims of armed conflict. In the words of the International Committee of the Red Cross, even wars have limits. In its modern treaty form, international humanitarian law began in 1864, with the first Geneva Convention for the amelioration of the condition of the wounded in armies in the field. It was adopted following the horrors of the Battle of Solferino of 1859 observed by Henry Dunant, one of the founders of the worldwide Red Cross and Red Crescent Movement. That Convention was adapted to apply to maritime warfare in 1906 and 1907 in the Convention for the wounded, sick and shipwrecked armed forces at sea, following such wars as those between Japan and Russia. The inadequacies of the Hague Regulations of 1899 and 1907 concerning the laws and customs of war led, after the Great War, to the preparation of the third Convention on the protection of prisoners of war. The plans for a conference to adopt a convention on the protection of civilians, especially in occupied territory, were tragically frustrated by the outbreak of the Second World War. The dreadful events of that war resulted in the adoption of the fourth Convention on the protection of civilians in time of war in 1949 when the other texts were also updated. All four Conventions also incorporate what is known as a mini convention stating basic obligations for wars not of an international character, reflecting inadequacies in the law which had been highlighted in the Spanish Civil War in the 1930s. That mini convention, among other things, stated an unqualified prohibition on torture.

I have briefly indicated some of the reasons for the adoption of each of those four Conventions to emphasise that they came out of the harsh realities of war. They are not theoretical constructs dreamt up in an ivory tower. They recognise the demands of military necessity. The recognition of both humanity and military necessity appears in the fact that the four Conventions have been adopted universally, by the governments of every State in the world, all 194.

Over the next 20 or more years, following the adoption of the four 1949 Conventions, the challenges of the increasing numbers of armed conflicts which were internal, not international, and the growing recognition of the impacts of new military technology developed over the century, especially in aerial warfare, on civilian populations (a rapidly increasing proportion of war deaths and casualties), led to the drafting and adoption of the 1977 Additional Protocols, one concerned with international armed conflicts and the other with non-international. They have been widely accepted, now by 168 and 164 States, respectively. (A third Additional Protocol dealing with the vexing problem of the emblem was adopted in 2005 and has now been accepted by 33 States including five from the Commonwealth.)

Those involved in preparing those treaty texts from 1864 through to the 1970s were concerned not only with updating the substance of the law to cover new and developing areas but also with the critical matter of getting better compliance with that law. The means within the Conventions and Protocols include: instruction and education for the military, in schools and more widely, through national societies as well as through governments;

prosecution and discipline of alleged offenders, nationally and internationally, in the case of certain grave breaches of the Conventions and Protocols (an obligation which includes the enactment of the necessary legislation); protecting powers; the services of the ICRC; inquiry; fact finding and good offices. To those methods have been added *ad hoc* international criminal tribunals, for instance at Nuremberg and Tokyo after the Second World War and for the former Yugoslavia and Rwanda in the 1990s, the International Criminal Court in 1998 and the hybrid tribunals for Sierra Leone, Cambodia, East Timor and Lebanon. Issues relating to international humanitarian law also arise in other international courts and tribunals, including the International Court of Justice in The Hague, for instance in judgments relating to warfare in the Balkans and in the Great Lakes area in central Africa and in the advisory opinion relating to the legality of the use of nuclear weapons. One very encouraging feature of this Special Issue of the *Commonwealth Law Bulletin* is the major emphasis it places on better implementation of this vital area of law.

That emphasis continues to be seen in the deliberations of international conferences, notably for present purposes at the Second Commonwealth Red Cross and Red Crescent International Humanitarian Law Conference. It was attended by more than 150 representatives of about 45 Commonwealth Governments and National Societies in Wellington, New Zealand, in August 2007 (www.redcross.org.nz/ihl/outcome). That meeting agreed among other things

> 5   to encourage National Societies to give greater priority to publicising, applying and promoting, both nationally and internationally, respect for international humanitarian law in their programmes of activity and their policies;
>
> ...
>
> 7   to encourage States to examine their existing legislation and, where necessary, to adopt effective legislative and other measures to implement those international humanitarian law treaties to which they are a party.

The Conference itself was a means of promoting better knowledge of international humanitarian law and as a consequence better compliance with it. So too are publications like this Special Issue. The emphasis of that meeting on getting better compliance with the law was to be seen just a few months later, in Geneva, in the deliberations and outcomes of the 30th International Conference of the Red Cross and Red Crescent Movement.

The Commonwealth Conference also gave close attention to the valuable, painstaking work of the ICRC and a wide range of experts and consultants it engaged, which led to the publication in 2005 of the ICRC Customary Law Study, again a topic considered in this Special Issue. The preparation of that study involved the gathering of relevant national, international and other practice supporting and developing the treaty texts, a process of collection which continues to this day. In the opinion of the authors of the study and the wider movement which supported it, the gathering and assessment of all that practice and its formulation in 161 rules of customary international law was important, for several reasons. One was to state in a much extended form the law applicable to non-international armed conflicts beyond that stated all too briefly in the 'mini convention' of 1949 and in the second Additional Protocol of 1977.

A second reason was the emphasis, in particular for the States which have yet to accept the 1977 Protocols, on the customary law status of the rules in those Protocols. That was particularly important so far as they updated the law regulating methods and means of warfare and the protection of the civilian population, especially from the effects of hostilities, and also the law for the protection of persons in the power of a party to the conflict. That last section includes provisions guaranteeing fundamental rights, stated in essentially the same terms as are found in the International Covenant on Civil and Political Rights. That statement again includes a prohibition on torture. That essential identity of statement is yet another recognition of the basis of international humanitarian law in human dignity, a matter which will no doubt receive added recognition in this year which marks the 60th anniversary of the Universal Declaration of Human Rights.

The Customary Law Study is valuable for a third reason: customary international law may help in the interpretation of treaty law. It also provides a much briefer statement of the essentials of the law than do the many pages and provisions of the four Conventions, the Protocols and many other treaties. That concentration has real value for the effective dissemination of the text, as does the brief 1978 statement of seven fundamental rules prepared by the ICRC. Different texts are appropriate for different audiences.

This foreword has so far emphasised the development of the Geneva texts from 1860 to the present. The law and practice regulating warfare may be traced back to much earlier times in all cultures and civilisations, and the Wellington Conference heard something of that. This law has a universal character; it forms part of the common heritage of humanity. Much of the law is also to be found in modern texts adopted outside the Geneva system such as the Ottawa Landmines Convention and very recently the Oslo Cluster Munitions Convention. Another new developing area is disaster relief law, also the subject of study by the International Law Commission of the United Nations.

This Special Issue considers subjects touched on above and others. It provides yet another recognition by a Commonwealth body of the essential mission of this body of law which places everyone affected by armed conflict, civilian and combatant alike, under the protection and authority of the written law, and the principles of international law derived from established custom, from the principles of humanity and from the dictates of public conscience. Those are the words of Frederic de Martens, a major Russian figure in the development of the law a century ago, as most recently repeated in the 1977 First Protocol.

K.J. Keith
Judge, International Court of Justice
Chair, Second Commonwealth IHL Conference
The Hague, 22 September 2008

Preface

Preface

International Humanitarian Law (IHL) differs from other branches of contemporary international law in that it currently develops independently from the framework of the United Nations, though in close association therewith. The International Committee of the Red Cross (ICRC), as an independent and neutral entity, has been concerned, from the beginning, with the development of modern IHL, and acts exclusively in the pursuit of humanitarian interests and the protection of vulnerable individuals when war rears its ugly head.

It is natural that the Commonwealth, with its commitment to dignity, humanity and the rule of law, should take an interest in IHL since this aspect of law helps to inculcate principles of humanity, limits violence and preserves global peace.

In this respect, the Commonwealth has engaged closely with the International Red Cross and Red Crescent Movement. Two Commonwealth Red Cross and Red Crescent International Humanitarian Law Conferences were organised, one in London (2003) and another in Wellington (2007), as well as a Meeting of Commonwealth National Committees on International Humanitarian Law in Nairobi (2005).

Since 1999, the ICRC's Advisory Service on IHL has worked with Commonwealth Member States in a variety of ways. It has encouraged Member States to ratify IHL treaties and has assisted in the adoption of national legislative and administrative measures.

Successive Commonwealth Heads of Government Meetings have likewise drawn attention to IHL issues, such as anti-personnel landmines, the International Criminal Court, children and armed conflict, the protection of civilians and small arms and light weapons. Indeed, the Abuja Communiqué of 2003 urged all countries to accede to the Ottawa Convention on the Prohibition of the Use, Stockpiling, Production and Transfer of Anti-Personnel Mines and on their Destruction, and the Malta Communiqué of 2005 urged States that have not yet done so to accede to the Rome Statute of the International Criminal Court.

The ICRC has also been regularly invited to present papers to Law Ministers and Senior Officials of the Commonwealth and, at the most recent Commonwealth Law Ministers Meeting, in Edinburgh (2008), the ICRC informed Ministers on the ratification and implementation status of the core IHL treaties by Commonwealth Member States, and on International Disaster Response laws, rules and principles.

This Special Issue of the *Commonwealth Law Bulletin* on International Humanitarian Law provides further attestation of the strong engagement between the Commonwealth and the International Red Cross and Red Crescent Movement. It aims to examine some of the key challenges facing the development of IHL today. The contributors are experts in their field and the focus is on the Commonwealth experience. It is hoped that you will find this Special

Issue a useful resource and, as such, that you will find it both an interesting and informative read.

Betty Mould-Iddrisu
Director, Legal and Constitutional Affairs Division
Commonwealth Secretariat
London, 15 September 2008

Chapters

Introduction to International Humanitarian Law

ALDO ZAMMIT BORDA

Legal and Constitutional Affairs Division, Commonwealth Secretariat

International Humanitarian Law (IHL) is that portion of international law which is inspired by considerations of humanity. It aims to minimize the suffering of those not, or no longer, taking part in hostilities and to render the fighting more humane by restricting the use of barbaric weapons. Although the origins of contemporary IHL can be traced back to the nineteenth century, it is based on principles and practices which are much older. The two principal sources of IHL are the Hague and Geneva Conventions, the former setting out restrictions on the means and methods of warfare and the latter providing protection to certain categories of vulnerable persons. It is generally accepted that a large portion of the principles permeating IHL reflect customary international law and, in some cases, peremptory law (*jus cogens*). As such, it is binding on all States, irrespective of whether they have acceded to the relevant treaties. Although IHL has made a difference in protecting vulnerable individuals and restricting the means and methods of warfare, tragically, there are countless examples of violations of IHL in armed conflicts around the world and a number of other challenges still remain.

Introduction

International Humanitarian Law (IHL), which is also known as the 'Law of War' and the 'Law of Armed Conflict', is that portion of international law which is inspired by considerations of humanity and is centred on the protection of certain vulnerable individuals in time of armed conflict and on rendering the fighting more humane.

Professor Jean Pictet, who played a major role in the work of developing IHL undertaken by the International Committee of the Red Cross (ICRC),[1] has argued that the provisions of IHL are in fact a transposition into international law of moral, and more specifically, humanitarian concerns:

> It is precisely because this law is so intimately bound to humanity that it assumes its true proportions, for it is upon this category of law, and no other, that the life and liberty of countless human beings depend if war casts its sinister shadow across the world.[2]

---

1   For a clear outline of the International Red Cross and Red Crescent Movement, and its three components, i.e. the International Committee of the Red Cross (ICRC), the International Federation of Red Cross and Red Crescent Societies and the recognized National Red Cross and Red Crescent Societies, refer to the article on: 'National Red Cross and Red Crescent Societies: Humanitarian Partner of Choice for Commonwealth States' *infra*.

2   Professor Pictet was vice president of the ICRC and chairman of the ICRC Law Commission. See Pictet, J. (1985) *Developments and Principles of International Humanitarian Law* (Boston: Martinus Nijhoff Publishers), p. 1.

This article aims to provide a general introduction to IHL. It will firstly outline the origins of contemporary IHL from the latter part of the eighteenth century and the nineteenth century. It will proceed to consider its sources, including treaties and customary law. The two areas covered by IHL, namely, means and methods of warfare; and protection of certain categories of persons are discussed next, followed by a discussion on IHL's application. The article concludes by setting out some challenges to the effective development and implementation of IHL.

Origins

Although the origins of contemporary IHL can be traced back to the nineteenth century, it is based on principles and practices which are much older.[3] In the sixteenth and seventeenth centuries, the rationale of the laws governing the conduct of hostilities was to minimize the harm inflicted in the exercise of the right of a sovereign to wage a 'just war':

> The balance of evil and good was sought to be struck by reference to the doctrine of necessity. It was held to be a 'general rule from the law of nature' that as long as the end pursued by the war was just, armed violence necessary to achieve that end ... was permissible. No distinction was drawn per se between soldiers and civilians, nor between military and civilian property, although reason dictated that the killing of civilians and the destruction of civilian property was usually unnecessary and therefore unlawful.[4]

The dominance of autonomous sovereign States in the latter part of the eighteenth century and the nineteenth century,[5] together with the growing influence of humanism, allowed for an increased focus on the conduct of warfare, and what is today known as IHL emerged as a set of independent rules[6] which represent a careful balance between the requirements of humanity and military necessity.[7]

The 1864 Diplomatic Conference, which was convened by the Swiss government and chaired by General Guillaume-Henri Dufour,[8] adopted the Geneva Convention for the Amelioration of the Condition of the Wounded on the Field of Battle (Red Cross Convention). This Convention laid the foundations for contemporary humanitarian law. It was chiefly characterized by:

1.   standing written rules of universal scope to protect the victims of conflicts;

2.   its multilateral nature, open to all States;

---

3   Doebbler, C. F. J. (2005) *Introduction to International Humanitarian Law* (Washington: CD Publishing), p. 5. See also Bantekas, I. (2002) *Principles of Direct and Superior Responsibility in International Humanitarian Law* (Manchester: Manchester University Press), p. 1; Elias, T. O. (1979) *New Horizons in International Law* (Leiden: Brill Publishers), p. 181.

4   O'Keefe, R. (2006) *The Protection of Cultural Property in Armed Conflict*, Cambridge Studies in International and Comparative Law (Cambridge: Cambridge University Press), pp. 5–6.

5   In this period, international law had very little to say about when sovereign States could wage war, and the distinction between 'just' and 'unjust' wars become increasingly blurred. See Kennedy, D. (2006) Reassessing International Humanitarianism: The Dark Sides, in A. Orford (Ed.) *International Law and its Others* (Cambridge: Cambridge University Press), p. 144.

6   Gardam, J. (2004) *Necessity, Proportionality and the Use of Force by States*, Cambridge Studies in International and Comparative Law (Cambridge: Cambridge University Press), p. 29.

7   International Committee of the Red Cross (ICRC), *What is International Humanitarian Law?*, Advisory Service on International Humanitarian Law, Geneva. Available at www.icrc.org.

8   One of the five founding members of the ICRC. The others were: Gustave Moynier, Henry Dunant, Dr Louis Appia and Dr Théodore Maunoir.

3. the obligation to extend care without discrimination to wounded and sick military personnel;

4. respect for and marking of medical personnel, transports and equipment using an emblem (red cross on a white background).[9]

Following adoption of this Convention, the First and Second Hague Peace Conferences, held in 1899 and 1907 respectively, aimed partly to prevent war and partly to define rules of warfare.

The 1899 First Hague Peace Conference was convened with the object of seeking the most effective means of ensuring to all peoples the benefits of a real and lasting peace, and, above all, of limiting the progressive development of existing armaments.[10] This Conference, which was summoned without reference to any particular war, was regarded as the culmination of the peace movement.[11]

The Conference adopted three Conventions and three Declarations.[12] In its Final Act,[13] the Conference also expressed the wish that a number of outstanding issues, such as the limitation and/or reduction of armaments and the rights and duties of neutrals, be considered by a subsequent Conference.

The 1907 Second Hague Peace Conference was thus convened for the purpose of giving a fresh development to the humanitarian principles which served as a basis for the work of the First Conference of 1899.[14] The Conference adopted 13 Conventions and two Declarations.[15]

---

9   ICRC (2002) *What are the Origins of International Humanitarian Law?*, Advisory Service on International Humanitarian Law, Geneva. Available at www.icrc.org.

10 Russian note of 30 December 1898/11 January 1899. Available at http://www.yale.edu/lawweb/avalon/lawofwar/hague99/hag99-02.htm.

11 Villiger, M. E. (1985) *Customary International Law and Treaties: A Study of Their Interactions and Interrelations with Special Consideration of the 1969 Vienna Convention on the Law of Treaties* (Boston: Martinus Nijhoff Publishers), p. 66.

12 These were: (a) Convention for the peaceful adjustment of international differences; (b) Convention regarding the laws and customs of war by land; and (c) Convention for the adaptation to maritime warfare of the principles of the Geneva Convention of the 22 August 1864. The three Declarations were: (a) To prohibit the launching of projectiles and explosives from balloons or by other similar new methods; (b) To prohibit the use of projectiles the only object of which is the diffusion of asphyxiating or deleterious gases; and (c) To prohibit the use of bullets which expand or flatten easily in the human body, such as bullets with a hard envelope, of which the envelope does not entirely cover the core, or is pierced with incisions.

13 *Final Act of the International Peace Conference; July 29, 1899*, The Avalon Project at Yale Law School, 1998. Available at http://www.yale.edu/lawweb/avalon/lawofwar/final99.htm.

14 *Final Act of the Second Peace Conference. The Hague, 18 October 1907*, International Committee of the Red Cross, Treaties Home. Available at http://www.icrc.org/ihl.nsf/FULL/185?OpenDocument.

15 These were: (a) Convention for the pacific settlement of international disputes; (b) Convention respecting the limitation of the employment of force for the recovery of contract debts; (c) Convention relative to the opening of hostilities; (d) Convention respecting the laws and customs of war on land; (e) Convention respecting the rights and duties of neutral powers and persons in case of war on land; (f) Convention relative to the status of enemy merchant ships at the outbreak of hostilities; (g) Convention relative to the conversion of merchant ships into warships; (h) Convention relative to the laying of automatic submarine contact mines; (i) Convention respecting bombardment by naval forces in time of war; (j) Convention for the adaptation to naval war of the principles of the Geneva Convention; (k) Convention relative to certain restrictions with regard to the exercise of the right of capture in naval war; (l) Convention relative to the creation of an International Prize Court; and (m) Convention concerning the rights and duties of neutral powers in naval war. The two Declarations were: (i) To prohibit the discharge of projectiles and explosives from balloons; and (ii) On compulsory arbitration. This Conference also gave rise to the Permanent Court of Arbitration, the oldest international legal institution in the Hague. See van Krieken, P. and McKay, D. (2005) *The Hague—Legal Capital of the World* (Cambridge: Cambridge University Press), p. 113.

Though not negotiated in the Hague, the 1925 Geneva Protocol for the Prohibition of the Use in War of Asphyxiating Gas, and for Bacteriological Methods of Warfare, is considered a further addition to the Hague Conventions.[16]

The 1899 and 1907 Peace Conferences have been hailed as 'landmarks' and an 'epoch in the history of international law',[17] and much of the law they gave rise to is accepted as customary international law.

Following the atrocities of World War II, four Geneva Conventions were concluded in 1949 to mitigate the effects of war by protecting people who do not take part in the fighting (civilians, medics, chaplains, aid workers) and those who can no longer fight (wounded, sick and shipwrecked troops, prisoners of war), known as *persons hors de combat*.[18] These Conventions recognize two types of violations, namely: 'grave breaches' and other prohibited acts not falling within the definition of grave breaches.[19]

The first Geneva Convention ('for the Amelioration of the Condition of the Wounded and Sick in Armed Forces in the Field') and the second Geneva Convention ('for the Amelioration of the Condition of Wounded, Sick and Shipwrecked Members of Armed Forces at Sea') are similar, covering land and sea respectively. They provide minimum standards of protection for members of the armed forces who become wounded or sick.

The third Geneva Convention ('Relative to the Treatment of Prisoners of War') lays down minimum standards of protection for members of the armed forces who are captured by the enemy. Prisoners of war must, *inter alia*, be treated humanely with respect for their persons and their honour and quickly released and repatriated when hostilities cease.

The fourth Geneva Convention ('Relative to the Protection of Civilian Persons in Time of War') covers all civilians who do not belong to the armed forces, take no part in the hostilities and find themselves in the hands of the Enemy or an Occupying Power. The Convention lays down minimum standards of protection for such civilians, which include protection against acts or threats of violence, insults and public curiosity, and protection from being used to shield military operations.

The 1949 Geneva Conventions were supplemented in 1977 with the addition of two Protocols on the Protection of Victims of International Armed Conflicts and Protection of Victims of Non-International Armed Conflicts, and in 2005 by the addition of a third Protocol on the Red Crystal as an additional distinctive emblem.

Sources

The corpus of international law devoted to IHL has expanded over the past decades, primarily because of renewed interest in international dispute resolution, the decline in the traditional doctrine of sovereignty and the related growth of norms recognizing the

---

16 See Zammit Borda, A. (2003) *The Threat and Use of Chemical and Biological Weapons under International Law*, LLD Thesis, p. 19. Available at the Peace Palace Library, The Hague.

17 Villiger, *op. cit.*, n 11, p. 66.

18 See ICRC (2006) *The Geneva Conventions: The Core of International Humanitarian Law*. Available at http://www.icrc.org/Web/eng/siteeng0.nsf/htmlall/genevaconventions.

19 The term 'grave breaches' is defined in Articles 50, 51, 130 and 147 of the I, II, III, and IV Geneva Conventions respectively, and includes wilful killing, torture or inhuman treatment, if committed against persons or property protected by the Conventions.

enforceability of rights of individuals against states for the violation of humanitarian legal norms.[20]

The sources of IHL are the same as those of international law generally, a basic description of which may be found in Article 38 of the Statute of the International Court of Justice,[21] namely:

1. international conventions;

2. international custom;

3. general principles of law; and

4. judicial decisions and the teachings of the most highly qualified publicists as subsidiary sources.

These sources of International Humanitarian Law have been considered at length in a number of other publications[22] and only a general outline is required here. As regards international conventions on IHL, in addition to the Hague and Geneva Conventions, and their Protocols,[23] one could add:

1. the 1954 Protection of Cultural Property in the Event of Armed Conflict Convention;

2. the 1972 Biological and Toxin Weapons Convention;

3. the 1976 Environmental Modification Convention;

4. the 1980 Conventional Weapons Convention (and its five Protocols);

5. the 1993 Chemical Weapons Convention;

6. the 1997 Ottawa Convention on Anti-Personnel Landmines;

7. the 1998 Rome Statue of the International Criminal Court; and

8. the 2000 Optional Protocol to the Convention on the Rights of the Child.[24]

As regards international custom, in December 1995, the 26th International Conference of the Red Cross and Red Crescent officially mandated the ICRC to prepare a report on customary rules of international humanitarian law applicable in international and non-international armed conflicts.[25] Following extensive research and widespread consultation

---

20 Martin, F. F. et al. (2006) International Human Rights and Humanitarian Law: Treaties Cases and Analysis (Cambridge: Cambridge University Press), p. 22.

21 Statute of the International Court of Justice, 59 Stat. 1005, T.S. 993, 26 June 1945.

22 See, for instance, Martin, op. cit., n 20; and Gardam, J. G. (1993) Non-combatant Immunity as a Norm of International Humanitarian Law (Boston: Martinus Nijhoff Publishers).

23 Some academic authors have tried to define IHL narrowly, and distinguish between the 'law of Geneva' and the 'law of the Hague'. However, it has been argued that this distinction has never been more than a convenient but imprecise simplification, which has progressively lost in significance. See Abi-Saab, G. (1984) The Specificities of Humanitarian Law, in C. Swinarski (Ed.) Studies and Essays on International Humanitarian Law and Red Cross Principles (Boston: Martinus Nijhoff Publishers), p. 265, fn 1.

24 See ICRC, Promotion of International Humanitarian Law within the Commonwealth, paper originally presented by the ICRC in collaboration with the British Red Cross at the Meeting of Law Ministers and Attorneys General of Small Commonwealth Jurisdictions, organized by the Legal and Constitutional Affairs Division of the Commonwealth Secretariat, on 4–5 October 2007. It is important to point out that this list is not exhaustive.

25 26th International Conference of the Red Cross and Red Crescent, Geneva, 3–7 December 1995, Resolution 1, International humanitarian law: from law to action; Report on the follow-up to the International Conference for the Protection of War Victims, International Review of the Red Cross 310 (1996), p. 58.

with experts, this report was published in 2005[26] and identified over 160 IHL rules of customary international law, categorized in six parts:

1. the Principle of Distinction;
2. Specifically Protected Persons and Objects;
3. Specific Methods of Warfare;
4. Weapons;
5. Treatment of Civilians and Persons Hors de Combat; and
6. Implementation.

Scope

IHL covers two areas:

1. means and methods of warfare; and
2. protection of certain categories of persons.

(1) Means and methods of warfare

The recognition that there have to be restrictions on the means and methods of warfare is ancient.[27] Article 22 of both the 1899 and 1907 Hague Conventions respecting laws and customs of war on land provide: 'The right of belligerents to adopt means of injuring the enemy is not unlimited'.

IHL prohibits means of warfare which:

1. fail to discriminate between those taking part in the fighting and those, such as civilians, who are not taking part in the fighting;[28]
2. cause superfluous injury or unnecessary suffering; and/or
3. cause severe or long-term damage to the environment.

On the basis of these criteria, a number of means of warfare have become prohibited under IHL, including asphyxiating gases and bacteriological methods of warfare; and certain

---

26 Henckaerts, J. M. and Doswald-Beck, L. (2005) *Customary International Humanitarian Law, 2 volumes, Volume I. Rules, Volume II. Practice (2 Parts)* (Cambridge: Cambridge University Press).

27 Consider Hugo Grotius's *De jure belli et pacis*, published in 1625, and mentioned in Doebbler, *op. cit.*, n 3, p. 40.

28 Foremost amongst such weapons should be nuclear weapons which, as was witnessed in Hiroshima and Nagasaki, not only fail to discriminate between combatants and non-combatants, but also cause mass suffering and destruction. However, when the International Court of Justice (ICJ) was asked to render its Advisory Opinion by the UN General Assembly on the following question: 'Is the threat or use of nuclear weapons in any circumstance permitted under international law?', the ICJ delivered the following opinion, by seven votes to seven, by the President's casting vote:

> [T]he threat or use of nuclear weapons would generally be contrary to the rules of international law applicable in armed conflict, and in particular the principles and rules of humanitarian law; However, in view of the current state of international law, and of the elements of fact at its disposal, the Court cannot conclude definitively whether the threat or use of nuclear weapons would be lawful or unlawful in an extreme circumstance of self-defence, in which the very survival of a State would be at stake.

conventional weapons which may be deemed to be excessively injurious or to have indiscriminate effects, such as laser-blinding weapons.

As regards prohibited methods of warfare, these include treachery, i.e. improper use of a flag of truce, of the national flag, or of the military insignia or uniform of the enemy, as well as the distinctive badges of the Geneva Convention; and destroying the property of the enemy, unless required by military necessity.

As technology advances, the potential for new means and methods of warfare which may cause superfluous injury or unnecessary suffering will continue to increase. Some conventions already protect against future developments. The 1972 Biological Weapons Convention and the 1993 Chemical Weapons Convention, for instance, contain a 'general purpose criterion' which allows the conventions to keep up with technological change.

(2) Protection of certain categories of persons

The basic guarantees of IHL may be said to start with Article 3, common to all four Geneva Conventions, which prohibits the following acts against non-combatants, including persons *hors de combat*:

(a) violence to life and person, in particular murder of all kinds, mutilation, cruel treatment and torture;

(b) taking of hostages;

(c) outrages upon personal dignity, in particular humiliating and degrading treatment; and

(d) the passing of sentences and the carrying out of executions without previous judgment pronounced by a regularly constituted court, affording all the judicial guarantees which are recognized as indispensable by civilized peoples.

This article also provides that the 'wounded and sick shall be collected and cared for'.

All four Geneva Conventions and the two Additional Protocols require that protected persons be treated in a non- ;discriminate manner in respect to their rights and that women be treated 'with all consideration due to their sex'.[29]

Each of the four Geneva Conventions and their 1977 Protocols moreover provide for additional basic fundamental guarantees to protect civilians generally, children, sick and wounded combatants, detainees and prisoners of war, medical and religious personnel, medical transports and facilities, registration, and the emblem and symbols.

Application

All Commonwealth Member States have ratified the 1949 Geneva Conventions and a number of other IHL treaties. However, it is generally accepted that a large portion of the principles permeating IHL reflect customary international law and, in some cases, peremptory law (*jus cogens*). This is true, at least, of the majority of the norms contained in the Hague and Geneva Conventions and 'all States can be held to have a legal interest in [their]

---

29 Doebbler, *op. cit.*, n 3, p. 50.

protection; they are obligations *erga omnes*.[30] Consequently, all States are bound by these rules of IHL, irrespective of whether they have acceded to the relevant treaties.

IHL only applies to armed conflict. It does not cover internal disturbances such as isolated acts of violence or other acts which do not amount to 'armed conflict'. However, international law does not provide a definition of armed conflict—the existence of such a conflict is essentially determined by the behaviour of the States or belligerents involved.[31] In the *Tadic* case, the Appeals Chamber of the International Criminal Tribunal for the former Yugoslavia (ICTY) ruled that: 'an armed conflict exists whenever there is resort to armed force between States or protracted armed violence between governmental authorities and organized armed groups or between such groups within a State'.[32] In such as case, the Appeals Chamber stated, 'International humanitarian law applies from the initiation of such armed conflicts and extends beyond the cessation of hostilities until a general conclusion of peace is reached; or, in the case of internal conflicts, a peaceful settlement is achieved'.[33]

However, it has been submitted that it is open to question whether all States have treated the threshold for armed conflict as being so low.[34] Indeed, the undefined nature of armed conflict in IHL could raise difficult questions about when violence has reached the threshold where there can be said to be armed conflict between the participants.[35]

IHL also distinguishes between international armed conflict and internal armed conflict. While an extensive range of rules apply to international armed conflict, a more limited range of rules apply to internal armed conflict. This distinction has been described as 'arbitrary', 'undesirable', 'difficult to justify', and that it 'frustrates the humanitarian purpose of the law of war in most of the instances in which war now occurs'.[36]

Already in 1948, the ICRC presented a report recommending that the Geneva Conventions apply the full extent of IHL '[i]n all cases of armed conflict which are not of an international character, especially cases of civil war, colonial conflicts, or wars of religion, which may occur in the territory of one or more of the High Contracting Parties'.[37]

---

30 *Jus cogens* refers to the legal status that certain international crimes reach, and *obligatio erga omnes* pertains to the legal implications arising out of a certain crime's characterization as *jus cogens*. Thus, these two concepts are different from each other. See Bassiouni, M. C. (1996) International crimes: *jus cogens* and *obligatio erga omnes*, Law & Contemp. Probs., 59(63), Autumn, Duke Law School, p. 63; and Bantekas, *op. cit.*, n 3, pp. 13 and 24.

31 Borelli, S. (2004) The Treatment of Terrorist Suspects Captured Abroad: Human Rights and Humanitarian Law, in A. Bianchi (Ed.) *Enforcing International Law Norms Against Terrorism* (Oxford: Hart Publishing), p. 40.

32 *The Prosecutor v. Dusko Tadic* ('Prijedor'), Case No. IT-94-1-AR77, Appeals Chamber, 2 October 1995, para. 70.

33 *Ibid.*

34 Kuper, J. (2005) *Military Training and Children in Armed Conflict: Law, Policy and Practice* (Boston: Martinus Nijhoff Publishers), p. 10.

35 See Ministry of Justice, *The Governance of Britain: War Powers and Treaties—Limiting Executive Powers*, Consultation Paper CP26/07, p. 25, para. 48. The undefined nature of 'armed conflict' is prone to give rise to differing interpretations, with the possible effect of excluding someone from the protection of IHL. See Orford, *op. cit.*, n 5, p. 23. Speaking about Guantanamo Bay, the author argues: 'While some US lawyers have argued that these detainees are properly outside the protection of international humanitarian law, this has been responded to with outraged virtue by the rest of the international humanitarian law community'.

36 See Stewart, J. G. (2003) Towards a single definition of armed conflict in international humanitarian law: a critique of internationalized armed conflict, *ICRC International Review of the Red Cross*, 85(850), June, p. 313.

37 Pictet, J. (Ed.) (1960) *Commentaries on the Geneva Conventions of 12 August 1949*, Vol. III: *Geneva Convention Relative to the Treatment of Prisoners of War* (Geneva: ICRC), p. 31.

Another distinction is between 'law on the use of force or law on the prevention of war' (*jus ad bellum*) and 'law in war' (*jus in bello*). While these two branches of the law are related, they remain independent. This is because the application of IHL does not involve the denunciation of guilty parties. Since each adversary would claim to be a victim of aggression, making IHL conditional on guilt or other considerations would be bound to arouse controversy and paralyse its implementation. IHL applies equally to all parties engaged in armed conflict, irrespective of the reasons for the conflict and whether or not the cause upheld by the parties is just.[38]

It is also important to distinguish between IHL and human rights law. These two branches of law have been said to constitute 'two distinct yet complimentary systems'.[39] A number of basic human rights are so fundamental that they are universal and must be respected at all times, whether in peacetime or war.[40] But the effective protection of the victims of armed conflict requires not only that they should enjoy certain basic human rights, but also that they should benefit from certain supplementary rights which are necessary precisely because of the armed conflict, such as medical care, the right of prisoners of war to correspond with their families, the right of repatriation in certain circumstances, etc. In these areas, the provisions of IHL go beyond the requirements of basic human rights law.

Challenges

Tragically there are countless examples of violations of IHL in armed conflicts around the world.[41] And the number of civilians amongst the victims and causalities of warfare is ever-increasing. Nevertheless, IHL has made a difference in minimizing the suffering of those not, or no longer, taking part in hostilities and in rendering the fighting itself more humane by restricting the use of barbaric weapons.

When it comes to punishing those responsible for violations, while as was mentioned above, all Commonwealth Member States have ratified the 1949 Geneva Conventions and a number of other IHL treaties, the implementation of the obligations that flow from these treaties into national law is sometimes lagging behind. Without such legislation, especially the implementation of appropriate criminal sanctions, States may be unable to effectively punish or deter the commission of serious violations of IHL.

Another challenge concerns the universalization of IHL treaties, such as the Chemical and Biological Weapons Convention, and the Rome Statute of the International Criminal Court, which has international jurisdiction to try and punish war crimes.

Yet another challenge, which falls within a wider conception of IHL, is the continuing development of international disaster response laws, rules and principles, in order to reduce human vulnerability by promoting legal preparedness for disasters. Despite over

---

38 ICRC, *What are jus ad bellum and jus in bello?*, 2002. Available at http://www.icrc.org/web/eng/siteeng0.nsf/html/5KZJJD.

39 Robertson, A. H. (1984), Humanitarian Law and Human Rights, in Swinarski (Ed.), *op. cit.*, n 23, p. 802. Historically speaking, there is no doubt that humanitarian law is a much older branch of international law, going back, as has been seen above, to the nineteenth century. Nevertheless, the author argues that human rights law is the genus of which IHL is the species. Human rights law relates to the basic rights of all human beings everywhere and at all times; IHL relates to the rights of particular categories of human beings in particular circumstances.

40 *Ibid.*

41 International Committee of the Red Cross (ICRC), *op. cit.* fn 7.

100 years of collective experience with international assistance operations in response to major disasters, the process of initiation frequently remains fraught with difficulty.[42]

These are some of the challenges that stand in the way of the effective application of IHL, and this Special Issue of the *Commonwealth Law Bulletin* on International Humanitarian Law will endeavour to examine a number of them in more detail.

---

42 International Federation of the Red Cross and Red Crescent Societies (2007) *Law and Legal Issues in International Disaster Response: A Desk Study*, p. 89.

The Inter-play between International Humanitarian Law and International Human Rights Law

RUONA IGUYOVWE

Criminal Law Section, Legal and Constitutional Affairs Division, Commonwealth Secretariat

While International Humanitarian Law and International Human Rights Law have traditionally been regarded as two distinct branches of law, recent developments in international law, national juris-prudence and national law have increasingly led to a recognition that these two bodies of law overlap substantially in practice. The concurrent application of these two bodies of law in certain contexts has been expressly recognised by various international courts and tribunals. This article examines the similarities and differences between International Humanitarian Law and International Human Rights Law, as well as the areas of their overlap and of concurrent applicability.

1. Introduction

Traditionally, International Humanitarian Law and International Human Rights Law were regarded as two distinct branches of law with distinct modes of application. International Human Rights Law was considered to be generally applicable during peace times whilst International Humanitarian Law was believed to be the applicable law during times of conflict. While human rights law is primarily concerned with the way a State treats those within its territory, humanitarian law regulates the conduct of parties during armed conflicts so as to diminish the effect of warfare.[1] Other distinctions between human rights and humanitarian law include the scope of beneficiaries, the range of rights protected, subjects of obligations, the institutions competent to determine violations, the period of application, the locus of application, and the source of obligations.[2]

Recent developments in international law, national jurisprudence, law and practice have increasingly led to a recognition that these two bodies of law overlap substantially in practice. International Human Rights Law not only applies during peace times but it can also apply in situations of occupation or non-international armed conflict to complement the protection provided by humanitarian law, for example in relation to the prohibition on torture, prohibition on death in custody, and right to a fair trial.

This paper[3] considers the similarities and differences between International Humanitarian Law and International Human Rights Law. It also examines the relationship between

---

1   ICTY: *Prosecutor v Kunarac, Kovac, and Vukovic*, Case no. IT-96-23-T and IT-96-23/1, Trial Chamber II, Judgment, para. 470 (22 February 2001); Cerone, John (2007) Jurisdiction and power: the intersection of Human Rights Law and the Law of Non-International Armed Conflict in an Extraterritorial Context, *International Law Forum*, Research Paper No 12-07, p. 5.

2   *Ibid.*, p. 5.

3   This paper is based in part on the contents of Droege, Cordula (2007) The interplay between International Law and International Human Rights Law in situations of armed conflict, *International Law Forum*, Research Paper No 14-07.

International Human Rights Law and International Humanitarian Law in times of armed conflict and the areas of overlap. It outlines some of the developments that have led to the increasing areas of overlap between these two bodies of law and considers how the interaction between both bodies of law works in practice.

2. Similarities and Differences between International Humanitarian Law and International Human Rights Law

- International Humanitarian Law and International Human Rights Law are both complementary. They both strive to protect the lives, health and dignity of individuals, albeit from a different angle. They share common humanist ideals of the protection of the dignity and integrity of the person, and many of their guarantees are identical, such as the protection of the right to life, freedom from torture and inhuman and degrading treatment, the protection of family rights, economic, and/ or social rights. However, there are notable differences between them such as their origin, the subjects of obligations, the nature and scope of obligations, the institutions competent to determine violations, the period of application, the scope of beneficiaries, the locus of application, the range of rights protected, and the source of the obligations.

- Human rights were in the beginning, essentially, laws to protect persons from abuse by State powers. They were a matter of constitutional law, an internal affair between the government and its citizens; humanitarian law, by its very nature, took its roots in the relation between States, in international law. While modern human rights can be traced back to the quest of visionaries for a more just relationship between the State and its citizens,[4] humanitarian law did not emanate from a struggle of human rights claimants, but from a principle of charity—'inter arma caritas'.[5] It was primarily based on the reciprocal expectations of two parties at war and the notions of chivalry and civilised behaviour.[6] The primary motivation for humanitarian law was a principle of humanity, not a principle of rights. Its legal development was borne out of the needs of military necessity, military strategy and the idea of reciprocity between States in the treatment of the other States' troops.[7]

- The scope of application of the two bodies of law is different. Human rights law governs the relationship between a State and its citizens. It is primarily concerned with the way a State treats those within its jurisdiction. Humanitarian law on the other hand, deals with the laws which regulate the conduct of parties to an armed conflict. Human rights laws generally bind States and States alone. Human rights treaties, such as the International Covenant on Civil & Political Rights (ICCPR), place responsibility for 'respecting and ensuring' human rights squarely upon States Parties.[8] While human rights law is primarily concerned with the way a

---

4 Droege, Cordula (2007) The interplay between International Humanitarian Law and International Human Rights Law in situations of armed conflict, *Isr. L. Rev.* 40(2), at p. 312.

5 *Ibid.*, at p. 313.

6 *Ibid.*, at p. 313 and see, for example, the Lieber Code: US War Department, Instructions for the Government of Armies of the United States in the Field, General Orders No 100, 24 April 1863, reprinted in Schlinder, Dietrich and Toman, Jiri (Eds) (1988) *The Laws of Armed Conflicts*, p. 3.

7 Droege, *op. cit.*, n 4, at p. 313.

State treats those within its domain, humanitarian law regulates the conduct of parties (State and non-State actors) during armed conflicts so as to diminish the effect of warfare on the victims of the hostilities.

Human Rights, for instance the European Convention on Human Rights (1950) (ECHR), is mainly concerned with setting limits on the ability of State authorities to interfere with individual rights. In this sense, the Convention defines the *negative obligations* of State authorities, i.e. obligations to refrain from certain action.[9] Even though only conduct (i.e. acts or omissions) attributable to the State can constitute an intentionally wrongful act under these human rights treaties, and only a State can be held responsible on the international plane for such violations, that is not to say that only acts of State officials can engage the international responsibility of the State under human rights law. Human rights law also imposes *positive obligations* on States. Thus, the failure to act may in certain instances also constitute a violation of human rights law.[10] Article 2(1) of the ICCPR States that 'each State Party to the present Covenant undertakes to respect and to ensure to all individuals within its territory and subject to its juris-diction the rights recognised in the present Covenant ...'.[11] In its General Comments, the Human Rights Committee has construed this provision to oblige States to protect the rights contained in the Covenant against non-State interfer-ence.[12] In General Comment 31, the Committee stated:

> However the positive obligations on States Parties to ensure Covenant rights will only be fully discharged if individuals are protected by the State, not just against violations of Covenant rights by its agents, but also against acts commit-ted by private persons or entities that would impair the enjoyment of Covenant rights in so far as they are amenable to application between private persons or entities. There may be circumstances in which a failure to ensure Covenant rights as required by article 2 would give rise to violations by States Parties of those rights, as a result of States Parties' permitting or failing to take appropriate measures or to exercise due diligence to prevent, punish, investigate or redress the harm caused by such acts by private persons or entities.[13]

The regional human rights institutions have interpreted comparable provisions[14] in their respective treaties.[15]

- Under human rights law, derogation is allowed in most general treaties in times of war or other public emergency threatening the life of the nation.[16] The African

---

8   Article 2, ICCPR: While the preambles of the ICCPR and the ICESR both speak of duties of individuals, no normatice content for this language has been determined. The idea of duties under human rights law is generally employed in the context of permissible restrictions on rights made through, e.g. claw-back clauses. See Article 19(3), ICCPR. Finally, although the African Charter on Human and Peoples Rights (ACHPR) sets forth duties in its operative text, these provisions have never been used by the African Commission to find individuals responsible for breaches of the Charter. Indeed there are no procedures for alleging a breach of these duties. ACHPR, adopted on 27 June 1981, OAU Doc. CAB/LEG/67/3 rev. 5, reproduced in 21 I.LM 58 and came into force on 21 October 1986.

9   European Human Rights Law Keir Starmer, p. 194, para. 5.1.

10 *Ibid.*, p. 194, para 5.2.

11 Emphasis added.

12 See, for example, General comment No. 31, Human Rights Committee General Comments 6, 10, 16, 17, 18, 20, 21, 27, 28 and 31. Human Rights Committee General Comments are available at: http://www.ohcr.org/english/bodies/hrc/comments.htm (last accessed 10 October 2008).

13 Human Rights Committee General Comment 31[80] Article 2 of the Covenant: The Nature of the General Legal Obligation Imposed on States Parties to the Covenant, UN Doc. CCPR/C/74/CRP.4/Rev.6 (2004) at para. 8.

(Banjul) Charter on Human and People's Rights (1986) (ACHPR), contains no derogation clause and is unique in that regard. Certain rights are considered to be so fundamental and of such importance that a State cannot derogate from these rights even in times of national emergency,[17] such as the right to life and the prohibition against torture or cruel, inhuman or degrading treatment or punishment. Moreover, unless and until a State has issued derogations in accordance with the relevant procedures, it is bound by its conventional obligations even in times of armed conflict.

Unlike human rights law, however, there is no concept of derogation in humanitarian law. No derogations are permitted under humanitarian law because it was conceived for wartime situations.

Derogation:

Article 4 of the ICCPR permits a State to derogate in 'time of public emergency which threaten the life of the nation and the existence of which is officially proclaimed ...'. A similar provision can be found in the regional conventions (Article 15 of ECHR; Article 27 of ACHR).

(Article 15 of ECHR; Article 27 of the American Convention on Human Rights 1978 (ACHR))

---

14 See Article 1 of the African Charter on Human & People's Rights, Article 1(1) of the American Convention on Human Rights, Article 1 of the European Convention for the Protection of Human Rights and Fundamental Freedoms: Article 1 of the European Convention requires the High Contracting Parties to 'secure' the rights contained in the Convention. The European Court has interpreted Article 1 to entail a scope of obligations similar to that encompassed by the phrase 'to respect and to ensure' as interpreted by the Human Rights Committee. The African Commission on Human and People's Rights has gone even farther, interpreting Article 1 of the African Charter, which obliges states to 'recognise' rights and to 'adopt ... Measures to give effect to them', to entail the obligations to respect, protect, promote, and fulfil the rights contained in the Charter. See Decision Regarding Communication 155/96 (Social and Economic Rights Action Center/Center for Economic and Social Rights v Nigeria). Case No. ACHPR/ COMM/A044/1, printed in *Fifteenth Annual Activity Report of the African Commission on Human and People's Rights* (2001), available at: http://www.achpr.org/english/activity-reports/activity (last accessed 10 October 2008)15-en.pdf.

15 *Ibid.*; Velasquez-Rodriguez, Case, Inter-Am Ct. H.R. 9Ser. C, No. 4 (1988); Applic. 15599/94, *A v. UK*, Eur. Ct. H.R. report of 18 September 1997; *Kilic v. Turkey*, Applic. No. 22492/93 (given 28 March 2000), available at: http://www.echr.coe.int (last accessed 10 October 2008); as stated by the Velasquez-Rodriguez Court, 'An illegal act which violates human rights and which is initially not directly imputable to a State (for example, because it is the act of a private person or because the person responsible has not been identified) can lead to international responsibility of the State, not because of the act itself, but because of the lack of due diligence to prevent the violation or to respond to it as required by the Convention'. Velasquez-Rodriguez case at para. 172. The 'due diligence' standard 'has been generally accepted as a measure of evaluating a State's responsibility for violation of human rights by private actors'. Preliminary report submitted by the Special Rapporteur on violence against women, its causes and consequences, Radhika Coomaraswamy, E/CN.4/1995/42, para. 103 [citing Moore, Int. Arb. 495 (1872)]. Application of the 'due diligence' standard can be seen in the reports of UN special rapporteurs, UN special representatives, and the secretary-General; comments, views and concluding observations of human rights treaty bodies; reports on expert group meetings; resolutions of the Commission on Human Rights and the Economic and Social Council; Declarations by the General Assembly, and the writings of publicists. See Cerone, John (2002) The human rights framework applicable to trafficking in persons and its incorporation into UNMIK regulation 2001/4, 7 *Int. Peacekeeping: Y. B. Int. Peace Op.* 43–98. See also Cerone, John (2007) Jurisdiction and power: the intersection of human rights law & the law of non-international armed conflict in an extraterritorial context, *Isr. L. Rev.*, 40(2), pp. 72–128.

16 Article 4 of the ICCPR; Article 15 of the ECHR; Article 27 of the American Convention on Human Rights 1969. The African Charter on Human and Peoples' Rights contains no derogation clause, but in general it has more far-reaching limitation clauses.

17 See for example Article 15(2) of the ECHR. This applies to the right to life in Article 2 ECHR (save to the extent that death is the result of a lawful act of war); the prohibition against torture and inhuman and degrading treatment or punishment in Article 3; the prohibition on slavery and servitude in Article 4(1) ECHR and the prohibition on the retrospective application of criminal law in Article 7 ECHR.

> In time of war or other public emergency threatening the life of the nation any High Contracting Party may take measures derogating from its obligations under this Convention to the extent strictly required by the exigencies of the situation, provided that such measures are not inconsistent with its other obligations under international law.

- Humanitarian law applies in situations of armed conflict, whereas human rights law protects individuals at all times, both in war and peace alike. The principal goal of human rights law is to protect individuals from arbitrary behaviour by their own governments. Humanitarian law on the other hand, aims to protect persons who do not or who are no longer taking part in hostilities. The concurrent application of these two bodies of law has been expressly recognised by various international tribunals, including the International Court of Justice, the UN Human Rights Committee, the European Court of Human Rights, the Inter-American Commission on Human Rights and, numerous national courts.[18]

- Unlike human rights law, humanitarian law (or the law of armed conflict) was designed to apply primarily in an *inter-state* context. The vast majority of its provisions apply to a State's *extraterritorial conduct*, specifically in the territory of the opposing state.[19] Human rights law was not primarily designed to apply extraterritorially but there are circumstances in which there is extraterritorial applicability of human rights (considered later in this article).

  International Human Rights Law still applies where there is an internal armed conflict; or where the existing State apparatus is replaced or removed following an international armed conflict. In the latter case, the occupying power assumes the responsibilities of the State and must ensure the protection of human rights not just for 'protected persons' as defined under the Geneva Conventions but for all those who fall under their jurisdiction. Although International Human Rights Law applies both during peacetime and during an armed conflict (both internal and international), it does not, however, govern the laws of war. When issues such as the conduct of hostilities or the treatment of prisoners of war are raised, International Humanitarian Law would address those issues as it deals with the application of human rights in an armed conflict. For this reason, in relation to International Humanitarian Law, there is a need to apply Conventions other than the Geneva Conventions and the Additional Protocols thereto. This is amply demonstrated by the decisions of human rights bodies such as the Inter-American Court of Human Rights.

- Human rights implementing mechanisms are complex, and unlike International Humanitarian Law, include regional systems. International Humanitarian Law provides for specific mechanisms that help its implementation. Notably, States are required to ensure respect also by other States. Provision is also made for an enquiry procedure, a Protecting Power mechanism, and the International Fact-Finding Commission. In addition, the ICRC is given a key role in ensuring respect for the humanitarian rules.

  However, a common feature is that the duty to implement International Humanitarian Law and International Human Rights Law lies first and foremost

---

18 See *Humanitarian Law, Human Rights and Refugee Law—Three Pillars*, available at: www.icrc.org/web/siteeng0.nsf/html/6T7G86 (last accessed 28 April 2008).

19 Cerone, *op. cit.*, n 1, p. 2.

with the States. International Humanitarian Law obliges States to take practical and legal measures, such as enacting penal legislation and disseminating International Humanitarian Law. Similarly, States are bound by International Human Rights Law to accord national law with international obligations.

- International Humanitarian Law and International Human Rights Law differ fundamentally in a number of procedural aspects: right to a remedy and individual standing, right to an investigation and the right to reparation:

Right to a remedy

While humanitarian law focuses on 'the parties to a conflict', human rights are built around the individual and are formulated as individual entitlements or rights such as the right to life, freedom of expression, freedom of association and right to private and family life. The human rights case-law has started to influence the understanding of humanitarian law. On occasion, there may not be any independent international remedy specifically foreseen for International Humanitarian Law. 'The fact that an individual has a remedy under human rights law gives additional strength to the rules of International Humanitarian Law corresponding to the human rights norm alleged to be violated'.[20] In some cases human rights jurisprudence can even provide greater protection for the victims or reinforce the protection by other mechanisms and institutions[21]. However, human rights law does not always afford higher protection to victims and the human rights courts do not always offer greater protection. In the case of restrictive rights, the human rights have to be balanced against the rights of others and can (with few exceptions) always be limited on grounds of security. Humanitarian law often does not allow for any limitation of its rights.

Investigations

In both human rights law and International Humanitarian Law, there are secondary obligations to protect the right to life. The most important are the obligations to investigate, prosecute, and punish violations of the right to life. However the International Human Rights Law and jurisprudence with regard to the obligation to investigate is far more advanced than in International Humanitarian Law.[22] In human rights law, the European Court of Human Rights has recognised that if the rights declared in the Convention are to be protected effectively, certain provisions have to be read as imposing positive obligations on the State. These positive obligations protect victims and potential victims of crime and others (notably witnesses) whose rights may be infringed during the criminal process. There are positive obligations on States to: prevent the infringements of rights under Articles 2 and 3; to have in place laws and effective

---

20 Bothe, Michael (2004) The Historical Evolution of International Humanitarian Law, International Human Rights Law, Refuge Law and International Criminal Law, in H. Fischer, Ulrike Froissart, Wolff Heintschel von Heinegg and Christian Raap (Eds) *Crisis Management and Humanitarian Protection*, p. 37.

21 Abresch, William (2005) A human rights law of internal armed conflict: the European court of human rights in Chechnya, 16 *Eur. J. Int.* 741; see also Bothe, n 20, at p. 90.

22 See the UN Principles on the Effective Prevention and Investigation of Extra-legal, Arbitrary and Summary Executions, recommended by Economic and Social Council resolution 1989/65 of 24 May 1989; Principles on the Effective Investigation and Documentation of Torture and Other Cruel, Inhuman or Degrading Treatment or Punishment; among the relevant body of jurisprudence see Human Rights Committee, Concluding Observations on Serbia and Montenegro, p. 9, UN Doc. CCPR/CO/81/SEMO, (12 August 2004); *Finucane v. the United Kingdom* [2003] VIII Eur. Ct. H.R. at para. 69 (summary of its constant jurisprudence).

criminal sanctions which penalise infringements of basic rights; there is a duty to investigate alleged breaches of Articles 2 and 3; obligation to prosecute where there is evidence or if decision taken not to prosecute, to give reasons for not doing so. Lastly there are procedural rights of victims and witnesses in the course of a prosecution and the rights of victims and their families in relation to the sentencing process.[23]

As its starting point in the judgment in *Osman v United Kingdom*[24] the Court made the following general statement:

> The Court notes that the first sentence of Article 2(1) enjoins the State not only to refrain from the intentional and unlawful taking of life, but also to take appropriate steps to safeguard the lives of those within its jurisdiction.[25] It is common ground that the State's obligation in this respect extends beyond its primary duty to secure the right to life by putting in place effective criminal law provisions to deter the commission of offences against the person backed up by law enforcement machinery for the prevention, suppression and sanctioning of breaches of such provisions. It is thus accepted by those appearing before the Court that Article 2 of the Convention may also imply in certain well-defined circumstances a positive obligation on the authorities to take preventive operational measures to protect an individual whose life is at risk from the criminal acts of another individual.[26]

The 'positive obligations' doctrine has significant implications for the rights of victims of crime.[27] The Court has held that the State is under a duty to adopt an adequate system of law to deter and punish individuals guilty of violating the Convention rights of others,[28] and that any available defences must not be cast in terms so wide as to undermine the effectiveness of the criminal sanction.[29] The authorities must have taken reasonable steps to secure the evidence, including any eye witness testimony, forensic evidence, and where appropriate, an autopsy which provides a complete and accurate record of the injury and an objective analysis of clinical findings. In order to maintain public confidence in the investigation, there must be a sufficient element of public scrutiny of the investigation. While the degree of public scrutiny may vary from case to case, the victim's relatives must in all cases be involved in the procedure to the extent necessary to safeguard their legitimate interests and they must be protected against any form of intimidation. The result of the investigation must be made public.

Where the right to life and the right to be protected from inhuman and degrading treatment are concerned, the police[30] and other relevant public bodies[31] are now

---

23 Emmerson QC, Ben, Ashworth, Andrew and Macdonald, Alison (2007) *Human Rights and Criminal Justice* (Sweet & Maxwell) by Ben Emmerson Q.C., Prof Andrew Ashworth and Alison Macdonald, Ch. 18 (especially at paras 18-01–18-02).

24 *Osman v United Kingdom* [2000] 29 EHRR 245.

25 The court referred here to its judgment in *LCB v United Kingdom* [1999] 27 EHRR 212, para. 36.

26 *Osman v United Kingdom* [2000] 29 EHRR 245 at para. 115.

27 Emmerson *et al.*, *op. cit.*, n 23, at p. 93, para. 2–59.

28 *Ibid.*, and *X and Y v Netherlands* [1985] 8 EHRR 235.

29 *A v United Kingdom* [1999] 27 EHRR 611.

30 *Mrs W v United Kingdom* [1983] 32 DR 190; *Mrs W v Ireland* [1983] 32 DR 211; *Osman v United Kingdom*, Judgment of 28 October 1998; *Z and others v United Kingdom*, Application No. 29392/95, Judgment 10 May 2001 (concerning the liability of the social services under Article 3 for failure to take an abused child into care).

31 *Deweer v Belgium* [1979–80] 2 EHRR 439 at para. 49.

recognised as being under a positive operational obligation to take reasonable measures to prevent a criminal violation of an individual's rights under Articles 2 and 3; and (where such violations have occurred) to carry out an effective and independent investigation[32] which is capable of leading to the identification and prosecution of the offender.[33]

- **Equality and no discrimination**

It is a fundamental principle of International Human Rights Law that all persons have a right to be recognised as persons before the law, and are to be treated as equal before the law, and are entitled without any discrimination, to equal protection of the law. Like International Human Rights Law, International Humanitarian Law is based on the premise that the protection accorded to victims of war must be without any discrimination. This is such a fundamental rule of human rights that it is specified not only in the United Nations Charter but also in all human rights treaties.[34] One example of this principle in humanitarian law is Article 27 of the Fourth Geneva Convention of 1949:

> ... all protected persons shall be treated with the same consideration by the Party to the conflict in whose power they are, without any adverse distinction based, in particular, on race, religion or political opinion.

- **Right to life**

The right to life is one of the absolute (non-derogable) rights in human rights law. Given the obvious risk to life in armed conflict, a great deal of humanitarian law is also devoted to its protection, thus having a direct beneficial effect on the right to life. There are protections set out in humanitarian law for victims of war in the power of the enemy. These persons are mainly protected by the 1949 Geneva Conventions, with some extension of this protection in 1977 Additional Protocol I. In respect of combatants who are still fighting, there is a rule that prohibits the use of weapons of a nature to cause superfluous injury or unnecessary suffering which is partly aimed at outlawing those weapons that cause an excessively high death rate among soldiers.[35]

The Protocol prohibits the starvation of civilians as a method of warfare and consequently the destruction of their means of survival.[36] Secondly, it offers the means for improving their chance of survival by, for example, providing for the declaration of special zones that contain no military objectives[37] and consequently may not be attacked. Thirdly, there are various stipulations in the Geneva Conventions and their Additional Protocols that the wounded must be collected and given the medical care that they need. In human rights treaties this would fall

---

32 *McCann, Savage and Farrell v United Kingdom* [1996] 21 EHRR 97 at para. 161.

33 *Aydin v Turkey* [1998] 25 EHRR 251 at paras 103–109. See also Emmerson *et al., op. cit.,* n 23, at p. 93, para. 2-59.

34 See Article 14 ECHR, Article 16 ICCPR, Article 7 UDHR.

35 The most recent codification of the prohibition of the use of weapons of a nature to cause unnecessary suffering is in Article 35(b) of 1977 Protocol I. The reasoning, however, is most clearly stated in the St Petersburg Declaration of 1868: '... the only legitimate object which States should endeavour to accomplish during war is to weaken the military forces of the enemy ... this object would be exceeded by the disabled men, or render their death inevitable ...'.

36 Article 54.

37 Articles 14 and 15 of the Fourth Geneva Convention and Articles 59 and 60 of 1977 Protocol I. It should be noted, however, that a non-defended area was protected from bombardment in customary law.

into the category of 'economic and social rights'.[38] Fourthly, the Geneva Conventions and their Protocols specify in considerable detail the physical conditions that are needed in order to sustain life in as reasonable a condition as possible in an armed conflict. Thus, for example, the living conditions required for prisoners of war are described in the Third Geneva Convention and similar requirements are also laid down for civilian persons interned in an occupied territory. With regard to the general population, an occupying power is required to ensure that the people as a whole have the necessary means of survival and to accept outside relief shipments if necessary to achieve this purpose.[39] There are also provisions for relief for the Parties' own populations, but they are not as absolute as those that apply in occupied territory.[40] Humanitarian law lays down restrictions on the imposition of the death penalty, in particular, by requiring a delay of at least six months between the sentence and its execution, by providing for supervisory mechanisms, and by prohibiting the death sentence from being pronounced on persons under 18 or being carried out on pregnant women or mothers of young children. Also, an occupying country cannot use the death penalty in a country which has abolished it.[41]

In Protocol I of 1977 there is the careful delimitation of what can be done during hostilities in order to spare civilians as much as possible. The balance between military necessities and humanitarian needs that was explained in the Lieber Code continues to be at the basis of this law, and the States that negotiated this treaty had this firmly in mind so as to codify a law that was acceptable to their military staff. The result is a reaffirmation of the limitation of attacks to military objectives and a definition of what this means[42] but accepting the occurrence of 'incidental loss of civilian life' subject to the principle of proportionality.[43]

'Proportionality' is considered to be a core principle in both International Humanitarian Law and in International Human Rights Law.[44] However, the concept of proportionality in human rights law is very different from the concept of proportionality in humanitarian law.

- **Prohibition against torture, cruel, inhuman or degrading treatment or punishment**

    Another absolute/non-derogable human right is the right not to be subjected to torture or to cruel, inhuman or degrading treatment or punishment. Humanitarian law also contains an absolute prohibition of such behaviour and states this prohibition explicitly in the relevant Conventions.[45] The Convention against Torture and other cruel, inhuman or degrading treatment 1984 (CAT) criminalises and

---

38 Article 12 of the ESC Covenant recognises that everyone has the right to 'the enjoyment of the highest attainable standard of physical and mental health'. This goes much further of course than what is provided for in humanitarian law, but it is the only human rights provision under which the right to receive medical treatment could be categorised.

39 Article 55 of the Fourth Geneva Convention and Article 69 of Additional Protocol I.

40 Article 23 of the Fourth Geneva Convention and Article 70 of Additional Protocol I.

41 Articles 68 and 75 of the Fourth Geneva Convention.

42 Articles 48 and 52.

43 Article 52(5)(b).

44 Delbruck, J. (1984) Proportionality, in *Encyclopaedia of Public International Law, Vol. 7* (Elsevier Science Publishers), p. 398.

45 For example, Article 3 common to the Geneva Conventions prohibits 'violence to life and person, in particular murder of all kinds, mutilation, cruel treatment and torture'.

provides for universal jurisdiction for torture committed by a State official in order to obtain information/confession. It also renders the evidence so obtained inadmissible. Equally, admissions obtained under torture in a third State may still be excluded by a court in the receiving country.[46]

- **Prohibition against slavery**

Both human rights law and humanitarian law have provisions prohibiting slavery.[47] As far as humanitarian law is concerned, this is explicitly laid down in 1977 Protocol II;[48] the possibility of slavery is furthermore precluded by the various forms of protection given elsewhere in the Geneva Conventions. It is interesting to note in particular that this prohibition was well established in customary law, and is reflected in the Lieber Code's articles on the treatment of prisoners of war, who are not seen as the property of those who captured them[49] and on the treatment of the population in occupied territory.[50]

- **Right to family life**

In human rights law, there is a right to respect for private and family life.[51] This is a qualified right.[52] The protection of children and family life is also given a great deal of importance in humanitarian law. It is taken into account in a number of different ways, such as the provision made for children's education and physical care, the separation of children from adults if interned (unless they are members of the same family), and special provisions for children who are orphaned or separated from their families.[53] The family is protected as far as possible by rules that help prevent its separation by keeping members of dispersed families informed of their respective situation and whereabouts and by transmitting letters between them.[54]

- **Freedom of religion**

There is a freedom of religious thought and conscience in human rights.[55] This is also a qualified right.[56] Respect for religious faith is also taken into account in humanitarian law, not only by stipulating that prisoners or war and detained civilians may practise their own religion,[57] but also by providing for ministers of

---

46 Commonwealth Manual on Terrorism. The common law (as well as international law) and 'the importance a civilized society attaches to proper behaviour by the police' compel the exclusion of 'evidence' obtained by torture. It is excluded as inherently unreliable, unfair, offensive to ordinary standards of humanity and decency and incompatible with principles which should inform a tribunal seeking to administer justice; A & Others v Secretary of State Home Affairs (UK House of Lords, December 2005); R v Mushtaq (UK House of Lords 2005); Lam Chi-Ming v The Queen (Privy Council, 1991). See also Article 69 Rome Statute (International Criminal Court) and the Rules of Procedure of the International Criminal Tribunals (Former Yugoslavia and Rwanda).
47 See for example Articles 4(1) and (2) of the ECHR.
48 Article 4(2)(f).
49 Article 74 in particular.
50 Articles 42 and 43 in particular.
51 See for instance Article 8(1) of the ECHR.
52 See Article 8(2) of the ECHR.
53 For further detail, see Plattner, D. (1984) Protection of children in international humanitarian law, IRRC, No. 240, May–June, pp. 140–152.
54 The articles are too numerous to list individually, but the majority are to be found in the Third and Fourth Geneva Conventions and their Additional Protocols.
55 See for instance Article 9(1) of the ECHR.
56 See Article 9(2) of the ECHR.
57 Article 34, Third Geneva Convention, and Articles 27 and 38(3), Fourth Geneva Convention.

religion who are given special protection.[58] In addition, the Geneva Conventions stipulate that if possible the dead are to be given burial according to the rites of their own religion.[59]

3. The Overlap between International Humanitarian Law and International Human Rights Law in Situations of Armed Conflict

Having looked at the origins and formulation of these two areas of law, one can now turn to their present method of interpretation and implementation and look at the ways in which they overlap with each other. There were significant historical developments which led to the recognition that human rights law applies in armed conflict and can and ought to be recognised in International Humanitarian Law, even if the detail of their interaction remains a matter of discussion.

3.1. Some important historical developments[60]

Outlined below are some examples of historical developments which have led to the converging development of International Humanitarian Law and International Human Rights Law.

Human rights in their beginning were a matter of constitutional law, an internal affair between the State and its citizens. They remained so until after the Second World War. With the conclusion of the Second World War and the adoption of the Universal Declaration of Human Rights in 1948, human rights became part of the international law.

After the Second World War, the protection of civilians in the Fourth Geneva Convention, especially with regards to those civilians in detention, added a dimension to humanitarian law that drew it much closer to the idea of human rights law.[61] Also, the codification of the Common Article 3 to the Geneva Conventions for situations of non-international armed conflict brought humanitarian law closer to human rights law because it concerned the treatment of the State's own nationals. The common Article 3 lays down the basic rules which States are required to respect when confronted with armed groups on their own territory. It thus diverges from the traditional approach of humanitarian law which, in principle, did not concern itself with the relations between a State and its nationals.[62] Such a provision would be more readily associated with the human rights sphere.

At the XIX International Conference of the Red Cross and the Red Crescent in New Delhi in 1957, the Conference adopted the Draft Rules for the Limitation of the Dangers

---

58 Articles 33 and 35–37, Third Geneva Convention, and Articles 38(3), 58 and 93, Fourth Geneva Convention.

59 Article 17, First Geneva Convention; Article 120, Third Geneva Convention; Article 130, Fourth Geneva Convention.

60 See Droege, *op. cit.*, n 4, pp 312–318 for more historical developments leading to the convergence of both IHL and IHRL.

61 *Ibid.*, p. 313.

62 Although the Lieber Code did make some mention of forms of protection that could be accorded in civil wars, treaty law did not do so until common Article 3 of the Geneva Conventions.

Incurred by the Civilian Population in Time of War[63] elaborated by the International Committee of the Red Cross; the initiative was not pursued.

At the United Nations, on the other hand, States were slowly starting to acknowledge that human rights were relevant in armed conflict[64]

In 1953, the General Assembly invoked human rights in the context of the Korean conflict.[65]

After the invasion of Hungary by the Soviet Troops in 1956, the Security Council called upon the Soviet Union and the authorities of Hungary 'to respect [...] the Hungarian people's enjoyment, of fundamental human rights and freedoms'.[66]

The situation in the Middle East triggered the will to discuss human rights in situations of armed conflict. In 1967, the United Nations Security Council in regard to territories occupied by Israel after the Six Day War had already considered that 'essential and inalienable human rights should be respected even during the vicissitudes of war'.[67]

In 1968, during the International Conference on Human Rights in Tehran, the United Nations for the first time considered the application of human rights in armed conflict. The delegates adopted a resolution inviting the Secretary-General of the United Nations to examine the development of humanitarian law and to consider steps to be taken to promote respect for it.[68]

Increasingly, human rights texts are expressing ideas and concepts typical of humanitarian law and vice versa hence the gap which still exists today between human rights and humanitarian law is diminishing. Influences from both sides are gradually tending to bring the two spheres together.[69]

In 1968, at the Tehran International Conference, the United Nations accepted the application of human rights in armed conflict. The first resolution of the International Conference, entitled Respect and Enforcement of Human Rights in the Occupied Territories, called on Israel to apply both the Universal Declaration of Human Rights and the Geneva Conventions in the occupied Palestinian territories.[70] Then followed the Resolution entitled Respect for Human Rights in Armed Conflict which affirmed that 'even during the periods of armed conflicts, humanitarian principles must prevail'. It was reaffirmed by the General Assembly Resolution 2444 of 19 December 1968 with the same title.[71] That resolution requested the Secretary General draft a report on measures to be adopted for the protection of all individuals in times of armed conflict. The two reports of the Secretary General conclude that human rights instruments, particularly the ICCPR (which had not even entered into force at the time) afforded a more comprehen-

---

63 Droit des conflits armes, reprinted in Schlinder, Dietrich and Toman, Jiri (Eds) (1996) *Droit des Conflicts Armes*, p. 251.

64 Droege, *op. cit.*, n 4, p. 314.

65 GA Res. 804 (VIII), UN Doc, A804/VIII (3 December 1953) (on the treatment of captured soldiers and civilians in Korea by North Korean and Chinese forces).

66 GA Res. 1312 (XIII), UN Doc. A38/49 (12 December 1958).

67 GA Res. 237, 2, UN Doc. A237/1967 (14 June 1967); see also GA Res. 2252 (ES-V), UN Doc. A2252/ESV (4 July 1967), which refers to this resolution.

68 Resolution XXIII, 'Human Rights in Armed Conflicts', adopted by the International Conference on Human Rights, Tehran, 12 May 1968.

69 Article 74 in particular.

70 Final Act of the International Conference on Human Rights, UN Doc. A/Conf. 32/41(22 April–13 May 1968).

71 Droege, *op. cit.*, p. 315.

sive protection to persons in times of armed conflict than the Geneva Conventions only.[72]

A further significant development was the Diplomatic Conference on the Reaffirmation and Development of International Humanitarian Law from 1974 to 1977. This Conference was a reaction to the United Nations process. The International Committee of the Red Cross (ICRC), in particular, could now re-launch the process of development of International Humanitarian Law for a better protection of civilians not only in international, but also non-international armed conflict. The Diplomatic Conference and the two Additional Protocols of 1977 made some rights which were derogable under human rights law non-derogable as humanitarian law guarantees. Both acknowledged the application of human rights in armed conflict. While the ICRC did not follow this route in the early stages of the discussion,[73] it later accepted that human rights continue to apply concurrently with International Humanitarian Law in time of armed conflict.[74] Since then the application of human rights in armed conflict is recognised in International Humanitarian Law, even if the detail of their interaction remains a challenge at times.

3.2. Developments in United Nations security resolutions

The interlinking of human rights and humanitarian law can also be seen in the work of bodies responsible for monitoring and implementing international law. In recent years the United Nations Security Council has been citing humanitarian law more and more frequently in support of its resolutions. One example of this tendency can be found in Resolution 808 (1993) on the conflict in the former Yugoslavia, in which the Security Council decided to establish an international tribunal 'for the prosecution of persons responsible for serious violations of International Humanitarian Law committed in the territory of the former Yugoslavia since 1991'.[75]

There have been a number of resolutions by the Security Council, the General Assembly, and the Commission on Human Rights reaffirming or implying the application of human rights in situations involving armed conflict.[76] The United Nations has also conducted investigations into violations of human rights, for example in connection with various conflict situations such as Iraq's military occupation of Kuwait,[77] the conflicts in Liberia[78] and Sierra-Leone,[79] and Israel's military occupation of the Palestinian territories.[80] More recently, the Security Council has condemned human rights violations by

---

72 Report on Respect for Human Rights in Armed Conflict, UN Doc. A/7729 (20 November 1969) see especially Ch. 3: Report on Respect for Human Rights in Armed Conflict, pp. 20–29, annex 1, UN Doc. A/8052 (18 September 1970).

73 ICRC, Draft Additional Protocols to the Geneva Conventions of 12 August 1949—Commentary131 (1973); see also Pictet, Jean S. (1975) Humanitarian Law and the Protection of War Victims, p. 15.

74 Sandoz, Y., Swinarski, C. and Zimmermann, B. (Eds) (1987) Commentary on the Additional Protocols, see especially para. 4429.

75 See also Security Council Resolutions 670 (1990) on Iraq's occupation of Kuwait and Resolution 780 (1992) establishing a Commission of Experts to enquire into breaches of humanitarian law committed in the territory of the former Yugoslavia. See also the interim Report of the Commission of Experts established pursuant to Security Council Resolution 780 (1992): S/25274.

'militias and foreign armed groups' in the Great Lakes region, implying human rights violations by troops abroad. Resolutions of the United Nations General Assembly and the
United Nations Commission on Human Rights have also sometimes referred to human
rights with regard to international armed conflict[81] and situations of occupation.[82]

3.3. Developments in some new international treaties and instruments

Some newer international treaties and instruments incorporate or draw from both human
rights and International Humanitarian Law provisions.[83] See for example Article 38 of the
Convention on the Rights of the Child of 1989,[84] 20 November 1989, 1577 UNTS 3
[hereinafter referred to as CROC].

An illustration of this can be seen in the adoption in 1977 of the two Protocols additional to the 1949 Geneva Conventions. The subjects and wording of Protocol I's Article
75, entitled 'Fundamental guarantees', are in fact directly inspired by the major human rights
instruments, for it lays down the principle of non-discrimination, the main prohibitions relating to the physical and mental well-being of individuals, the prohibition of arbitrary detention
and the essential legal guarantees. The same could be said of Articles 4, 5 and 6 of Protocol
II, which in situations of non-international armed conflict, are the counterpart to the afore-
said article in Protocol I.

Another example appears in the 1989 Convention on the Rights of the Child. Although
this is a human rights treaty, in Article 38, it makes a general reference to the humanitarian
law provisions applicable to children and lays down rules itself that are applicable in the
event of armed conflict.[85]

---

76 S.C. Res. 1019, UN Doc. S/Res/1019 (9 November 1995); and S.C. Res. 1034, UN Doc. S/Res/1034
    (21 December 1995) (in regard to former Yugoslavia); S.C. Res. UN Doc S/Res/1635 (28 October 2005)
    and S. C. Res 1653, UN Doc. S/Res/1653 (27 January 2006) (Great Lakes region); G.A. Res. 50/193, UN
    Doc. A/Res/50/193 (22 December 1995) (Former Yugoslavia); G.A. Res. 325 (XXX), UN Doc. A/3525
    (15 December 1975) (territories occupied by Israel); G.A. Res. 46/135, UN. Doc. A/Res/46/135
    (19 December 1991) (Kuwait under Iraqi occupation); G.A. Res. 52/145, UN Doc. A/Res/52/145
    (12 December 1997) (Afghanistan); Commission on Human Rights Resolutions and Decisions see, e.g.,
    Resolutions and: UN Docs. E/CN.4/1992/84 (3 March 1992) (Iraq); E/CN.4/2003/77 (25 April 2003)
    (Afghanistan); A/E/CN.4/Res/2003/16 (17 April 2003) (Burundi); E/CN.4/Res/2001/24 (20 April 2001)
    (Russian Federation); E/CN.4/Res/2003/15 (17 April 2003) (Congo); OHCRH/STM/CHR/03/2 (2003)
    (Colombia); OHCHR/STM/CHR/03/3 (2003) Timor-Leste; see also the Report of the Special Rappor-
    teur of the UN Commission on Human Rights on the Situation of Human Rights in Kuwait under Iraqi
    occupation, UN Doc. E/CN.4/1992/26 (16 January 1992).
77 Commission on Human Rights Resolution, UN Doc. E/CN.4/1991/67 (6 March 1991).
78 The Secretary-General, Progress Report on UNOMIL, UN Doc. S/1996/47 (23 January 1996).
79 The Secretary-General, Progress Report on UNOMSIL, UN Doc. S/1998/750 (12 August 1998).
80 Commission on Human Rights Resolution, UN Doc. E/CN. 4/S5/1 (19 October 2000).
81 G.A. Res. 804 (VIII), UN Doc. A804/VIII (3 December 1953) (on treatment of captured soldiers and civil-
    ians in Korea by North Korean and Chinese forces).
82 G.A. Res. 2546 (XXIV), UN Doc. A/Res/2546/XXIV (11 December 1969); G.A. Res. 3525 (XXX), UN
    Doc. A/ Res/46/135 (19 December 1991) (Kuwait under Iraqi occupation); see also the Report of the
    Special Rapporteur of the UN Commission on Human Rights on the situation of human rights in Kuwait
    under Iraqi occupation, UN Doc. E/CN.4/1992/26 (16 January 1992).
83 Droege, op. cit., n 4, at p. 317.
84 Ibid., p. 314. See also the Rome Statute of the International Criminal Court, 1 July 2002, 2187 UNTS 3;
    see also The Optional Protocol to the Convention on the Rights of the Child on the Involvement of
    Children in Armed Conflict, the Basic Principles and Guidelines on the Right to a Remedy and Reparation
    for Victims of Gross Violations of International Human Rights Law and Serious Violations of International
    Humanitarian and the Draft Convention on the Rights of Persons with Disabilities adopted by G.A. Res.
    61/106, UN Doc. A/Res/61/106 (13 December 20006), especially Article 11.

Several United Nations General Assembly resolutions also mingle references to humanitarian law and human rights within one and the same text. The General Assembly often States that it is 'guided by the principles embodied in the Charter of the United Nations, the Universal Declaration of Human Rights, the Universal Declaration of Human Rights, the International Covenants on Human Rights and accepted humanitarian rules as set out in the Geneva Conventions of 12 August 1949 and the Additional Protocols thereto, of 1977'.[86]

3.4. Developments in the international jurisprudence of universal and regional human rights bodies

A further important development leading to the recognition that human rights law applies to situations of armed conflict is the vast body of jurisprudence by universal and regional human rights bodies. Human rights bodies have been prepared to scrutinise situations involving armed conflicts though it is a matter of challenge whether they have the mandate and the necessary expertise to evaluate military operations.[87]

Although it may be thought that the pronouncements of human rights bodies would seem to be generally limited to violations of human rights as contained in their respective treaties, as opposed to pronouncing on violations of International Humanitarian Law, there may be possibilities for such bodies to discuss International Humanitarian Law, since most of the treaties do contain references to other applicable law, for instance in articles covering derogation.[88] Some human rights bodies have been less willing to make overt use of International Humanitarian Law, and direct reference to it has rarely appeared although they have made use of the humanitarian law principles to interpret specific situations.[89] On the other hand, human rights bodies established through the mechanisms of the UN Charter do not have the same restrictions and are therefore more easily able to refer directly to violations of International Humanitarian Law.[90] This can be seen in the reports on thematic procedures, such as those by the Special Rapporteur on Extrajudicial Executions, and in reports on country-specific procedures when dealing with countries involved in armed conflict, such as those compiled by the Special Rapporteurs on Iraq, the former Yugoslavia, and Sudan.[91]

United Nations Human Rights Committee

In its concluding observations on country reports such as the concluding observations on the democratic Republic of Congo as well as its opinions on individual cases, the UN Human

---

85 Council of Europe (1991) Convention on the Rights of the Child, in *Human Rights in International Law* (Strasbourg: Basic Texts).

86 Resolution 46/136 on the situation of human rights in Afghanistan. See also Resolution 46/135 on the situation of human rights in Kuwait under Iraqi occupation and the Declaration 47/133 on the protection of all people against forced disappearances.

87 See Lubell, Noam (2005) Challenges in applying human rights law to armed conflict, *International Review of the Red Cross*, 87(860), December, at p. 742.

88 See discussion of this approach in Reidy, A. (1998) The approach of the European Commission and Court of Human Rights to international humanitarian law, *International Review of the Red Cross*, No. 324, September, pp. 514–516; see also Lubell, *op. cit.*, n 87, at p. 742.

89 ECHR, Ergi v Turkey.

90 See also Lubell, *op. cit.*, n 87, at pp. 742–743.

91 See also *Ibid.*, at p. 743. Examples of these and others are cited in O'Donnell, D. (1998) Trends in the application of international humanitarian law by United Nations human rights mechanisms, *International Review of the Red Cross*, No. 324, September, p. 481.

Rights Committee has applied the ICCPR in non-international armed conflict, including situations of occupation.[92] The same is true for the concluding observations of the UN Committee of Economic and Social Rights, the Committee on the Elimination of Racial Discrimination, the Committee on the Elimination of Discrimination against Women[93] and the Committee on the Rights of the Child.[94] The Human Rights Committee has stated that it can take other branches of law into account in considering the lawfulness of derogations.

The Human Rights Commission

The Human Rights Commission on Human Rights, a body more specifically concerned with the implementation of human rights, has been known to invoke humanitarian law to back up its recommendations.[95] The 'Report on the Situation of Human Rights in Kuwait under Iraqi Occupation' presented at its 48th session is a clear example.[96]

To establish the law applicable to the situation in Kuwait, the Special Rapporteur begins by pointing out, in a chapter entitled 'Interaction between human rights and humanitarian law', that 'there is consensus with the international community that the fundamental human rights of all persons are to be respected and protected both in times of peace and during periods of armed conflict'.[97] The Rapporteur further considers that the rules of customary law applicable to the occupation of Kuwait include Article 3 common to the 1949 Geneva Conventions, Article 75 of the 1977 Additional Protocol I thereto and the 1948 Universal Declaration of Human Rights. In terms of positive law, he considers that the 1966 International Covenant on Civil and Political Rights, the 1966 International Covenant on Economic, Social and Cultural Rights and the 1949 Geneva Conventions can also be applied.

---

92 Droege, *op. cit.*, n 4, at p. 320; and see Concluding Observations on: Democratic Republic of Congo, UN Doc. CCPR/C/COD/CO/3 (26 April 2006); Belgium, 6, UN Doc. CCPR/CO/81/BEL (12 August 2004); Colombia, UN Doc. CCPR/CO/80/COL (26 May 2004); Sri Lanka, UN Doc. CCPR/CO/79/LKA (1 December 2003); Israel, 11 UN Doc. CCPR/CO/78/ISR (21 August 2003); Guatemala, UN Doc. CCPR/CO/72/GTM (27 August 2001); Netherlands, 8, UN Doc. CCPR/CO/72/NET (27 August 2001); Belgium, 14 UN Doc CCPR/C/79/Add 99 (19 November 1998); Israel, 10, UN Doc. CCPR /C/79/Add. 93 (18 August 1998); UN Doc. CCPR A/46/40 (1991); UN Doc. CCPR A/46740 (1991); United States of America, UN Doc. CCPR/C/USA/CO/NON/ENCORE PUBLIE; *Sarma v Sri Lanka*, UN Doc. CCPR/C/78/D/950/2000 (31 July 2003); *Bautista v Colombia*, UN Doc. CCPR/C/55/D/563/1993 (13 November 1995); *Guerrero v Colombia*, UN Doc. CCPR/C/157D/45/1979 (31 March 1982).
93 Concluding Observations on: Sri Lanka, pp. 256–302, UN Doc. A/57/38 (Part I) (7 May 2002); Democratic Republic of the Congo, pp. 194–238, UN Doc. A/55/381 (February 2000); Colombia, pp. 337–401 UN Doc. A/54/38 (4 February 1999).
94 Committee on Economic, Social and Cultural Rights, Concluding Observations on Guatemala, UN Doc. E/C.12/1/Add. 93 (12 December 2003); Concluding Observations on Guatemala, UN Doc. E/C.12/1/Add. 93 (12 December 2003); Concluding Observations on Israel, pp. 14–15, UN Doc. E/C.12/1/Add.90 (23 May 2003); Committee on the Elimination of Racial Discrimination: Concluding Observations on Israel, UN Doc. CERD/C/304/Add. 45 (30 March 1998); Committee on the Rights of the Child: Concluding Observations on the Democratic Republic of Congo, UN Doc. CRC/C/15/Add. 153 (9 July 2001); Concluding Observations on Sri Lanka, UN Doc. CRC/C/15/Add. 207 (2 July 2003); Concluding Observations on Colombia, UN Doc. CRC/C/cOL/CO/3 (8 June 2006).
95 Among some examples, see the Report of the Working Group on Enforced or Involuntary Disappearances (E/CN.4/1993/25 paras 508–510) and its Addendum on the situation in Sri Lanka (E/CN.4/1993/25/Add. I para. 40.42), and the Report on Extrajudicial, Summary or Arbitrary Executions (E/CN.4/1993/46 paras 60, 61, 664 and 684).
96 Report on the situation of human rights in Kuwait under Iraqi occupation, prepared by Mr Walter Kalin (E/CN.4/1992/26).
97 *Ibid.*, para. 33.

The Commission on Human Rights is no longer concerned with marking an overly clear distinction between human rights and humanitarian law. Although it was set up to promote the implementation of human rights, it does not hesitate to invoke humanitarian law when the situation so requires. It now seems to consider that its mandate is no longer confined to human rights but takes it in a larger area comprising 'the principles of the law of nations derived from the usages established among civilized peoples, from the laws of humanity and the dictates of the public conscience'.[98] This view of its terms of reference enables it to draw upon the rules of humanitarian law in order to make pronouncements on the situations it is asked to examine.

The European Court of Human Rights

The European Court of Human Rights has recognised the application of human rights both in situations of non-international armed conflict[99] and in situations of occupation in inter-national armed conflict.[100] The Inter-American Commission and Court have done the same with regard to the American Declaration on the Rights and Duties of Man and the American Convention on Human Rights.[101]

The Inter-American Commission and the Inter-American Court on Human Rights

The Inter-American Commission on Human Rights has also shown a similar tendency as the Human Rights Commission in its approach to some cases. In 1983, the organisation Disabled Peoples' International filed a complaint with the Commission, accusing the United States of violating the right to life guaranteed by Article 1 of the American Declaration on the basis of the principles of humanitarian law. The Commission declared the petition to be admissible. In dealing with the fundamental aspects of the issue, the Commission had to base its decision on a provision drawn up in the spirit of human rights in order to apply that provision to an armed conflict.[102] In the *Tablada (Abella) case*,[103] the Commission made direct use of humanitarian law and in particular of Article 3 common to the four Geneva Conventions of 1949, stating that human rights law did not give them enough tools to analyse the case in hand. The Commission repeated this in

---

98 As in Articles 63, 62, 142 and 158 common to the four 1949 Geneva Conventions. The Rapporteur considers that the principles set out in these articles are relevant to the case he is examining and that they belong both to human rights and to humanitarian law.

99 See for example, *Isayeva, Yusupova and Basayea v Russia, Isayeva v Russia*, at paras 172–178; *Ergi v Turkey* [1998] IV Eur. Ct. H.R at paras 79–81; *Ozkan v Turkey* [2004] Eur. Ct. H.R., Judgment of 6 April 2004, at para. 297, available at: http://cmiskp.echr.coe.int/tkp197/view.

100 *Cyprus v Turkey*, for an overview see Reidy, *op. cit.*, n 88, pp. 513–529.

101 *Bamaca Velasquez v Guatemala*, Case 10. 11/129, Inter-Am. C.H.R. para. 209; *Coard v. the United States of America*, Case 10.951, Inter-Am. C.H.R., OEA/ser.L/V/II.106 doc.3rev (1999), at para. 37; *Alejandre v. Cuba*, Case 11.589, Inter-Am. C.H.R., Report No. 86/99, OEA/Ser.L/V/IIIII, doc. 20 rev at 289 (1998), at para. 18; *Rafael Ferrer-Matorra and others v the United States*, Case No. 9903, Inter-Am. C.H.R., Report No 51/01, OEA/Ser.L/V/IIIII, doc 20 rev 289 (1980), at para. 179; Request for Precautionary Measures Concerning the Detainees at Guatanamo Bay, Cuba, Inter-Am. C.H.R. decision of 12 March 2002, 41 ILM 532 (2002).

102 For further details on the Grenada affair, see Weissbrodt, D. and Andrus, B. (1988) The right to life during armed conflict: Disabled Peoples' International v United States, *Harvard International Law Journal*, 29, p. 59.

103 Inter-Am. CHR, *Juan Carlos Abella v Argentina*, Case No. 11.137, Report No. 55/97, 18 November 1997, para. 271.

the *Las Palmeras Case*, declaring that Colombia had violated the said Common Article 3. But the Inter-American Court was not pleased with this outcome and ruled that neither the Commission nor the Court had the mandate to make direct pronouncements on violations of International Humanitarian Law.[104] It left open the possibility of using International Humanitarian Law to interpret human rights law obligations in situations of armed conflict, albeit without directly making pronouncements on International Humanitarian Law obligations. In a later case, Bamaca Velasqez,[105] the Inter-American Court applied humanitarian law by interpreting the American Convention on Human Rights in the light of the Geneva Conventions because of their overlapping content.[106] The Inter-American Commission is the only body that has expressly assigned itself the competence to apply humanitarian law.[107]

The International Court of Justice

The International Court of Justice has re-affirmed the jurisprudence of human rights bodies. In its Advisory Opinion on the Legality of the Threat of Use of Nuclear Weapons of 1996 with respect to the ICCPR, it made its first statement on the application of human rights in situations of armed conflict:

> The Court observes that the protection of the International Covenant of Civil and Political Rights does not cease in times of war, except by operation of Article 4 of the Covenant whereby certain provisions may be derogated from in a time of national emergency. Respect for the right to life is not, however such a provision. In principle, the right not arbitrarily to be deprived of one's life applies also in hostilities. The test of what is an arbitrary deprivation of life, however, then falls to be determined by the applicable lex specialis, namely, the law applicable in armed conflict which is designed to regulate the conduct of hostilities. Thus whether a particular loss of life, through the use of a certain weapon in warfare, is to be considered an arbitrary deprivation of life contrary to Article 6 of the Covenant can only be decided by reference to the law applicable in armed conflict and not deduced from the terms of the Covenant itself.[108]

In its advisory opinion on the Legal Consequences of the Construction of a Wall in the Occupied Palestinian Territory, the International Court of Justice expanded this argument to the general application of human rights in armed conflict:

> more generally, the Court considers that the protection offered by human rights conventions does not cease in case of armed conflict, save through the effect of provisions for derogation of the kind to be found in Article 4 of the International Covenant on Civil and Political Rights. As regards the relationship between International Humanitarian Law and human rights law, there are thus three possible situations: some rights may be exclusively matters of International Humanitarian Law; others may be exclusively matters of human rights law; yet others

---

104 Inter-Am. CHR, *Las Palmeras v Colombia*, Case No. 67, Judgment on Preliminary Objections, 4 February 2000.

105 Inter-Am. CHR, *Bamaca Velasqez v Guatemala* Judgment, Case No. 70, 25 November 2000.

106 *Bamaca Velazquez v Guatemala*, Case 10. 11/129, Inter-Am. C.H.R, at paras 207–209. The Human Rights Committee has stated that it can take other branches of law into account to consider the lawfulness of derogations: Human Rights Committee, General Comment No. 29: States of Emergency (Article 4), p. 10, UN Doc. CCPR/C/21/Rev.1/Add 11 (24 July 2001).

107 In *Abella v Argentina*, Case 11.137, Inter-Am. C.H.R. Report No. 55/97, OEA/Ser.L/V/?II.98, doc 6 rev, (1997) at paras 157–171.

108 Legality of the Threat or Use of Nuclear Weapons, advisory Opinion, 1996 I.C.J. 226–593 (8 July) at para. 25 [hereinafter referred to as the 'Nuclear Weapons Case'].

may be matters of both these branches of international law. In order to answer the question put to it, the Court will have to take into consideration both these branches of international law, namely human rights law and, as lex specialis, International Humanitarian Law.[109]

It confirmed this statement in the Case Concerning the Territory in Eastern Congo occupied by Uganda. In this judgment, it also repeated the holding of the advisory opinion on the Legal Consequences of the Construction of a Wall in the Occupied Palestinian Territory that International Human Rights Law applies in respect of acts done by a State in the exercise of its jurisdiction outside its own territory and particularly in occupied territories,[110] making clear that its previous advisory opinion with regard to the occupied Palestinian territories cannot be explained by the long-term presence of Israel in those territories,[111] since Uganda did not have such a long term and consolidated presence in the eastern Democratic Republic of the Congo. Rather there is a clear acceptance of the Court that human rights apply in time of belligerent occupation.[112]

By and large, States have not objected to the interpretation of international bodies, with the exception of some States who contest the application of human rights in times of armed conflict.[113]

3.5. Derogations from human rights during times of armed conflict and their limits

In order to understand the application of human rights during times of armed conflicts and the limits, it is a useful starting point to consider the texts of the international human rights treaties. The Universal Declaration of Human Rights is silent in regard to armed conflict. The question of the extent of application of human rights during situations of armed conflict only later arose with the drafting of human rights treaties.

Most human rights can be derogated from in times of public emergency, which includes situations of armed conflict.

Article 15(1) of the ECHR provides that:

In time of war or other public emergency threatening the life of the nation any High Contracting Party may take measures derogating from its obligations under this Convention to the extent strictly required by the exigencies of the situation, provided that such measures are not inconsistent with its other obligations under international law.

---

109 Legal Consequences of the Construction of a Wall in the Occupied Palestinian Territory, Advisory opinion, 2004 I.C.J. (9 July) at para. 106 [hereinafter Wall case]. See also Droege, op. cit., n 4, at pp. 322–323.
110 Case Concerning Armed Activities on the Territory of the Congo (DRC v Uganda), 2005 ICJ 116, (19 December) at para. 119 [hereinafter DRC v Uganda].
111 As argued by Dennis, Michael J. (2005) Application of human rights treaties extraterritorially in times of armed conflict and military occupation, Am. J. Int. L. 99, pp. 119, 122.
112 See Droege, op. cit., n 4, at p. 323.
113 Summary Legal Position of the Government of Israel, Annex I to the Report of the Secretary-General Prepared pursuant to GA Res, ES-10713, p. 4, UN Doc. A/ES -10/248 (24 November 2003) (relating to the construction of a wall in the occupied Palestinian territory); Annex I: Territorial Scope of the Application of the Covenant, 2nd and 3rd periodic Reports of the United States of America, Consideration of Reports Submitted by States Parties under Article 40 of the Covenant, UN Doc. CCPR/C/USA/3 (28 November 2005); Summary Record of the 2380th Meeting: United States of America, at 2, UN Doc. CCPR/C/SR. 2380 (27 July 2006).

See also Article 4 of the ICCPR and Article 27 of the American Convention on Human Rights 1969. The African Charter on Human and Peoples' Rights contains no derogation clause, but in general it has more far-reaching limitation clauses.

Certain rights are of such high importance that no derogation from them is permitted even in times of national emergency.[114] This applies to the right to life (save to the extent that a death is the result of a lawful act of war); the prohibition on torture and inhuman and degrading treatment; the prohibition on slavery and servitude; and the prohibition on the retrospective application of criminal law.

Derogations, where permitted, merely limit the application of the human rights in question and they are strictly interpreted against the derogating State. In *Yaman v Turkey* [2005] EHRR 49, paras 65–70, the geographical limits of derogation were strictly applied. Derogations do not have the effect of dismissing the application of human rights in times of armed conflict or entirely suspending the right.[115] Human rights take effect in domestic law subject to any 'designated derogation'.[116]

Article 15 of the ECHR for instance permits contracting States to derogate from their obligations under the Convention in times of war or 'other public emergency threatening the life of the nation'; providing the derogation is 'strictly required by the exigencies of the situation'[117] and is consistent with the State's other obligations under international law. Not only has the State got to show that there is a public emergency threatening the life of the nation within the meaning of the provisions relating to derogation, it is necessary to show that the measures to be applied by means of the derogation are 'strictly required by the exigencies of the situation'. In *A and others v Secretary of State for the Home Department* [2005] 2 AC 68, a derogation order was quashed by a majority House of Lords decision in the UK because it failed to meet the requirements of Article 15 of the ECHR. All of their Lordships except Lord Hoffman considered that the Special Immigration Appeals Commission (SIAC) (which had seen all the material available to the Government[118]) had been entitled to reach the conclusion it reached that there was a *'public emergency threatening the life of the nation'* within the meaning of Article 15 ECHR, but seven of their Lordships held that the measures applied to foreign nationals under Part IV of the UK Prevention of Terrorism Act 2001 in that case, were not *'strictly required by the exigencies of the situation'* as required by that article, primarily because the Government had not demonstrated that the steps taken in relation to UK nationals who represented a similar threat (steps which did not involve detention), would not suffice to counter the threat from foreign nationals.[119]

Article 14 remained in full force despite the derogation. Seven of their Lordships also held that the Part IV measures unjustifiably discriminated against the appellants in violation of Article 14 on the basis of their immigration status, which it was accepted, fell within 'other status' under Article 14. Lord Bingham also found a violation of the free-standing non-discrimination requirement in Article 26 of the ICCPR, which was part of the UK's international obligations under Article 15. The submissions that the Convention and international law sanctions the differential treatment, including the detention of aliens as

---

114 See Article 15(2) of the ECHR and Article of the African Charter of Human Rights.

115 Droege, *op. cit.,* n 4, at p. 318.

116 See for example Section 1(2) of the Human Rights Act 1998 and Emmerson *et al.,* *op. cit.,* n 23, paras 3–24.

117 Article 15(1) of ECHR.

118 This included some 'closed' material not shown to the Appellants. The Attorney General was invited to show the 'closed material' to the House but expressly declined to do so.

119 Emmerson *et al.,* *op. cit.,* n 23.

compared with nationals in times of war or public emergency were rejected.[120] Accordingly, the Derogation Order was quashed, and a declaration of incompatibility was made in respect of s.23 of the 2001 Act. Lord Bingham in this case emphasised the primacy of the courts as arbiters of fundamental human rights. In response to the decision, the Government did not seek to renew Part IV of the 2001 Act but instead it introduced control orders under the Prevention of Terrorism Act 2005, which applies to both foreign nationals and British citizens alike.

In order for a derogation to be lawful, there are two formal requirements that the State is required to comply with. Derogations must be officially proclaimed and other States party to the treaty must be notified of them.

In conclusion, derogation clauses, where they exist, not only permit the suspension of rights, but also limit the suspension and prohibit the suspension of other rights. Derogations are only permissible to the extent that they are strictly required by the exigencies of the situation and provided that such measures are not inconsistent with a State's other international law obligations and do not involve discrimination solely on the grounds of race, colour, sex, language, religion or social origin.[121] They ensure that during times of armed conflict, human rights continue to apply and to be respected, albeit in a modified manner.[122]

4. The Extraterritorial Application of Human Rights

Developments in international jurisprudence and state practice have shown that human rights apply not only in non-international armed conflict, but also in international armed conflict, including situations of occupation. This means that there is extraterritorial application of human rights.[123] What are the requirements for extraterritorial application of human rights and what are the limits?

In order to consider the requirements for extraterritorial application of human rights, one possible starting point is the wording of the international human rights treaty as many of the treaties have specific application clauses[124] which determine the basis of their extraterritorial reach. However, there are others which have no application clauses at all but there is relevant human rights jurisprudence which can be found in the decisions of the Human Rights Committee, the European Court of Human Rights and the American Commission of Human Rights which sets out the basic requirements for extraterritorial application of human rights.

These requirements are effective control, either over a territory or over a person.

---

120 Paras 55–70.
121 Article 4 ICCPR, Article 15 ECHR and Article 27, American Convention on Human Rights.
122 See Droege, *op. cit.*, n 4, at p. 320.
123 For a detailed analysis of case-law and views on extraterritorial applicability of human rights see the examination of the case-law contained in The High Court of Justice; Queen's Bench Division, Divisional Court, R *(Al-Skeini and others) v Secretary of State for Defence*, 14 December 2004; see also Hampson, Francoise and Salama, Ibrahim (2005) Working paper on the relationship between human rights law and international humanitarian law, UN Sub-Commission on the Promotion and Protection of Human Rights, E/CN.4/Sub.2/2005/14 (21 June), paras 78–92.
124 See Article 2(1) ICCPR, Article 1 ECHR, Article 1 ACHR, Article 2(1) Convention Against Torture, 10 December 1984, 1465 UNTS 85 [hereinafter (CAT)].

4.1. Effective control over a territory

Human rights obligations can extend to areas under the *effective control* of the State. Occupied territories over which authority has been clearly established by a State can come within the ambit of the human right obligations of the State. This was the case in Northern Cyprus and in the occupied Palestinian territories.[125] This view is supported by human rights bodies and was stated by the International Court of Justice.[126] The UN Human Rights Committee (HRC) speaks of protecting 'anyone within the power or effective control of that State Party, even if not situated within the territory of the State Party'.[127]

Occupied territory is in effect under the authority and control of the occupying state so the situation can be said to be analogous to national territory. Where a State exercises *de facto* control over another state's territory,[128] or where agents of a contracting state detain an individual abroad,[129] any person affected by the action may bring a complaint against the State concerned.[130] As was stated by the European Court of Human Rights in cases such as *Loizidou v Turkey*,[131] *Cyprus v Turkey*,[132] effective control, however, does not mean control over every act or part of the territory, but 'effective overall control'.

It justified the effective control argument by saying that:

> Any other finding would result in a regrettable vacuum in the system of human-rights protection in the territory in question by removing from individuals there the benefit of the Convention's fundamental safeguards and their right to call a High Contracting Party to account for violation of their rights in proceedings before the Court.[133]

Article 1 of the ECHR

The protection afforded by Article 1 of the ECHR extends to any person within the *jurisdiction* of the contracting state, or of any overseas territory for whose international relations that state is responsible under Article 56.

In terms of extraterritorial application, the European Court requires effective control over a territory which is fulfilled in the case of military occupation:

> Bearing in mind the object and purpose of the Convention, the responsibility of a Contracting Party may also arise when as a consequence of military action—whether lawful or unlawful—it exercises effective control of an area outside its national territory. The obligation to secure, in such an area, the rights and freedoms set out in the Convention derives from the fact of

---

125 *Ibid.*, at p. 739.

126 Legal Consequences paras 107–112; Concluding Observations on the Human Rights Committee: Israel, 18 August 1998, CCPR/C/79/Add. 93; Loizidou case.

127 General Comment 31, Nature of the General Legal Obligation on States Parties to the Covenant, UN Doc. CCPR/C/21/Rev. 1/Add 13 (2004), para. 10.

128 *Loizidou v Turkey* [1997] 23 EHRR 513; *Ilascu v Moldova and Russia* [2005] 40 EHRR 46; *Issa v Turkey* [2005] 41 EHRR 27, paras 65–82.

129 *Reinette v France* [1989] 63 DR 189.

130 Emmerson *et al., op. cit.*, n 23, paras 1–75.

131 *Loizidou v Turkey* [1996] VI Eur. Ct. H.R. 2216, 2234–2235, para. 52.

132 *Cyprus v Turkey*, Appl. No. 6780/74 & 6950/75, Eur. Ct. H.R. Dec. & Rep. 125; European Court of Human Rights: *Cyprus v Turkey* [2001] IV Eur. Ct. H.R. para. 77.

133 *Cyprus v Turkey* [2001] IV Eur. Ct. H.R. para. 77.

such control whether it be exercised directly, through its armed forces, or through a subordinate local administration.[134]

Member States of the Council of Europe have unanimously accepted this jurisprudence through their resolutions on execution of judgments in the Committee of Ministers.[135]

In *Bankovic v Belgium*,[136] the European court held that the NATO States had not exercised effective control over Serbia during its bombing campaign, and that therefore Serbia did not, during that period, fall within the territorial ambit of the Convention. The case dealt with NATO's bombardment of the Serbian Radio-Television station. It was a case that involved the conduct of hostilities as opposed to occupation or detention situation. The Court took the view that such bombardments did not mean that the attacking States had jurisdiction within the meaning of Article 1 of the ECHR. The Court stated that 'had the drafters of the Convention wished to ensure jurisdiction as extensive as that advocated by the applicants, they could have adopted a text the same as or similar to the contemporaneous Articles 1 of the four Geneva Conventions of 1949'.[137] It clearly felt there was a difference between warfare in an international armed conflict, where one state has no control over the other at the time of the battle, and the situation of occupation. It also used a rather obscure geographical argument, arguing that the former Yugoslavia did not fall in the 'European legal space'.[138]

This led to some speculation as to whether any act committed by a State Party outside the geographic area covered by the Convention would fall outside the jurisdiction of the State.[139] However such argument was laid to rest by the subsequent judgment in *Ocalan v Turkey* which contradicted such a conclusion. In *Ocalan v Turkey*, the European Court of Human Rights found Turkey responsible for the detention of the applicant by Turkish authorities in Kenya: it considered the applicant to be within the jurisdiction of Turkey by virtue of his being held by Turkish agents[140]. This approach was confirmed later in the *Issa and other v Turkey case*.[141] Reconsidering the *Bankovic* decisions in the light of these later cases, it is clear that the decisive argument was not whether the territory was within the European geographic territory but rather that the Court simply did not find that the States had effective control over the territory they were bombarding, nor did they have persons in their power so that no 'jurisdiction' arose.

Occupied territories over which authority has been clearly established can come within the ambit of the human rights obligations of the State.

134 *Loizidou v Turkey* [1995] 310 Eur. Ct. H.R. (ser A) at paras 62–64 (1995) (GC) (Preliminary Objections) [hereinafter Loizidou (Preliminary Objections)].

135 Interim Resolution ResDH (2005) 44, concerning the judgment of the European Court of Human Rights of 10 May 2001 in the case of Cyprus against Turkey (adopted by the Committee of Ministers on 7 June 2005 at the 928th meeting of the Ministers' Deputies); Interim Resolution ResDH (2006) 26 concerning the judgment of the European Court of Human Rights of 8 July 2004 (Grand Chamber) *Ilascu v Moldova and Russia*, (adopted by the Committee of Ministers on 10 May 2006 at the 964th meeting of the Ministers' Deputies).

136 [2001] XII Eur. Ct. H.R. 333 (GC); 11 B.H.R.C. 435.

137 *Bankovic v Belgium* [2001] 12 Eur. Ct. H.R. 333 (GC).

138 Ibid., at para. 80.

139 See Leach, P. (2005) The British military in Iraq—the applicability of the Espace Juridique doctrine under the European Convention on Human Rights, *Pub. L.*, p. 448 with further references; Condorelli, L. (2005) La protection des droits de l'homme lors d'actions militaries menees a l'etranger, *Collegium*, 32(89), p. 100.

140 *Ocalan v Turkey*, Eur. Ct. H.R. Judgment of 12 May 2005; confirmed in *Issa v Turkey* [2004] 41 Eur. Ct. H.R. 27 at para. 71.

141 Ibid.

Occupied territories, in which significant hostilities are occurring, as was the case in parts of Iraq, remain controversial with regard to the human rights obligation of the State as was evidenced in the case of *Al-Skeini*.[142]

In the *Al-Skeini* case, the proceedings arose from the deaths of six Iraqi civilians and the brutal maltreatment of one of them causing his death, in Basra. Each of the deceased was killed (or, in one case, is said to have been killed) and the maltreatment was inflicted by a member or members of the British Armed Forces. In each case, a close relative of the deceased applied in the High Court in London for an order of judicial review against the Secretary of State for the Defence, seeking to challenge his refusal to order an independent enquiry into the circumstances of this maltreatment and these deaths, and his rejection of liability to afford the claimants redress for causing them. The claimants found their claims in the English Court on the UK Human Rights Act 1998 (HRA). In order to succeed, each claimant had to show:

1. That a public authority had acted unlawfully, that is in a manner incompatible with a Convention right under the ECHR of the claimant or the deceased contrary to Section 6(1) of the HRA;

2. That he or the deceased was a victim, i.e. a victim of the unlawful act (Section 7(1)(3) of the Human Rights Act 1998. This particular requirement gave rise to no issue in this case.

3. That the complaint fell within the scope of the ECHR since the claim could not fall under the Human Rights Act 1998 if it did not fall within the Convention.

In the ordinary run of claims under the Human Rights Act 1998, the last condition gives rise to no difficulty as the claim would normally relate to conduct within the borders of a contracting State such as the UK and the question would usually be whether a claimant's Convention rights had been violated and if so, by whom. But in this case, the substantial violations alleged did not take place within the borders of a contracting State. They took place in Iraq, which is not part of the UK and is not a contracting State. This fact is an important fact since the focus of the ECHR is on what is done or not done within the borders of contracting States and not outside. To this rule there are certain limited exceptions, recognised by the jurisprudence of the ECHR. The claimants stated that in each case, because of the special circumstances in which the British troops were operating in Basra, the conduct complained of although taking place outside the borders of the UK (and for that matter, any other contracting State) fell within the exceptions recognised by the ECHR.

The Queen's Bench Divisional Court[143] held that although the claims of the first five claimants fell outside the scope of the Convention that of the sixth claimant, Mr Mousa, did not. The Secretary of State accepted this ruling, the first five claimants challenged this ruling (supported by interveners).

The Court of Appeal[144] held on grounds somewhat differing from those of the Divisional Court that the first five claims fell outside the scope of the Convention, but the sixth fell within it. The Secretary of State supported this conclusion, though he criticised the basis upon which the Court of Appeal held the sixth claimant's case to fall within the Convention.

---

142 See opinions of the House of Lords in *Al-Skeini and others (Respondents) v Secretary of State for Defence* (Appellant); *Al-Skeini and others (Appellants) v Secretary of State for Defence* (Respondent) (Consolidated Appeals) [2007] UKHL 26. Note the distinction made by the Court between the first five claimants and the sixth claimant. Al-Skeini, paras 284–285.

143 [2007] QB 40.

144 [2006] EWCA Civ. 1609; [2007] QB 140 [Brooke, Sedley and Richards LJJ].

Both Courts held that the claims of the first five claimants fell outside the scope of the Human Rights Act 1998 but that Mr Mousa's case fell within the scope of the Act. The Secretary of State challenged the conclusion that Mr Mousa's case fell within the scope of the Human Rights Act 1998. He submitted that the Human Rights Act 1998 has no extraterritorial application. He therefore submitted that the claim of the first five claimants and the sixth claimant could not succeed under the Human Rights Act 1998. The claimants on the other hand argued that the Human Rights Act 1998 *does extend* to cover the conduct of the British forces given the special circumstances in which they were operating and what they did. If and to the extent that the claimants could show that their cases fell within the scope of the Convention and the Human Rights Act 1998, the success of their claim would have depended on their satisfying another condition that a Convention right had in each case been violated. The violation alleged consisted primarily of a failure to investigate a violent death caused or allegedly caused by agents of the State, as the Convention has been held to require.

The Divisional Court found such a violation in the case of Mr Mousa and would have found violations in the case of the first five claimants if they had fallen within the scope of the Convention and the Act.

The Court of Appeal agreed with the latter conclusion, i.e. that they would have found violations in the case of the first five claimants but in the case of Mr Mousa there had been factual developments of potential significance since the date of the Divisional Court's judgment and the Court of Appeal concluded that this question, should in his case be remitted to the Divisional Court. It was common ground between the parties that the order should stand if the first two issues were resolved in Colonel Mousa's favour.

The Secretary of State resisted the finding of violation, provisional though it was, in the case of the first five claimants. The first five claimants appealed to the House of Lords against the dismissal of their claims and the Secretary of State cross-appealed against the ruling that Mr Mousa's case fell within the scope of the Human Rights Act 1998.

In the House of Lords, as in the courts below, the case of the sixth claimant, Mr Mousa, was distinguished from that of the first five claimants. His case was remitted back to the Divisional Court. The actions giving rise to the six killings took place between the cessation of major combat operations and the handover of sovereignty to the Iraqi interim government. Mr Mousa's case was wholly different from that of the first five claimants. He died as a result of appalling treatment in a detention facility occupied and run by British military personnel.

The Secretary of State's cross-appeal and the appeals of the first five claimants were dismissed. The opinion of the court was that the relatives of the first five claimants were not within the jurisdiction of the UK when they were killed in Iraq. The evidence of senior British officers indicated that on the ground, the British troops faced formidable difficulties due to terrorist activity and a volatile situation and the lack of any effective Iraqi security forces. In the circumstances of this case, their Lordships did not consider that the UK was in *effective control* of Basra and the surrounding areas for the purposes of jurisdiction under Article 1 of the Convention at the relevant time. The Court said in paragraph 83: leaving other rights and freedoms aside, with all its troops doing their best, the United Kingdom did not even have the kind of control of Basra and the surrounding area which would have allowed it to discharge the obligations, including positive obligations of a contracting state under Article 2 as described for instance in *Osman v UK* [1998] 29 EHRR 245, 305; paras 115–116. It was undisputed that while there was occupation of British troops in the Al Basrah and Maysan provinces of Iraq at the material time,[145] the United Kingdom possessed

---

145 Al-Skeini (CA) at para. 119.

no executive, legislative, or judicial authority in Basrah city. It was simply there to maintain security in a situation on the verge of anarchy.

The majority of the Court of Appeal therefore found that there was no effective control for the purpose of application of the European Convention on Human Rights.[146] Sedley LJ, on the contrary found that while the United Kingdom might not have had enough control to ensure all Convention rights, it had at least control over its own use of force when it killed the five civilians.[147]

The opinion of the House of Lords[148] was that there was no effective control for the purpose of the application.

Even in other situations in which the State does not control the whole territory, there may be circumstances in which human rights obligations do still extend extraterritorially, for instance when the State is running a detention facility outside its borders[149] as in the case of Mr Mousa in the Al-Skeini case.[150]

The meaning of 'effective control' in human rights law is different from its meaning in humanitarian law

Human rights law applies extraterritorially where the authorities have 'effective control' over a territory so that they can effectively and practically ensure respect for human rights. This notion of effective control in human rights is different from the meaning of effective control in humanitarian law.

The notion of effective control in human rights resembles the term 'established and exercised' authority in Article 42 of the Hague Regulations of 1907 that stipulates that 'territory is considered occupied when it is actually placed under the authority of the hostile army. The occupation extends only to the territory where such authority has been established and can be exercised'.

Both the regime of occupation and the human rights regime are based on the idea that to ensure law enforcement and the well-being of the persons in a territory, a State must wield the necessary amount of control.[151]

Effective control for the purposes of human rights, however, appears to be broader and much more flexible than for the purpose of occupation in humanitarian law. In human rights law, the threshold is lower and indeed the human rights obligations are flexible: with varying degrees of control. The state has varying obligations, ranging from the duty to respect, to the duties to protect and fulfil human rights.[152] In the case of *Ilascu and Others v Moldova and Russia*,[153] there was effective control, short of occupation triggering the application of human rights law. The European Court of Human Rights found Russia to be responsible for

---

146 *Ibid.*, at para. 124.

147 *Ibid.*, at paras 195–197.

148 [2007] UKHL 26.

149 Lubell, *op. cit.*, n 87, at p. 740.

150 See *Al-Skeini and others (Respondents) v Secretary of State for Defence* (Appellant); *Al-Skeini and others (Appellants) v Secretary of State for Defence* (Respondent) (Consolidated Appeals) [2007] UKHL 26.

151 See Articles 64 and 65 of the Fourth Geneva Convention; Sassoli, M. (2005) Legislation and maintenance of public order and civil life by occupying powers, *Eur. J. Int.* 16(661), pp. 663–667.

152 Ben-Naftali, Orna and Shany, Yuval (2003) Living in denial: the application of human rights in the occupied territories, *Isr. L. Rev.* 37(17), p. 64.

153 *Ilascu v Moldova and Russia* [2004] VII Eur. Ct. H.R. at para. 392.

human rights violations on the basis of the presence of a relatively small number of troops—not enough to amount to occupation in the sense of Article 42 of the Fourth Hague Regulation. Indeed, the Court found that the separatist regime had been:

> set up in 1991–92 with the support of the Russian Federation, vested with organs of power and its own administration, remained under the effective authority, or at the very least under the decisive influence, of the Russian Federation, and in any event that it survived by virtue of the military, economic, financial and political support given to it by the Russian Federation.[154]

In conclusion, in humanitarian law control over a territory is a notion pertaining to the law of occupation and triggers a number of absolute obligations of the occupying power. In International Human Rights Law, the notion of 'effective control' has a much broader meaning since human rights obligations are more flexible and vary with varying degrees of control. Effective control for the application of human rights, albeit not all human rights in all their aspects, can be said to exist even in a situation below the threshold of occupation.[155]

4.2. Power over a person

Jurisprudence of human rights bodies

According to the jurisprudence of various human rights bodies, States may be held accountable for violation of the human rights and freedoms of persons in the power of the authorities. International human rights bodies agree that where a State has effective control over a territory or over a person, their respective human rights treaties apply. Typical examples of control over a person would be abduction, detention, or ill-treatment.

UN Human Rights Committee

According to the UN Human Rights Committee:

> State Parties are required by Article 2, paragraph 1, [of the ICCPR] to respect and to ensure the Covenant rights to all persons who may be within their territory and to all persons subject to their jurisdiction. This means that a State party must respect and ensure the rights laid down in the Covenant to anyone *within the power or effective control* of that State Party, even if not situated within the territory of the State Party ... This principle also applies to those within the *power or effective control of the forces of a State Party acting outside its territory*, regardless of the circumstances in which such power or effective control was obtained, such as forces constituting a national contingent of a State Party assigned to an international peacekeeping or peace-enforcement operations.[156]

The constant jurisprudence of the UN Human Rights Committee has confirmed this approach to Article 2(1) of the ICCPR. The Committee has applied the Covenant to situations of military occupation[157] and in relation to troops taking part in peacekeeping

---

154 *Ibid.*

155 Droege, *op. cit.*, n 4, at p. 332.

156 Human Rights Committee, General Comment No. 31 on Article 2 of the Covenant: The Nature of the General Legal Obligation Imposed on States Parties to the Covenant, 10, UN Doc. CCPR/C/74/CRP.4/Rev. 6 (2004) [hereinafter General Comment No. 31] (emphasis added CD).

157 Concluding Observations on: Cyprus, p. 3, UN Doc. CCPR/C/79/Add.39 (21 September 1994); Israel, p. 10, CCPR/C/79/Add 93 (18 August 1998); Concluding Observations on Israel, 11, UN Doc. CCPR/CO/78/ISR (21 August 2003).

operations.[158] In the Wall case, the International Court of Justice adopted the Human Rights Committee's approach with regard to the ICCPR.[159]

While most States accept the jurisprudence of the Human Rights Committee, a small number of States have contested it.[160] As noted by Cordula Droege,[161] the objection of these governments does not necessarily reflect internally coherent state practice by the State including all state organs (the executive, the legislature and the judiciary) because national courts in some of these States such as in Israel[162] and the United Kingdom[163] have applied human rights extraterritorially (since the ICCPR and the ECHR are incorporated as domestic law into the respective national systems).

In a case not related to armed conflict but concerning the abduction of dissidents by agents of the secret service outside the State, the UN Human Rights Committee had to consider allegations of violations of the ICCPR by state agents on foreign territory. The applicant had been kidnapped in Buenos Aires by Uruguayan forces and was secretly detained in Argentina before being clandestinely transported to Uruguay. Had the UN Human Rights Committee applied the Covenant according to the literal meaning of Article 2, it could not have held Uruguay responsible. Rather than adopting a strictly literal approach, the UN Human Rights Committee applied a teleological approach in its interpretation of Article 2 of the ICCPR and took the view that: 'it would be unconscionable to so interpret the responsibility under article 2 of the Covenant as to permit a State party to perpetrate violations of the Covenant on the territory of another State, which violations it could not perpetrate on its own territory'.[164]

European Court of Human Rights

The European Court of Human Rights followed exactly the same argument in the case of *Ocalan v Turkey* and the case of *Issa and others v Turkey*. The Court stated clearly that control over an individual also engages the State's responsibility:

> A State may also be held accountable for violation of the Convention rights and freedoms of persons who are in the territory of another State but who are found to be under the former State's authority and control through its agents operating—whether lawfully or unlawfully— in the latter State. Accountability in such situations stems from the fact that Article I of the

---

158 Concluding Observations on: Belgium, p. 17, CCPR/C/79/Add 99 (19 November 1998); Netherlands, p. 8, CCPR/CO/72/NET (27 August 2001); Belgium, p. 6, CCPR/CO/81/BEL (12 August 2004).

159 Wall case at paras 108–111.

160 See Droege, *op. cit.*, n 4, at pp. 326–327. See also Replies of the Government of the Netherlands to the Concerns Expressed by the Human Rights Committee, p. 19, UN Doc. CCPR/CO/72/NET/Add. 1 (29 April 2003); Second Periodic Report of Israel to the Human Rights Committee, p. 8, UN Doc. CCPR/C/ISR/2001/2 (4 December 2001); Second Periodic Report of Israel to the Committee on Economic, Social and Cultural Rights, p. 5, UN doc.E/1990/6/Add 32 (16 October 2001); Conclusions and Recommendations on the United Kingdom, p. 4(b), UN Doc. CAT/C/SR. 703 (12 May 2006); annex 1: Territorial Scope of the Application of the Covenant, 2nd and 3rd periodic reports of the United States of America, Consideration of Reports submitted by States Parties under Article 40 of the Covenant, UN Doc. CCPR/C/USA/3 (28 November 2005).

161 Droege, *op. cit.*, n 4, at p. 326.

162 See e.g. *Marab v IDF Commander in the West Bank* [2002] Isr. SC 52(2) at 349.

163 *Al-Skeini v Secretary of State for Defence* [2004] EWHC 2911 (admin); *Al-Skeini v Secretary of State for Defence* [2005] EWCA (Civ) 1609, para. 48 at paras 3–11, 48–53, 189–190; *Al-Jedda v Secretary of State for Defense* [2006] EWCA (Civ) 327.

164 *Lopez Burgos v Uruguay*, Comm. No. 52/1979, UN Doc. CCPR/C/13/D/52/1979 (1981) at para. 12.3; *de Casariego v Uruguay*, Comm. No. 56/1979, UN Doc. CCPR/C/13/D/56/1979 (1981) at para 10.3.

Convention cannot be interpreted so as to allow a State party to perpetrate violations of the Convention on the territory of another State, which it could not perpetrate on its own territory.[165]

In both *Ocalan* and the *Issa* case, the Court recognised that States have 'jurisdiction' over persons who are in the territory of another state but who are found in the hands of state agents.

The Inter-American Commission on Human Rights

As previously mentioned, the Inter-American Commission on Human Rights applies the American Declaration to any person subject to a State's authority and control,[166] so that evidently, any person in the hands of the authorities falls under this requirement. The Inter-American Commission has also had to decide on the killings of persons without their being 'in the hands of the authorities'.[167] It condemned the assassination of Orlando Letelier in Washington and Carlos Prats in Buenos Aires by Chilean agents as a violation of the right to life.[168] Similarly it condemned attacks of Surinamese citizens by Surinamese State agents in the Netherlands.[169]

Authorised agents of a State such as its armed forces or diplomatic and consular authorities not only remain the subject of the State's jurisdiction abroad, but bring any other persons or property over which they have authority within the State's jurisdiction.[170] A state may be vicariously liable even for unauthorised acts of government servants exercising official functions.[171] The HRC case of Lopez Burgos and the Ocalan case of the European Commission of Human Rights indicate that human rights obligations can be attached to the extraterritorial actions of State agents in which they have authority and control over an individual.[172]

There has been some controversy over the drafting history of the ICCPR especially between the United States and the Human Rights Committee.[173] The United States argues that the *travaux préparatoires* show that the Covenant was not meant to be applied extra-territorially.[174] As noted by Cordula Droege,[175] the drafting history provides a number of

---

165 *Issa v Turkey* [2004] 41 Eur Ct. H.R. 27 at para. 71.

166 *Coard v the United States*, Case 10.951, Inter-Am. Commission H.R., OEA/ser.L?V/II.106.doc.3rev (1999) at para. 37.

167 Report on the Situation of Human Rights in Chile, OEA/Ser.L/V/II.66, Doc. 17 (9 September 1985) and Second Report on the Human Rights Situation in Suriname, OEA/Ser.L/V/II.66, doc 21 rev. 1 (2 October 1985) at ch. V, E.

168 Report on the Situation of Human Rights in Chile, OEA/Ser.L/V/II.66, Doc. 17 (9 September 1985).

169 Second Report on the Human Rights Situation in Suriname, OEA/Ser.L/V/II.66, doc 21 rev. 1 (2 October 1985) at ch. V, E.

170 *Mrs W v Ireland* [1983] 32 DR 211 at para. 14.

171 Emmerson *et al.*, *op. cit.*, n 23, paras 1–75.

172 HRC, 29 July 1981, UN Doc. A/36/40, 176, Communication No. 52/1979; ECHR 46221/99, Judgment 12 March 2003; Grand Chamber Judgment, 12 May 2005.

173 Annex 1: Territorial Scope of the Application of the Covenant, 2nd and 3rd Periodic Reports of the United States of America, Consideration of reports submitted by States parties under Article 40 of the Covenant, UN Doc. CCPR/C/USA/3 (28 November 2005); Summary Record of the 2380th Meeting, 18 July 2006, Second and third periodic reports of the United States of America, UN Doc. CCPR/C/SR. 2380 (27 July 2006); Human Rights First, Submission to the Human Rights Committee, (18 January 2006), at p. 7, available at: http://www.ohchr.org/english/bodies/hrc/87ngo_info.htm. See comments by Droege, *op. cit*, n 4, at pp. 326–327.

174 *Ibid.*, at pp. 326–327.

175 *Ibid.*, at p. 327.

contradictory conclusions but the *travaux preparatoires* are but one among several methods of interpretation. According to Article 31(1) of the Vienna Convention on the Law of Treaties 'a treaty shall be interpreted in good faith in accordance with the ordinary meaning to be given to the terms of the treaty in their context and in the light of its object and purpose'. The Human Rights Committee adopted this approach and held that in good faith the Covenant must apply extraterritorially:[176]

> The State party should review its approach and interpret the Covenant in good faith in accordance with the ordinary meaning to be given to its terms in their context including subsequent practice, and in the light of its object and purpose.

The Inter-American Commission of Human Rights has also asserted jurisdiction over acts committed outside the territory of a State.[177] The Commission's approach to human rights is a teleological one that since human rights are inherent to all human beings by virtue of their humanity, States have to guarantee it to any person under their jurisdiction, i.e. any person 'subject to its authority and control'.[178] The Commission took a broader view with respect to military operations than the European Court of Human Rights did in the Bankovic case. While the European Court rejected jurisdiction in that case, the Inter-American Commission, in the case of the invasion of Panama by the United States in 1989 stated:

> Where it is asserted that a use of military force has resulted in non-combatant deaths, personal injury, and property loss, the human rights of the noncombatants are implicated. In the context of the present case, the guarantees set forth in the American Declaration are implicated. This case sets forth allegations cognizable within the framework of the Declaration. Thus, the Commission is authorized to consider the subject matter of this case.[179]

5. Ways in Which the Interplay between International Humanitarian Law and International Human Rights Law Can Work in Practice

5.1. Principle of complementarity

The concurrent application of International Human Rights Law and International Humanitarian Law to all situations of armed conflict has the potential to offer the individual greater protection but it also raises some challenges as to how the relationship between the two bodies of law should be defined in such situations.

In the Wall case, the International Court of Justice set out a framework for this and stated:

---

176 Concluding Observations on the United States of America, Advanced Unedited Version, p. 10, UN Doc. CCPR/C/USA/Q/3/CRP.4 (2006).

177 For an overview of its jurisprudence see Cerna, C. (2004) Extraterritorial Application of the Human Rights Instruments of the Inter-American System, in F. Coomans and M.T. Kamminga (Eds) *Extraterritorial Application of Human Rights Treaties*, pp. 141–174; and Cassel, Douglas in *Ibid* at pp. 175–181.

178 *Coard v the United States*, Case 10.951, Inter-Am. Commission H.R., OEA/ser.L?V/II.106.doc.3rev (1999) at para. 37.

179 *Salas v the United States*, Case 10.573, Inter-Am. C.H.R., Report No. 31/93, OEA/Ser/L/V.85, Doc 9 rev (1994), at para. 6. However the case has been pending since 1993 and has not yet been decided on its merits.

Some rights may be exclusively matters of International Humanitarian Law; others may be exclusively matters of human rights law; yet others may be matters of both these branches of international law.[180] Some examples of rights which may be exclusively matters of humanitarian law, for instance are those of prisoners of war. Rights which are typically matters of human rights law are such rights as freedom of expression or the right of assembly. Some rights which may be matters of both bodies of law are such rights as the right to life, rights of persons deprived of liberty and the prohibition against torture and other cruel, inhuman or degrading treatment or punishment.

In those situations where there is overlap between the two bodies of law, the principles that govern their relationship are the principles of *Complementarity* and *Lex Specialis*.

Meaning of 'Complementarity'

Complementarity means that human rights law and humanitarian law do not contradict each other but, being based on the same principles and values can influence and reinforce each other mutually. It conveys the idea that despite their distinguishing features, they are complementary and not mutually exclusive and affirms the possibility of the simultaneous application of both bodies of law. In this sense, complementarity reflects a method of interpretation enshrined in Article 31(3)(c) of the Vienna Convention on the Law of Treaties which allows, in interpreting a norm, to take into account 'relevant rule of international law applicable in the relation between the parties'. This principle in a sense enshrines the idea of international law understood as a coherent system.[181] It sees international law as a regime in which different sets of rules cohabit in harmony. Thus human rights can be interpreted in the light of International Humanitarian Law and *vice versa*.[182] Frequently however, the relationship between the two branches of law is described as a relationship between general and specialised law, in which humanitarian law is the *lex specialis*.[183]

Complementarity: mutual influence and reinforcement

In view of their common ideals of preserving human dignity and protecting persons from abuses of power by those in authority, whether they are state authorities in the case of human rights law or parties to a conflict in the case of humanitarian law, there is an area of considerable overlap between International Humanitarian Law and International Human Rights Law. There is therefore scope for mutual influence and reinforcement when they are both relevant to a situation.

How might mutual influence and reinforcement work in practice? There are several ways in which this might work. There is mutual influence in interpretation and also mutual influence in the development of law. Human rights law is broader in its scope of application. As it enshrines the more general rules it can often benefit from the more narrowly applicable,

---

180 Legal Consequences of the Construction of a Wall in the Occupied Palestinian Territory Advisory Opinion, 2004 I.C.J. (9 July), at para. 106.

181 McLachlan, Campbell (2005) The principle of systemic integration and Article 31(3)(c) of the Vienna Convention, *ICLQ*, 54, pp. 279–320; International Law Commission, Report of the Study Group on Fragmentation of International Law: Difficulties Arising from Diversification and Expansion of International Law, p. 27, UN Doc. A/CN.4/L.676 (29 July 2005); see also Sands, Philippe (1999) Treaty, custom and the cross-fertilization of international law, *Yale Hum. Rts. Dev. LJ.*, 1, pp. 85 and 95.

182 Droege, *op. cit.*, n 4, at p. 337.

183 *Ibid.*, at p. 337.

but often more precise rules of humanitarian law. On the other hand, human rights law has become increasingly specific and refined through a vast body of jurisprudence and the details of interpretation can influence the interpretation of humanitarian law, which has less interpretative jurisprudence at its disposal.[184]

One example where human rights law has had an influence on humanitarian law is Article 75(4) of Additional Protocol I, which was drafted on the basis of Article 14 of the ICCPR,[185] and whose interpretation can therefore draw on the right to fair trial in human rights law. Conversely, humanitarian law has provided a threshold for minimum rights below which no derogation of human rights can reach. Derogations by States must be consistent with the States' other obligations under international law,[186] which includes humanitarian law. To this extent, humanitarian law can provide minimum obligations. The right to a fair trial, for instance, is derogable under human rights law, but its core has been considered to be non-derogable, based on Article 75 of the Additional Protocol I.[187]

Another example where human rights law has had an influence in the interpretation of humanitarian law is in the definition of 'Torture' but the definition has been adapted to suit the specific requirements of humanitarian law. There is an absolute prohibition against torture both in human rights law[188] and in humanitarian law.[189] The only written international definition is found in Article I of the Convention against Torture and Other Cruel, Inhuman or Degrading Treatment or Punishment (CAT).[190] Applying Article 31(3)(c) of the Vienna Convention on the Law of Treaties to the norms of humanitarian law prohibiting torture allows interpretative recourse to the definition of torture set out in Article I CAT. There is, however an important difference with humanitarian law. Human rights law and humanitarian law traditionally bind different entities. In general, human rights law binds state authorities and humanitarian law binds 'parties to a conflict', i.e. both state and non-state actors. Human rights law, based on Article I of CAT, defines torture as an act committed 'by or at the instigation of or with the consent or acquiescence of a public official or other person acting in an official capacity'. Under International Humanitarian Law, torture can also be committed by armed opposition groups, so that the definition must be adapted to fit the humanitarian law rationale.[191]

A more recent example of the influence of humanitarian law on human rights is in the Convention for the Protection of All Persons from Enforced Disappearance.[192] Certain

---

184 *Ibid.*, at p. 341.

185 Sandoz *et al.*, *op. cit.*, n 74, at para. 3092.

186 Article 4 ICCPR; Article 15 ECHR, and Article 27 ACHR.

187 The Human Rights Committee has stated that it can take other branches of law into account to consider the lawfulness of derogations: Human Rights Committee, General Comment 29: States of Emergency (Article 4), p. 10, UN Doc. CCPR/C/21/Rev.1/Add. 11 (24 July 2001) at para. 16.

188 Article 7 ICCPR, Article 2 Convention Against Torture, 10 December 1984, 1465 UNTS 85, Article 3 ECHR, Article 5 ACHR, Article 5 of the African Charter on Human and People's Rights, adopted 27 June 1981, OAU Doc. CAB/LEG/67/3 rev. 5, 21 ILM 58 (1982), entered into force 21 October 1986 [hereinafter ACHPR].

189 Common Article 3, Article 147 of the Geneva Convention (IV) relative to the Protection of Civilian Persons in Time of War, Articles 40, 55 & 56, 12 August 1949, 75 UNTS 287.

190 Article 2(1), Convention Against Torture, 10 December 1984, 1465 UNTS 85 [CAT].

191 See ICTY *Prosecutor v Kunarac and Others*, Case Nos. IT-96-23 & IT-96-23/1, Trial Chamber (22 February 2001) at para. 491; confirmed by the Appeals chamber judgment, (12 June 2000) at para. 148; *Prosecutor v Kvocka and Others*, Case No. IT-98-30/1-A, Appeals Chamber (28 February 2005) at para. 284; ICTR: *The Prosecutor v Laurent Semanza*, ICTR -97-20 (15 May 2003) at para. 32–343; Rome Statute, at Articles 7(1)(f) (Crimes against Humanity) and 8(2)(c)(i) and (ii) (War Crime). See also Droege, *op. cit.*, n 4, at p. 342.

192 Adopted by General Assembly Resolution 61/177 (20 December 2006).

provisions that have been included in the Convention such as the right to know (Article 24(2)) and communication and information rights of families (Article 18) have been influenced by humanitarian law.[193] These provisions have also influenced the jurisprudence of human rights bodies with regard to enforced disappearances.

As outlined above, there are many instances in which human rights law and humanitarian law do not contradict each other, but rather regulate different aspects of a situation or regulate a situation in more or less detail, and can therefore mutually reinforce each other. In other words, for the protection of persons in the power of a party to a conflict, human rights law (within its application limits) can reinforce the applicable provisions of humanitarian law, especially where there is relevant law or jurisprudence to flesh out the obligations.[194] Conversely, humanitarian law can reinforce human rights law through the absolute nature of its obligations and its greater detail.[195]

Complementarity: limits on the areas of mutual influence between both norms

There are limits on the areas of mutual influence of both bodies of law. Human rights law and humanitarian law differ fundamentally in a number of procedural aspects: right to a remedy and individual standing, right to an investigation and the right to reparation.

All major human rights treaties have a form of individual complaint mechanism which has led to case-law on the right to a remedy and the right to an investigation and the right to reparation. Humanitarian law does not know such individual standing at international level.

The nature of International Humanitarian Law, which is not, or at least not exclusively, conceived around individual rights, makes it difficult to imagine that it could integrate all procedural rights that have developed in human rights law. However, increasing awareness of the application of human rights in armed conflict, and also an increasing call for transparency and accountability in military operations can influence the understanding of certain rights under International Humanitarian Law.[196]

In both human rights law and International Humanitarian Law, there are secondary obligations to protect the right to life. The most important are the obligations to investigate, prosecute, and punish violations of the right to life. In the case of re McKerr,[197] it was stated that the Convention right of a relative under Article 2 of the ECHR to insist on an inquiry being held where a death has been caused by agents of the State is procedural or adjectival. As noted above, International Human Rights Law and jurisprudence with regard to the obligation to investigate is far more advanced than in International Humanitarian Law.[198] In human rights law all serious human rights violations must be subject to a prompt, impartial, thorough and independent official investigation. The investigation must be independent from those who are implicated in the events giving rise to the alleged violations. In order to ensure public confidence in the investigation, there must be a sufficient element of public scrutiny of the investigation. The elements of human rights jurisprudence relating to

---

193 The right to know is enshrined in Article 32 of Additional Protocol I and communication and information rights of families are enshrined in the fourth Geneva Convention. These have both influenced similar rights in the Convention for the Protection of All Persons from Enforced Disappearances.

194 Droege, op. cit., n 4, at pp. 343–344.

195 Ibid., at pp. 343–344.

196 Ibid., at pp. 354–355.

197 [2004] 1 WLR 807.

a public hearing capable of scrutiny and the requirements for the effective participation of victims are all elements that are new to the situations of armed conflict.

It is clear that if such investigations are to be fair, and to command the confidence of the public, they must comply with the requirements of independence and impartiality. Independence means independence of the parties, including those in the chain of command. Military investigations have been shown to pose particular challenges as far as independence is concerned.[199] Also investigations in situations of armed conflict can only be conducted if practically possible under the prevailing security situation and will have to take into account the reality of armed conflict, but all this does not preclude an investigation as such.[200]

Human rights bodies have not hesitated to apply these requirements to investigations in situations of armed conflict.[201] There is scope for the influence of human rights and humanitarian law in this respect. However, this is not without some challenges or difficulties.

As far as remedies at international level are concerned, courts do not hesitate to pronounce themselves on the lawfulness of acts committed in armed conflict— whether in purely human rights terms or in humanitarian law terms depends on the jurisdiction.[202] However, this has sometimes led to inconsistency and some criticism[203] for instance that human rights bodies might not have the mandate or required expertise to deal with the armed conflict situations,[204] though from the points of view of victims of human rights violations, it is difficult to argue that in the absence of any independent international remedy specifically foreseen for International Humanitarian Law recourse to tribunals and other human rights bodies is not a valid path. Instead, as has been stated, 'the fact that an individual has a remedy under human rights law gives additional strength to the rules of International Humanitarian Law corresponding to the human rights norm alleged to be violated'.[205] In some cases the human rights jurisprudence can even provide greater protection for the victims or reinforce the protection by other mechanisms and institutions.[206] On the other hand, there may be times when humanitarian law affords higher protection than human rights. Some human rights are limited and have to be balanced against the rights of others and can (with few exceptions) always be limited for security reasons. Humanitarian law often

---

198 See the UN Principles on the Effective Prevention and Investigation of Extra-legal, Arbitrary and Summary Executions, recommended by Economic and Social Council resolution 1989/65 of 24 May 1989; Principles on the Effective Investigation and Documentation of Torture and Other Cruel, Inhuman or Degrading Treatment or Punishment; among the relevant body of jurisprudence see Human Rights Committee: Concluding Observations on Serbia and Montenegro, p. 9, UN Doc. CCPR/CO/81/SEMO (12 August 2004); *Finucane v the United Kingdom* [2003] VIII Eur. Ct. H.R. at para. 69 (summary of its constant jurisprudence).

199 Report of the Special Rapporteur on Extrajudicial, Summary or Arbitrary Executions, Sections 33–38, UN Doc. E/CN. 4/2006/53m (8 March 2006) at para. 37.

200 Watkin, Kenneth (2004) Controlling the use of force: a role for human rights norms in contemporary armed conflict, *Am. J. Int.* 98(1), p. 34.

201 *Isayeva, Yusupova and Bazayeva v Russia, op. cit.*, n 4, at paras 208–213; *Myrna Mack-Chang v Guatemala, op. cit.*, n 163; Human Rights Committee: Concluding Observations on Colombia, Section 32, UN Doc. CCPR/C/79/Add. 76 (5 May 1997).

202 See Droege, *op. cit.*, n 4, at p. 350.

203 See some of the criticisms raised in the ICRC report on *International Humanitarian Law and the Challenges of Contemporary Armed Conflicts*, 28th International Conference of the Red Cross and Red Crescent, ICRC, Geneva, 2003, pp. 59–60. See also Lubell, *op. cit.*, n 87, at p. 743.

204 Hampson and Salama, *op. cit.*, n 123.

205 Bothe, *op. cit.*, n 20, at p. 45, who writes that 'their very idealism and naiveté are their greatest strength'.

206 Abresch, *op. cit.*, n 21. See also the discussion in Michael Bothe, Humanitares Volkerrecht und Schutz der Menschenrechte: Auf der Suche nach Synergien und Schutzlucken, in *Essays in honour of C. Tomuschat*, 63 at p. 90.

does not allow for limitation of rights since security considerations are already taken into account. Also many very precise rules of the Geneva Conventions exceed the protection afforded by human rights.[207] The provisions on notification of detention and information of the family no later than a week after internment in the Fourth Geneva Convention,[208] for instance, are such precise rules that they are more protective than the general prohibition of arbitrary detention or the right to family life in human rights law. Another example is the right of families to know the fate of their missing relatives in Article 32 of Protocol I, a rule that is only now finding its way into a binding human rights treaty.[209]

In human rights, the individual has a right to an effective procedural remedy before an independent body, for all violations of civil and political rights, no such individual right exists in International Humanitarian Law.[210] Similarly while every violation of a human right entails a right of reparation,[211] the equivalent norms on reparation in the law of international armed conflict award this right, or at least the possibility to claim it, to the State.[212] The law on non-international armed conflict is silent on reparation.

Nothing in International Humanitarian Law, however, precludes the right to a remedy and to reparation.[213] Many serious violations of humanitarian law will also constitute serious violations of human rights at the same time. In recognition of this, there is an increasing tendency by States to recognise that they should afford full reparation for violations of humanitarian law as well.[214] In the advisory opinion on the *Wall*, the International Court of Justice held that Israel was under an obligation to make reparation for the damage caused to all natural or legal persons affected by the construction of the wall.[215] Also there is a practice of reparation mechanisms by some UN bodies such as the United Nations Claims Commission or the Eritrea–Ethiopia Claims Commission, in which individuals can file claims directly, participate to varying degrees in the claims review process and receive compensation directly.[216] There is also a wealth of practice in National Law[217] in relation to National Reparation Programmes. Article 75 of the Rome Statute of the International

---

207 See Droege, *op. cit.*, n 4, at p. 350.

208 Article 106 of the Geneva Convention (IV), relative to the Protection of Civilian Persons in Time of War, Articles 40, 55 & 56, 12 August 1949, 75 UNTS 287.

209 See Article 24(2) of the Convention for the Protection of All Persons from Enforced Disappearance, UN Doc. A/Res/61/177 (20 December 2006) [not yet in force].

210 Zegveld, Liesbeth (2003) Remedies for victims of violations of International Humanitarian Law, *Int. Rev. Red Cross*, 851, pp. 497–528.

211 See the UN Principles and Guidelines on the Right to a Remedy and Reparation for Victims of Gross Violations of Human Rights and Serious Violations of International Human Rights Law.

212 Convention (IV) respecting the Laws and Customs of War on Land and its annex: Regulations Concerning the Laws and Customs of War on Land, Article 43, 18 Octover 1907, USTS 539, Article 3; Protocol I Additional to the Geneva Conventions of 12 August 1949, Relating to the Protection of Victims of International Armed Conflicts, Articles 77(2) and 4(3)(d), 12 December 1977, 1125 UNTS 3, Article 91; see Gillard, Emanuela-Chiara, Reparation for violations of International Humanitarian Law, *Int. Rev. Red Cross*, 851, pp. 529–554.

213 Hampson and Salama, *op. cit.*, n 123, at paras 20, 49.

214 See the Principles and Guidelines on the Right to a Remedy and Reparation for Victims of Gross Violations of Human Rights and Serious Violations of International Human Rights Law, adopted by the General Assembly in 2005, GA Res. 60/147 of 16 December 2005.

215 Legal Consequences of the Construction of a Wall in the Occupied Palestinian Territory, Advisory Opinion, 2004 I.C.J. (9 July), at para. 106.

216 See Gillard, *op. cit.*, n 212, at p. 540.

217 On Germany see Bank, Roland (2001) The new programs for payments to victims of national socialist injustice, *German Y.B. Int. L.*, 44, pp. 307–352; the most comprehensive description of national reparations programmes can be found in the *Handbook on Reparations* (Pablo de Greif fed, 2006).

Criminal Court marks an important development in that it recognises the rights of victims of international crimes to reparation (but with a margin of discretion for the court).

In cases involving large-scale violations of humanitarian law, the main argument against the individual right to reparation is that violations can be so massive and widespread and the damage done so overwhelming that it defies the capacity of States, both financially and logistically speaking, to ensure adequate reparation to all victims.[218] Even though admitting individual claims to reparation for victims of violations of humanitarian law committed on a large scale does bring some real problems of implementation, there is still a need to secure justice for victims in such circumstances. It may be that such reparation will take the form of lump-sum type compensation measures or community-based reparation measures to reach the widest possible number of victims.[219] As Cordula Droege notes, while it is now clear that the simple statement that there is no individual right to reparation for violations of International Humanitarian Law is not adequate anymore in the light of evolving law and practice, there remain many uncertainties as to the way in which widespread reparations resulting from armed conflict can be adequately ensured.[220]

There is the danger that if human rights bodies completely disregard humanitarian law, especially where it is the *lex specialis* for a situation, or where they distort human rights by implicitly but not openly employing humanitarian law language, this could lead to a weakening of both bodies of law. As Cordula Droege suggests,[221] there is a need for clarity as to which law is being applied to a certain situation as it would be a preferable manner to protect victims of armed conflict in the long run.

5.2. The principle of *lex specialis*

The principle of *lex specialis* is an accepted principle of interpretation in international law. It stems from a Roman principle of interpretation, according to which in situations especially regulated by a rule, this rule would displace the more general rule (*lex specialis derogat leges generalis*).

This principle can be found in the writings of early writers such as Vattel[222] or Grotius.

Grotius writes:

> What rules ought to be observed in such cases, i.e. where parts of a document are in conflict? Among agreements which are equal ... that should be given preference which is most specific and approaches most nearly to the subject in hand, for special provisions are ordinarily more effective than those that are general.[223]

In its advisory opinions on the *Nuclear Weapon case* and on the *Wall case* reiterated in the *DRC v Uganda case*, the International Court of Justice used the principle of *lex specialis* to describe the relationship between the right to life in human rights and in International

218 See Schwager, Elke and Bank, Roland, An individual right to compensation for victims of armed conflicts?, Paper submitted to the ILA Committee on the Compensation for Victims of War, see pp. 45–48; d'Argent, P. (2006) Wrongs of the past, history of the future, Eur. J. Int., 17, pp. 279, 286.
219 Droege, op. cit., n 4, at p. 354.
220 Ibid., at p. 354.
221 Ibid., at pp. 350–351.
222 Vattel, Emerich De (1758) Le Droit Des Gens Ou Principes De La Loi Naturelle, Bk II, ch xvii, at para. 316 (reproduction of Books I and II ed 1758, Geneva, Slatkine Reprints, Henry Dunant Institute, 1983).
223 Grotius, Hugo, De Jure Belli AC Pacis, bk II, sect XXIX.

Humanitarian Law. In *Coard v the United States*, at para. 42, the Inter-American Commission followed the jurisprudence of the International Court of Justice.[224]

Neither the African Commission on Human and People's Rights nor the European Court of Human Rights have yet expressed a position on the matter. The Human Rights Committee has avoided the use of the *lex specialis* formulation and has instead found that 'both spheres of law are complementary, not mutually exclusive'.[225] The International Court of Justice itself did not repeat the passages on *lex specialis* in its judgment on *Congo v Uganda* which begs the question whether to maintain the *lex specialis* approach.[226]

A number of commentators have criticised the lack of clarity of the principle of *lex specialis*. Most importantly, it has been said that international law as opposed to national law, has no clear hierarchy of norms and no centralised legislator, but a 'variety of *fora* many of which are disconnected and independent from each other creating a system different from the more coherent domestic legal order',[227] that the principle of *lex specialis* was originally conceived for domestic law and is not readily applicable to the highly fragmented system of international law.[228] Secondly, critics note that nothing indicates which of the two norms is the *lex specialis* or the *lex generalis*, particularly between human rights law and humanitarian law.[229] It has been suggested that human rights law might well be the prevailing body of law for persons in the power of an authority.[230] Critics have proposed alternative models to the *lex specialis* approach that they have called a 'pragmatic theory of harmonisation',[231] 'cross-pollination',[232] or 'cross-fertilisation',[233] or a 'mixed model'.[234] These approaches have in common that they emphasise harmony between the two bodies of law rather than tension.[235] Lastly there appears to be a lack of consensus in legal literature about the meaning of the *lex specialis* principle.[236]

Lex specialis: *resolving conflicts between the norms*

Where human rights law and humanitarian law are incompatible or there is a genuine conflict of norms, one of the two norms must prevail.[237] In such situations, the *lex specialis*

---

224 *Coard v the United States*, Case 10.951, Inter-Am. Commission H.R. OEA/serL/V/II.106. doc.3rev (1999) at para. 42.

225 Human Rights Committee, General Comment No. 31 on Article 2 of the Covenant: The Nature of the General Legal Obligation Imposed on States Parties to the Covenant, p. 10, at para. 11 UN Doc. CCPR/C/74/CRP.4/Rev. 6 (2004) [hereinafter General Comment No 31] (emphasis added CD).

226 *DRC v Uganda* [2005] ICJ 116 (19 December) at para. 216.

227 Lindroos, A. (2005) Addressing the norm conflicts in a fragmented system: the doctrine of lex specialis, *Nordic J. Int. L.*, 74, pp. 24, 28.

228 See e.g. International Law Commission's Study Group, note 108; Lindroos, *op. cit.*, n 227, note 115 at 27–28.

229 Prud'homme, Nancie (2007) Lex specialis: oversimplifying a more complex and multifaceted relationship? *Isr. L. Rev.*, 40(2), p. 356.

230 Doswald-Beck, Louise (1997) International Humanitarian Law and the International Court of Justice on the legality of the threat or use of nuclear weapons, *Int. Rev. Red Cross*, 316, p. 35.

231 Prud'homme, *op. cit.*, n 229, at p. 14.

232 Provost, Rene (2005) *International Human Rights and Humanitarian Law*, p. 350.

233 Sands, *op. cit.*, n 181, at pp. 85–105.

234 Kretzmer, David (2005) Targeted killing of suspected terrorists: extra-judicial executions or legitimate means of defence? *Eur. J. Int.*, 16, pp. 171, 185 at p. 171.

235 Droege, *op. cit.*, n 4, at p. 340.

236 *Ibid.*, at p. 339.

principle, in its narrow sense, i.e. as a means to solve the conflict of the two norms, is very useful to provide answers.

One instance where a conflict arises between the two bodies of law is the right to life. In human rights law, lethal force can only be resorted to if there is an imminent danger of serious violence that can only be averted by such use of force. The danger cannot be merely hypothetical, it must be imminent.[238] On the other hand, humanitarian law accepts the use of lethal force and permits the incidental killing and wounding of civilians not directly participating in hostilities, subject to proportionality requirements. Under human rights law, the planning of an operation with the purpose of killing is never allowed. This is not to say that intentional killing is never allowed. It may be when it is strictly unavoidable to protect life.

Also, the principle of proportionality in humanitarian law is different from proportionality in human rights law.[239] While human rights law requires that the use of force be proportionate to the aim to protect life, humanitarian law requires that the incidental loss of civilian life, injury to civilians, damage to civilian objects, or a combination thereof caused by armed attack must not be excessive in relation to the *concrete and direct military advantage* anticipated.[240]

The two principles can lead to different results. One therefore has to decide whether in a situation of armed conflict, humanitarian law or human rights law applies, because certain killings that are justified under humanitarian law are not justified under human rights law. Even in armed conflict, a killing can be governed by human rights law if the situation is one of law enforcement. Where the difficulty lies is in deciding which body of law to apply. This issue can be a factual issue not a legal one. While the applicable principles of either humanitarian law or human rights law are clear, it can be a matter of dispute whether a situation was in fact one of law enforcement or conduct of hostilities. For instance in a situation of occupation, which by definition presupposes effective authority and control, most use of force will be a function of law enforcement. However, in practice it may be necessary to differentiate between situations of occupation: there may be in reality situations of occupation where the territory is not entirely under control.[241] This is the scenario mentioned in the *Al-Skeini case*.[242] While hostilities are ongoing or hostilities break out anew, humanitarian law on the conduct of hostilities must prevail over the application of human rights, which presuppose control for their respect and enforcement. The question is, of course, when hostilities can factually be said to have broken out again.

---

237 See International Law Commission, Report of the Study Group on Fragmentation of International Law: Difficulties Arising from Diversification and Expansion of International Law, p. 27, UN Doc. A/CN.4/ L.676 (29 July 2005).

238 See Articles 9 and 10 of the UN Basic Principles on the Use of Force and Firearms by Law Enforcement Officials, adopted by the Eighth United Nations Congress on the Prevention of Crime and the Treatment of Offenders, Havana, 27 August–7 September 1990, Report prepared by the Secretariat (United Nations publication, Sales No. E.91.IV.2), Ch. 1, sect. B.2, annex [hereinafter UN Basic Principles]; see also Rodley, Nigel (2000) *The Treatment of Prisoners Under International Law*, pp. 182–188; Kretzmer, *op. cit.*, n 234, at p. 179.

239 *Ibid.*

240 See the codification in Article 51 5(b) of Additional Protocol 1, to the Geneva Conventions of 12 August 1949, Relating to the Protection of Victims of International Armed Conflicts, Articles 77(2) and 4(3)(d), (12 December 1977), 1125 UNTS 3.

241 Droege, *op. cit.*, n 4. See also the discussion in Bothe, *op. cit.*, n 206.

242 *Al-Skeini v Secretary of State for Defence* [2005] EWCA (Civ) 1609, para. 48.

In a number of cases concerning the conduct of hostilities and the right to life, the European Court of Human Rights clearly relied on principles close to humanitarian law but outwardly only applying the European Convention on Human Rights in cases concerning non-international armed conflict. It held that the right to life would be violated in security operations involving the use of force if the State agents omitted 'to take all feasible precautions in the choice of means and methods of a security operation mounted against an opposing group with a view to avoiding and, in any event, to minimising incidental loss of civilian life'.[243]

In situations where both bodies of law are incompatible, the object and purpose of the bodies of law give some guidance as to which body of law should provide the prevailing rule, the *lex specialis*. Humanitarian law was specially conceived for the conduct of hostilities and for the protection of persons in the power of the enemy. Human rights law on the other hand was designed to protect persons in the power of the State from abuse and does not rest, in principle, on the idea of conduct of hostilities, but on law enforcement. It is thus fair to say that for the conduct of hostilities, humanitarian law is the more refined body of law[244] whereas for law enforcement human rights law is the more refined version.[245] There will clearly be instances of overlap. In such situations, the closer a situation is to the battlefield, the more humanitarian law will prevail over human rights law, whereas for law enforcement, human rights law prevails.[246] As a general rule, humanitarian law is the most appropriate for the conduct of hostilities, because its norms on the use of force are based on the assumption that military operations are ongoing and that the armed forces have no definite control over the situation.

Conversely, where the situation is remote from the battlefield and the State authorities have enough control over a situation to be able to carry out law enforcement operations, human rights law provides the most appropriate framework.[247]

Generally speaking for the protection of persons in the hands of the authorities, there is usually no contradiction between the norms subject to the differences outlined above, especially with regard to non-state actors. Where the use of force is at stake, the focus of the use of force on conduct of hostilities or law enforcement can give some guidance as to which body of law prevails. For the conduct of hostilities, humanitarian law will allow for the use of lethal force in a manner that human rights law will not, and will be the *lex specialis*.

6. Conclusion

Traditionally, International Human Rights Law and International Humanitarian Law were regarded as two distinct bodies of law. While IHRL was considered to be generally applicable during peace times, IHL was believed to be the only applicable law during times of conflict. It is now generally accepted that there are areas of significant overlap between

---

243 *Ozkan v Turkey* [2004] Eur. Ct. H.R. Judgment of 6 April 2004 at para. 297; *Ergi v Turkey* [1998] IV Eur. Ct. H.R. at para 79; *Isayeva v Russia* [2005] Eur. Ct. H.R. Judgement of 14 October 2005. The Court uses a similar, but not identical formulation, in *Isayeva, Yusupova and Bazayeva v Russia* [2005] Eur. Ct. H.R. Judgement of 24 February 2005 at paras 176–177.

244 See Meron, Theodor (2000) The humanization of humanitarian law, *Am. J. Int.*, 94, p. 239 at p. 241.

245 See Droege, *op. cit*, n 4, p. 344.

246 *Ibid.*

247 *Ibid.*, at p. 347.

both. International Human Rights Law not only applies during peace times but it can also apply in situations of occupation or non-international armed conflict.

The concurrent application of these two bodies of law has been expressly recognised by various international tribunals, including the International Court of Justice, the UN Human Rights Committee, the European Court of Human Rights, the Inter-American Commission on Human Rights, and numerous national courts.[248]

It is also now clearly established that human rights law has extraterritorial effect but international jurisprudence has yet to produce a clearly defined criteria for when the extra-territorial effect will be triggered or clear parameters for determining the scope of such human rights obligations for a State when it acts outside its own territory. In order to ascertain whether human rights law is applicable in the context of transnational conflicts with non-state groups, it is essential to consider the extent to which the State has exercised 'effective control' over a territory or power over a person. The State's negative human rights obligations will be triggered in relation to the State's conduct and the individual affected by that conduct, while the positive human rights obligations will be based upon the degree of control exercised by the State and subject to a standard of reasonableness.

The law of armed conflict was designed to apply primarily in an inter-state context and the vast majority of its provisions clearly apply to its extraterritorial conduct, specifi-cally in the territory of the opposing state. There is, however, now growing acceptance of the application of the Common Article 3 in the context of a transnational armed conflict. This is a branch of humanitarian law which has developed to regulate non-international (i.e. non-inter-state) armed conflict: the Law of Non-international Armed Conflict. Article 3 of the 1949 Geneva Convention applies to 'armed conflicts not of an international character occurring in the territory of one of the High Contracting Parties'. It applies in non-international armed conflict, and protects only against the most serious abuses. The implications of its application, however, remain unclear.

Even though it is now accepted that International Humanitarian Law and International Human Rights Law cannot be compartmentalised, there are however challenges[249] in the way these two bodies of law interact with each other.

A useful framework for the interplay of both norms is the *Complementarity* and *Lex Specialis* principle. *Complementarity* gives rise to mutual influence and reinforcement while *Lex Specialis* is a useful tool for resolving conflicts between both norms. Human rights law has more advanced procedural safeguards for the protection of individual rights than humanitarian law, particularly in relation to the right to an individual remedy, the right to an independent and impartial investigation and to individual reparation. While these procedural rights are not entirely transferable to humanitarian law due to the nature of each body of law, increasing awareness of the application of human rights in armed conflict and increasing transparency and accountability in military operations can in future, have an influence on the understanding of certain rights under International Humanitarian Law.[250]

The fact that an individual has a remedy under human rights law gives additional strength to the rules of International Humanitarian Law corresponding to the human rights norm alleged to be violated.[251] In some cases human rights jurisprudence can even provide

248 See *Humanitarian Law, Human Rights and Refugee Law—Three Pillars*, available at: www.icrc.org/web/siteeng0.nsf/html/6T7G86 (last accessed 28 April 2008).

249 See Challenges in applying human rights to armed conflict, *International Review of the Red Cross*, 87(860), December 2005, p. 741.

250 See Droege, *op. cit.*, n 4, at p. 355.

greater protection for the victims or reinforce the protection by other mechanisms and institutions.[252]

Also, the ICRC continues to play a key role in ensuring respect for the humanitarian rules.

In conclusion, the question of whether, and if so, which of these two bodies of law applies to conduct outside a State's territory, goes to the purpose of the creation of the norms and the values underlying such norms.[253] As both norms share the common humanist ideals of the protection of health, life and dignity of the individual, and as both strive to protect individuals from abuses of state power, this will lead to application coextensive with the projection of that power. As has been suggested, while the exact contours of such application may not yet be settled, the traditional principles of good faith and reasonableness in the circumstances provide ample guidance for shaping those contours.[254]

251 Bothe, *op. cit.*, n 20.
252 Abresch, *op. cit.*, n 21. See also Bothe, *op. cit.*, n 20, at p. 90.
253 See Cerone, *op. cit.*, n 15, pp. 72–128, available at: http://lsr.nellco.org/nesl/neslfwps/papers/2.
254 *Ibid.*

Promoting International Humanitarian Law: The Work of the Commonwealth Secretariat

MELISSA KHEMANI[a] & JOSHUA BRIEN[b]

[a]LLM Candidate, International Legal Studies and Human Rights, Georgetown University Law Center, Washington, DC; [b]Economic and Legal Section, Special Advisory Services Division, Commonwealth Secretariat

International humanitarian law has been recognised by Commonwealth Heads of Government as a matter of continuing critical importance and has accordingly been the focus of work by the Commonwealth Secretariat. This article outlines the work carried out by the Commonwealth Secretariat in relation to such issues as countering the proliferation of small arms and light weapons, and the use of anti-personnel mines, and promoting the implementation of the Rome Statute of the International Criminal Court, including through the formulation of Model Laws. Possible future work for the Secretariat, including in the area of International Disaster Relief Laws, is also explored.

Background

The importance of the adoption and implementation of accepted rules and principles of international humanitarian law ('IHL') in Commonwealth member countries has been identified by Commonwealth Heads of Government as a matter of continuing and critical importance, and has accordingly been the focus of work by the Commonwealth Secretariat pursuant to the outcomes of meetings of Commonwealth Heads of Government and Law Ministers. In this regard, the emphasis of much of the work carried out to date to promote the effective implementation of IHL in Commonwealth member countries has focused on issues such as the proliferation of small arms and light weapons, the use of anti-personnel mines, cluster munitions and the protection of civilians, particularly children, in armed conflict, as well as the importance of Commonwealth member countries acceding to the Rome Statute of the International Criminal Court.

In this regard, the commitment of the Commonwealth to implementation of IHL in Commonwealth member countries was reaffirmed at the most recent Commonwealth Heads of Government Meeting (CHOGM) held in Kampala, Uganda in November 2007.

The terms of the Final 2007 CHOGM Communiqué reflect the general support by Commonwealth member countries for complete disarmament, the UN Firearms Protocol and, the 2001 UN Programme of Action to Prevent, Combat and Eradicate the Illicit Trade in Small Arms and Light Weapons in All Its Aspects. In addition, Heads of Government have expressed their support for the Ottawa Convention on the Prohibition of the Use, Stockpiling, Production and Transfer of Anti-Personnel Mines and on their Destruction, and took note of the ongoing discussions towards a comprehensive Arms Trade Treaty.

Importantly, Commonwealth Heads of Government have also recognised the nexus that exists between the proliferation of small arms and light weapons and the exacerbation of conflicts, the growth of international terrorism, increased drug trafficking, armed violence and other criminal activities throughout the world, and have reaffirmed their shared concern at the threat that this activity poses to national, regional and global peace and security.

Small Arms and Light Weapons and the Arms Trade Treaty

The proliferation of small arms and light weapons ('SALW') has particular significance for the Commonwealth of Nations as a number of its member countries have been affected by internal conflicts. The indiscriminate use of such weapons by non-State actors and organised gangs has led to the displacement and targeting of civilians and has had tragic consequences for children, many of whom have suffered not only as victims of armed conflict but, in certain instances, have been forced to become child soldiers.

The issue of SALW has been on the agenda of the Commonwealth Secretariat for a number of years. Commonwealth Law Ministers considered a paper presented by the Commonwealth Secretariat on the proliferation of SALW at their Meeting in Accra, Ghana in 2005.[1] The Paper highlighted the tragic impact and consequences of the proliferation of SALW, which are subject to fewer controls than larger conventional weapons. Law Ministers acknowledged that the proliferation of SALW threatens the security and stability of States and exacerbates problems in regions affected by internal conflicts.

In addition, Commonwealth Law Ministers noted that there had been little positive action in the Commonwealth to deal with this problem, and directed the Commonwealth Secretariat to engage in the following activities:

1. prepare a comprehensive summary of all the obligations undertaken by Common-wealth member countries;

2. draft model legislative provisions concerning the marking, tracing and brokering of SALW;

3. capacity building to ensure implementation; and

4. work closely with the International Committee of the Red Cross ('ICRC') to encourage IHL considerations in draft regulations on the transfer of SALW.

The first of these initiatives was commenced by the Criminal Law Section of the Commonwealth Secretariat's Legal and Constitutional Affairs Division, with the view to providing a basis for developing a comprehensive approach to SALW issues, including the convening of regional meetings and working groups, and ultimately helping to develop model licensing criteria for arms transfers and brokering, and guidelines for the application of such licensing criteria for application in Commonwealth member countries.

At their most recent meeting in July 2008, Commonwealth Law Ministers requested the Commonwealth Secretariat to continue providing assistance to member countries in relation to the implementation of the United Nations Programme of Action on SALW ('UN POA') and to the ongoing negotiations concerning the development of an Arms Trade Treaty.

---

1   Report on the Proliferation of Small Arms and Light Weapons within the Commonwealth (2005).

However, the international response to the proliferation of SALW to date has been largely piecemeal and fragmented. There are a number of international, regional and sub-regional initiatives aimed at addressing the problem, including the UN POA, which contains measures to be implemented at the national, regional and global levels, which include:

1. putting in place adequate national laws, regulations and administrative procedures to exercise control over the production, export, import, transfer and re-transfer of SALW and regulating dealers and brokers of SALW and the marking of firearms;

2. creating criminal offences under domestic law relating to the illegal manufacture, possession, stockpiling and trade of SALW and for violations of United Nations Security Council arms embargoes;

3. encouraging regional measures such as trans-border customs co-operation; and

4. ensuring effective implementation of Security Council arms embargoes, ratification of the relevant international conventions and post-conflict measures.

On 6 December 2006, the UN General Assembly adopted Resolution 61/89: 'Towards an arms trade treaty: establishing common international standards for the import, export and transfer of conventional arms' ('UNGA Res. A/Res/61/89 of 6 December 2006'), which was sponsored by the United Kingdom and received the support of 27 Commonwealth member countries.

The Resolution requests the UN Secretary-General to:

1. seek the views of Member States on the feasibility, scope and draft parameters for a comprehensive, legally binding instrument establishing common international standards for the import, export and transfer of conventional arms, and to submit a report on the subject to the General Assembly at its sixty-second session;

2. establish a group of governmental experts, on the basis of equitable geographical distribution, to examine, commencing in 2008, the feasibility, scope and draft parameters for a comprehensive, legally binding instrument establishing common international standards for the import, export and transfer of conventional arms, and to transmit the report of the group of experts to the Assembly for consideration at its sixty-third session; and

3. provide the group of governmental experts with any assistance and services that may be required for the discharge of its tasks.

In response to the direction of Commonwealth Law Ministers to provide assistance on the implementation of the UN POA and the ongoing Arms Trade Treaty negotiations, the Criminal Law Section proposed a two-tiered approach for consideration by Commonwealth member countries during the Meeting of Senior Officials of Commonwealth Law Ministries in October 2007.

The proposed approach provided as follows:

1. overall support to the UN initiative for a global legally binding instrument on the trade in conventional arms in pursuance of UN GA Res A/Res/61/89 of 6 December 2006; and

2. a Commonwealth initiative aimed at dealing with particular issues of concern for Commonwealth Member States.

The Criminal Law Section suggested this approach as it is unclear at this stage whether the proposed Arms Trade Treaty will result in a comprehensive treaty or a framework agreement (which would likely be narrower both in scope and effect). Furthermore, the scope of the proposed Arms Trade Treaty is unlikely to be confined solely to SALW and will likely take many years to conclude having regard to political issues, the interests of arms customers, suppliers and manufacturers, and the need for the establishment of an effective but not overly burdensome monitoring mechanism and the potential for linking technical assistance and development aid with enforcement.

With this in mind, the Criminal Law Section proposed that Commonwealth member countries consider the drafting of a Commonwealth instrument specifically addressing SALW, focusing on the following issues:[2]

- the eradication of illicit brokering and dealing of SALW;
- marking and tracing of SALW;
- transfer controls; end user certificates;
- controlling the flow and availability of weapons from post-conflict zones;
- control of ammunition and SALW already in existence (measures may include seizure and destruction, including the use of SALW as instrumentalities in the commission of a crime, amnesty and in appropriate instances registration);
- addressing the prevalence of and ease of access to SALW in parts of non-governable areas of States or regions;
- preventing the flow of SALW to non-State actors; and
- the link of SALW to corruption; one of the key responses to countering the illicit spread of SALW is the introduction and strengthening of anti-corruption measures.

This proposal secured little support from Member States during the Meeting of Senior Officials of Commonwealth Law Ministries 2007. It does, however, continue to provide a viable option for further consideration in the Commonwealth.

Implementation of the Rome Statute of the International Criminal Court

Underlying the work of the International Criminal Court is a clear understanding of IHL. Since the establishment of the International Criminal Court ('ICC') in 2002, Commonwealth Heads of Government have repeatedly urged Commonwealth member countries that have not yet acceded to the Rome Statute to do so in a timely manner.

In July 2004, a Commonwealth Expert Working Group was convened at Marlborough House to consider the issues surrounding the development of implementing legislation for the Rome Statute of the International Criminal Court. The Expert Working Group set out drafting instructions that could be used by legislative drafters in developing domestic legislation, and subsequently drafted a Model Law to Implement the Rome Statute of the ICC that was made available to Member States.

The ICC is now engaged in substantive work, and has launched formal investigations into four areas: Darfur, the Democratic Republic of Congo, the Central African Republic and Uganda. It has therefore become important that effective domestic implementing

---

2   The list is indicative rather than exhaustive.

legislation be enacted by Commonwealth member countries to support effective co-operation with the ICC.

In carrying out work to promote accession to the Rome Statute, the Criminal Law Section has however encountered a general lack of understanding of the Rome Statute and the ICC amongst policy- and decision-makers, prosecutors, judges, and the general public which could, if not properly addressed, hinder the adoption of effective implementing legislation.

In pursuance of the CHOGM mandate, the work of the Criminal Law Section is directed towards the adoption of appropriate legislation and enhancing knowledge to promote the effective implementation of that legislation.

In December 2006, in response to a request from the Government of Sierra Leone, the Commonwealth Secretariat together with partner organisations, arranged a National Stakeholders Consultative Seminar on the Domestic Implementation of the International Criminal Court and the Rome Statute in Freetown, Sierra Leone. Draft national implement-ing legislation was submitted to Parliament for consideration and enactment, which included provisions on ICC crimes, principles of liability and responsibility, arrest and surrender, privileges and immunities, offences against the administration of justice and requests for assistance.

To avoid duplication of resources in this area, the Commonwealth Secretariat works closely with other organisations, namely the International Criminal Court, International Committee for the Red Cross ('ICRC'), British Red Cross, and national governments.

Possible Future Work: International Disaster Relief Law

An area of possible future work for the Commonwealth Secretariat concerns collaboration with the International Federation of Red Cross and Red Crescent Societies in ongoing work to promote the establishment and promotion of a more coherent system of international rules and principles to support international disaster relief operations. While International Disaster Relief Law ('IDRL') is a distinct legal regime from IHL in that it is limited to non-armed conflict related disasters, the two regimes share a common bond by virtue that they both seek to regulate humanitarian assistance to certain categories of victims and protect basic rights.

The International Federation of Red Cross and Red Crescent Societies commenced a programme in 2001 entitled the *International Disaster Response Laws, Rules and Principles ('IDRL') Program,* as part of the Federation's mission to reduce human vulnerability by promoting legal preparedness for disasters. The aim of the programme is to explore the role of law in the response to disasters, with an emphasis on the impact on international disaster relief. The establishment of the IDRL Program followed the completion of a study undertaken by the Federation, which found that the existing body of national and interna-tional rules, principles and standards concerning disaster relief is incomplete, disparate and poorly understood, and that significant improvements would be required in order to establish a framework that would support effective disaster relief efforts at the national and international level.

On 30 November 2007, the 30th International Conference of the Red Cross and Red Crescent unanimously adopted Guidelines for the domestic facilitation and regulation of international disaster relief and initial recovery assistance (the 'IDRL Guidelines'). The IDRL Guidelines are designed to assist governments to address the range of legal problems that may arise in connection with international response operations, and to enable governments to take legal, policy and institutional measures to improve coordination and avoid unnecessary delays in the delivery of humanitarian and disaster relief.

The importance of the IDRL Guidelines and ongoing work under the IDRL Program has received considerable international recognition and attention in view of the important practical impact it may have upon disaster relief operations. An opportunity exists for the Commonwealth Secretariat to collaborate with the Federation to promote the IDRL Guidelines through legal training, assistance and the delivery of special advisory services, in order to improve national legal frameworks that impact upon disaster preparedness throughout the Commonwealth. In this regard, it may be noted that an Information Paper concerning the IDRL Program and possible collaboration in the promotion of the IDRL Guidelines was presented and discussed at the most recent Commonwealth Law Ministers Meeting held in July 2008.

Implementation of International Humanitarian Law within the Commonwealth

LEONARD BLAZEBY

Common Law Legal Adviser, International Committee of the Red Cross

Commonwealth States have a reasonable record in their accession to international humanitarian law (IHL) treaties, however, ratification is only the first step. In order for countries to be able to fulfil the obligations that flow from IHL treaties, they must put in place the required national legal, regulatory and administrative measures, including the prohibition of certain acts and penalties for offenders. This article examines various of the IHL treaties, the obligations on States that they create, and the efforts undertaken by Commonwealth States to incorporate these instruments into national law. It also outlines the support available for States to ensure that IHL rules are fully respected.

International humanitarian law (IHL) is a set of detailed rules that seek to limit the effects of armed conflict. In particular, it protects those who are not, or are no longer, taking part in the fighting, and sets limits on the means and methods able to be used in warfare. A number of international treaties have been developed that aim to protect people and certain property in armed conflict and restrict or prohibit the use of certain weaponry. There are also general IHL principles or practices, which States accept as legal obligations, often referred to as customary international law.

There are some 28 treaties that form the core of IHL and within the States of the Commonwealth there is somewhat of a disparity in the level of ratification of the different instruments. Some treaties are well represented, such as the universally ratified Geneva Conventions of 1949 (53), and the Chemical Weapons Convention,[1] which has also been ratified by almost all Commonwealth Member States (52), however some treaties, such as the Conventional Weapons Convention[2] (19) and the Hague Cultural Property Convention[3] (18) have many fewer States Parties from within the Commonwealth. In order for the rules of IHL to be truly effective, it is important that States consider becoming parties by ratification or accession to these instruments that make up the body of IHL. Ratification of these treaties, however, is only the first step.

Most of these IHL treaties create implementation obligations, which require States to undertake certain actions of compliance. As an example, the States that are parties to the 1949 Geneva Conventions are required firstly to respect and ensure respect for the Conventions in all circumstances.[4] They are further obliged to undertake to enact any legislation necessary to provide effective penal sanctions for persons committing or ordering to

---

1   1993 Convention on the Prohibition of the Development, Production, Stockpiling and Use of Chemical Weapons and on their Destruction.
2   1980 Convention on Prohibitions or Restrictions on the use of Certain Conventional Weapons which may be deemed to be Excessively Injurious or to have Indiscriminate Effects.
3   1954 Hague Convention for the Protection of Cultural Property in the event of Armed Conflict.
4   Geneva Conventions on the Protection of War Victims of 12 August 1949, Article 1.

be committed, any of the grave breaches of the Conventions, as well as to search for such persons and bring them before their courts or extradite them.[5] All of the States of the Commonwealth, then, indeed of the world, given the truly universal nature of the Geneva Conventions, are expected to undertake the necessary actions to execute these requirements. The fulfilment of these obligations entails the creation of legal, regulatory and administrative measures to ensure that the rules are fully respected.

In addition to the treaty obligations to prevent and punish violations of IHL treaties, there is also an obligation to ensure compliance with rules of customary international law.[6] Even though with respect to customary international law there is no actual requirement to enact penal legislation or to punish offenders, legislation is probably the best method of complying with the obligations that arise under the customary rules in situations of both international and non-international armed conflict.[7]

The Commonwealth shares a commonality in many areas, one of which is a common legal system, built on what is known as the 'common law', a system developed through decisions of courts and tribunals, rather than through legislative statutes or executive action. The way that the Commonwealth's members deal with the implementation of IHL is therefore often similar and, generally, States have adopted separate, instrument-specific, Acts to give effect to the different IHL treaties, as the treaties are not normally directly applicable in the domestic law of States Parties.

The most fundamental of the IHL treaties requiring adoption into domestic legislation are the Geneva Conventions and their Additional Protocols.[8] The provision, as mentioned above, relating to the obligation to adopt domestic law for the Geneva Conventions, is echoed in Additional Protocol I,[9] which demands that States shall 'take all measures for the execution of their obligations under the Conventions and this Protocol'. The provisions dealing with grave breaches of these instruments, set out in the Conventions and Protocol I,[10] refer to a number of acts which are prohibited and are required to be repressed and punished on the basis of universal jurisdiction, regardless of where the act takes place or the nationality of the offender. Additional Protocol I also requires the repression of those grave breaches that 'result from a failure to act when under a duty to do so'.[11] The term 'grave breaches' refers to serious contraventions of the Geneva Conventions and Additional Protocol I occurring in international armed conflicts.

As well as the grave breaches, States have a duty to suppress all other acts that are contrary to the Conventions.[12] States should therefore fulfil this obligation by also providing for the punishment of contraventions, which are not listed as grave breaches. The term 'grave breach' does not exist in the instruments dealing with armed conflicts of a non-international character, common Article 3 to the Geneva Conventions or in Additional Protocol II, however, it is accepted that individual criminal responsibility attaches to these

---

5   Geneva Convention for the Amelioration of the Condition of the Wounded and Sick in Armed Forces in the field of 12 August 1949, Article 49.
6   See Henckaerts, Jean-Marie and Doswald-Beck, Louise (2005) *Customary International Humanitarian Law* (Cambridge: Cambridge University Press), Vol. 1, Rule 158, p. 607.
7   *Ibid.*
8   Geneva Conventions I–IV 49/50/129/146, Additional Protocol I 85 (1).
9   Protocol Additional to the Geneva Conventions of 12 August 1949 and relating to the Protection of Victims of International Armed Conflicts (Protocol I) of 8 June 1977.
10   Articles 50/51/130/147 common to the four Conventions; Articles 11 (4) and 85 of Protocol I.
11   Additional Protocol I, Article 86 (1).
12   Geneva Conventions I–IV 49/50/129/146, Additional Protocol I 85 (1).

violations, as illustrated in particular in the Rome Statute for an International Criminal Court (ICC).[13]

The ICC Statute specifically states that a person who commits a crime within the jurisdiction of the Court shall be individually criminally responsible and liable for punishment in accordance with the Statute.[14] It also contains offences of war crimes in Article 8 (c) and (e) that occur in non-international armed conflicts, using the term 'serious violations'. The fact that individual criminal responsibility exists for these violations, and that they have been articulated as war crimes in the ICC Statute, lends strong support to the need to incorporate serious violations other than grave breaches as crimes in domestic law. Some common law countries for example, Fiji, Mauritius and Nigeria, have incorporated non-grave breaches of the Conventions and Protocols into their Geneva Conventions Acts, and Australia has catered for them in its Criminal Code.[15] A provision for the prosecution of non-grave breaches is provided in a model Geneva Conventions Act produced by the International Committee of the Red Cross (ICRC).

According to information available to the ICRC,[16] to date 32 Commonwealth States[17] have implemented the Geneva Conventions into domestic law, a number of them through succession on independence to the UK Geneva Conventions Act 1957 and its application to overseas territories through the UK Geneva Conventions Act (Colonial Territories) Order in Council, 1959. Only a few Commonwealth States have, however, incorporated the Additional Protocols, or provided for violations other than grave breaches.[18] In comparison to the Geneva Conventions only 12 Commonwealth States have either amended their law or put in place new implementing legislation to incorporate the Additional Protocols of 1977. The importance of the need to undertake this task can be seen in the fact that there is a requirement to incorporate the grave breaches which are set out in Additional Protocol I,[19] and further, the annex to Protocol I outlines the signs and signals that need to be protected in domestic law, either in a Geneva Conventions Act, or sometimes in National Society legislation, that deal with protection of the emblems. States who have ratified the Additional Protocols should revisit their pre-existing Geneva Conventions Acts to update them.

Besides the punishment of violations, States are required to provide for the judicial guarantees that are mentioned in the Geneva Conventions and their Protocols, such as the service of notice of the trial of the accused, the accused's representation by counsel, an appeal's provision, and a reduction of sentence for time served.[20] A Geneva Conventions Act should also include provisions relating to the misuse of the red cross and other emblems, signs, signals, identity cards, insignia and uniforms, as the Geneva Conventions[21] strictly regulate the use of the emblems and States need to repress and punish any

---

13 Rome Statute of the International Criminal Court, 17 July 1998.
14 Rome Statute, Article 25 (2).
15 International Criminal Court (Consequential Amendments) Act 2002, no. 42 of 2002.
16 Information on the individual country legislation is based on ICRC archival information and individual country legislation websites.
17 Antigua and Barbuda, Australia, Bahamas, Barbados, Belize, Botswana, Canada, Cyprus, Dominica, Fiji, India, Jamaica, Kenya, Lesotho, Malawi, Malaysia, Nigeria, New Zealand, Papua New Guinea, Seychelles, Singapore, St. Kitts and Nevis, St. Lucia, St. Vincent and the Grenadines, Solomon Islands, Sri Lanka, Trinidad and Tobago, Tuvalu, Uganda, the United Kingdom, Vanuatu and Zambia.
18 Fiji, Mauritius and Nigeria.
19 Articles 11 (2) and 85 (2), (3) and (4).
20 Geneva Convention III, Articles 99–108.
21 GC I, Articles 38–44; GC II, Articles 41–44; and AP I, Article 38.

misuse.[22] This section of a domestic Geneva Conventions Act usually deals with the use of the emblem by those entities entitled to do so and provides a penalty for misuse of the emblem. It is worth noting that the crime of perfidy is, within itself, a war crime.

The implementation in Commonwealth States varies. Mauritius,[23] for example, has amended its earlier Geneva Conventions Acts to incorporate the grave and non-grave breaches and to cover the signs and signals referred to in Additional Protocol I, and Namibia[24] passed its Geneva Conventions Act in 2003, covering the Geneva Conventions and 1977 Additional Protocols and providing punishment for the grave breaches and protecting the signs and signals. Australia on the other hand amended its Criminal Code Act 1995[25] to cater for violations, as a result of implementing the Statute of the International Criminal Court, but has dealt with the Additional Protocol I emblem provisions in its Geneva Conventions Act.[26]

The ICRC has developed a model law for the implementation of the Geneva Conventions and all three Protocols to assist States in their implementation efforts. The model has clauses on the creation of crimes and penalties, judicial guarantees and on the protection of the emblems.

In 2005 the international community adopted a third protocol to the Geneva Conventions dealing with the protection of a new distinctive emblem. The Third Additional Protocol to the Geneva Conventions also requires States to adopt provisions in their law to protect this emblem explicitly and to prevent violations of the Protocol, the instrument itself compelling States to 'take measures necessary for the prevention and repression, at all times, of any misuse of the distinctive emblems mentioned in Articles 1 and 2 and their designations, including the perfidious use'.[27]

Few Commonwealth countries have ratified the third Additional Protocol to the Geneva Conventions,[28] and, though all of those that have ratified have implemented the Protocol into domestic law, it has been undertaken in different ways. Canada for example has amended its Canada Red Cross Society Act, but Fiji on the other hand has amended its Geneva Conventions Act to cater for the protection of the Third Protocol emblem. The ICRC model law for the Geneva Conventions includes the requirements for implementing Additional Protocol III.

Another international instrument whose subject matter includes the repression of war crimes is the Rome Statute of the International Criminal Court, which was adopted in 1998.[29] This Statute creates requirements for States Parties to allow for cooperation with the International Criminal Court. Interestingly, the Statute does not explicitly require States to put in place domestic law to incorporate the core crimes under the Statute, crimes against humanity, genocide and war crimes, however, it is important when implementing the ICC Statute that States consider implementing these core crimes into domestic law, as the intention of the ICC statute is to end impunity and this can be done most effectively by having a mechanism to prosecute domestically. The Statute is also based on the principle of complementarity, that national prosecution has primacy and that the

---

22   GC I, Article 54; GC II, Article 45.
23   Geneva Conventions Act 1970, Geneva Conventions (Amendment) Act 2003.
24   Geneva Conventions Act 2003, no. 3109.
25   International Criminal Court (Consequential Amendments) Act 2002, no. 42 of 2002.
26   Geneva Conventions Act 1957 as amended, Article 15.
27   Article 6 (1).
28   Belize, Canada, Cyprus, Fiji and Singapore.
29   Rome Statute of the International Criminal Court, 17 July 1998.

ICC will only prosecute if a State is not willing or able to prosecute. The absence of national law on the core crimes would be seen as an inability to prosecute.[30] As the Court focuses on the prosecution of the most serious crimes and most serious offenders, it may also be the case that some violators may escape prosecution as a result.

Currently, nine Commonwealth countries have implementing law for the ICC Statute.[31] All of these States have included the incorporation of the crimes into their domestic law. Most have undertaken this task in the simplest way, that is, to make reference to the crimes in the Statute as set out in Articles 6–8 and to annex the Statute. Some States have also not limited themselves to the crimes as reflected in the Statute and have added other crimes, such as violations of the Geneva Conventions and Protocol I, which do not appear in the Statute. Some States have even incorporated the Statute's elements of crime.[32] The ICC Statute also details a number of defences that are available to the accused.[33] In the common law these are often already incorporated without the need for further legislation but it is necessary to make sure that all of these defences are reflected in domestic legislation.

It is also vital that the concepts of superior orders[34] and command responsibility[35] are catered for in domestic law and that there is no Head of State immunity from prosecution. Another aspect to be taken into account is the temporal jurisdiction for prosecution and whether to make it prospective or retrospective. There is an argument for retrospective jurisdiction on the basis of Article 15 (2) of the International Covenant on Civil and Political Rights, which allows for the trial and punishment of someone for committing an act 'which, at the time when it was committed, was criminal according to the general principles of law recognized by the community of nations'.[36] The core crimes can be seen as falling under the category of crimes outlined in Article 15 (2) and as a result retrospective jurisdiction for these crimes would be permissible.[37] It is also important to determine whether to provide for prosecution by means of universal jurisdiction, to provide for universal jurisdiction with a link with the territory of the State, or to have jurisdiction based on nationality and territoriality. There are examples of these various types of jurisdiction in the domestic law enacted by Commonwealth States.[38] There is a strong argument for providing universal jurisdiction for the crimes of the ICC in domestic law on the basis that war crimes require universal jurisdiction, flowing from the Geneva Conventions, and it would therefore be contradictory for there to be a more restricted jurisdiction for the same crimes when they are to be prosecuted under the ICC Statute.

A domestic ICC law also requires States to be able to prosecute the administration of justice offences, which are found in Article 70 of the Statute. Usually, each sub-paragraph of Article 70 is reflected in the domestic Act.[39] States must also provide for cooperation with

---

30 Rome Statute of the International Criminal Court, Article 17.
31 Australia, Canada, Cyprus, Malta, New Zealand, Samoa, South Africa, Trinidad and Tobago, and the United Kingdom.
32 See Australia, Criminal Code Act 1995.
33 Article 31.
34 See Article 28 of the ICC Statute.
35 Ibid.
36 International Covenant on Civil and Political Rights, adopted and opened for signature, ratification and accession by General Assembly Resolution 2200A (XXI) of 16 December 1966.
37 See Report of the Commonwealth Expert Group on Implementing Legislation for the Rome Statute of the International Criminal Court, Marlborough House, London, 7–9 July 2004.
38 For example Australia, Canada, Cyprus and New Zealand, universal jurisdiction; Malta and the United Kingdom, nationality and territoriality; South Africa, link to territory but including passive personality.
39 See Samoa International Criminal Court Act 2007, Act no. 26 of 2007.

the Court and this involves sections covering a range of issues such as requests for assistance from the Court, arrest and surrender of persons to the ICC, assistance in the taking of evidence and the protection of witnesses and victims, and the enforcement of sentences and orders of the ICC in the State. There is also need to provide for the sitting of the ICC in the territory of the State and the legal status, privileges and immunities of ICC officials. The incorporation of the cooperation requirements is common to most Commonwealth domestic Acts. The Commonwealth Secretariat has produced a model for the implementation of the International Criminal Court Statute.

Outside the IHL instruments that deal with the issue of repression of crimes, obligations arise for States from their adherence to other IHL treaties. The 1954 Hague Cultural Property Convention[40] and its two Protocols[41] from 1954 and 1999, respectively, deal with the protection of cultural property in the event of armed conflict. The second Additional Protocol has an explicit obligation for States to take necessary legislative measures to establish its jurisdiction over serious violations set out in Article 15 of the Protocol, which demands that the jurisdiction over the crimes should be on the basis of territoriality and nationality.[42]

A number of States of the civil law tradition have implemented into domestic law the 1954 Convention and Protocols, however in the common law this has been a late development and no country currently has an Act, though the UK and New Zealand have draft bills, which, at the time of writing are before their respective parliaments.

A number of treaties relating to the prohibition or restriction of various weapons also require States to undertake implementing measures to enable them to fulfil their obligations under these treaties. The 1972 Biological Weapons Convention[43] (BWC), for example, requires States to prohibit the production, acquisition, development, stockpiling and transfer of biological weapons and the destruction of such weapons and systems of delivery.[44] The Convention aims at a complete ban of these weapons and obliges States to take, in accordance with its constitutional processes, any necessary measures, to prohibit and prevent the acts specified under Article 1 of the Convention, in terms of territorial and nationality jurisdiction.[45] The Convention should be read along with the 1925 Gas Protocol,[46] which prohibits the use of asphyxiating and poisonous gases and bactreiological methods of warfare.

Relatively few Commonwealth States[47] have implementing legislation for this treaty, but those which have implemented it have in the main employed a similar style. These national laws deal with the prohibition of the acts detailed in Article 1 of the Convention, as well as the prohibition on use, which stems from the 1925 Protocol, with regard to microbial or biological agents or toxins and their means of delivery, reinforced by penal sanctions. The criminal offences created include the commission of acts by State agents. A

---

40 1954 Convention on the Protection of Cultural Property in the Event of Armed Conflict.
41 1954 Protocol to the Convention for the Protection of Cultural Property in the Event of Armed Conflict; 1999 Second Protocol to the Hague Convention of 1954 for the Protection of Cultural Property in the Event of Armed Conflict.
42 *Ibid.*, Article 16 (1).
43 1972 Convention on the Prohibition of the Development, Production and Stockpiling of Bacteriological (Biological) and Toxin Weapons and on their Destruction.
44 *Ibid.*, Article 1.
45 *Ibid.*, Article IV.
46 1925 Protocol for the Prohibition of the Use in War of Asphyxiating, Poisonous or Other Gases, and of Bacteriological Methods of Warfare.
47 Australia, Mauritius, New Zealand, Singapore, St. Kitts and Nevis, and the United Kingdom.

number of States have also set up a licensing scheme to prevent unauthorised dealings in these microbial and biological agents and toxins and provide for measures of domestic enforcement through an inspection regime. An information collection system is also provided for, which enables States to obtain information for reporting internally, to other States or to the Committee that has been established under United Nations Security Council Resolution 1540[48] that requires States to adopt legislation with regard to non-State actors in relation to biological, chemical and nuclear weapons. There is also a model law, produced by the ICRC and the Verification Research, Training and Information Centre (VERTIC), which provides guidance for the domestic measures required under the Biological Weapons Convention.

Another instrument dealing with related weaponry is the 1993 Chemical Weapons Convention.[49] This Convention benefitted from the developments in international treaties since the adoption of the BWC and is stronger in many respects including the legal implementation provisions. The Convention requires States to adopt necessary measures to implement its obligations under the Convention including the enactment of penal legislation, using more robust language than that of the BWC.[50] The Organisation for the Prohibition of Chemical Weapons (OPCW) has developed guidelines for States to implement the Convention. This is probably one of the most technical instruments to implement as the Convention itself is quite technical and there are annexes that deal with several of the chemical compounds. The Convention aims to prevent the possibility to use chemical weapons by requiring States to undertake not to, under any circumstances, use, develop, produce, stockpile, retain or transfer chemical weapons while still promoting the chemical industry for peaceful purposes. Riot control agents used as a method of warfare are also prohibited.

To fully implement the Chemical Weapons Convention, States must also undertake to destroy chemical weapons and their production facilities, enacting law to prohibit certain activity and provide penalties for violations, as well as giving effect to cooperation and legal assistance requirements, particularly in the prevention and suppression of prohibited activities. States must designate or establish a national authority to ensure effective liaison with the OPCW and other States Parties, provide for the transfer of information needed to prepare national declarations of chemical facilities, and for the facilitation of inspections by the OPCW. States, such as Australia,[51] have also incorporated a permit system for the operation of chemical facilities. Within the Commonwealth, this Convention has been implemented by a relatively high number of States (13),[52] with most not only providing for penal sanctions but also for the supply of information to the State inspection regimes.

A Convention that has received little attention in terms of legal implementation within the Commonwealth is the Conventional Weapons Convention (CCW),[53] which has been ratified by 19 States, none of which have comprehensive implementing legislation. This Convention aims to prohibit the use of some conventional weapons and restrict the use of others. A framework Convention provides the scope of application and deals with technical issues and the various weapons form the basis of a series of protocols. Although only Article

---

48 UN Doc. S/RES/1540 (28 April 2004).
49 1993 Convention on the Prohibition of the Development, Production, Stockpiling and Use of Chemical Weapons and on their Destruction.
50 Ibid., Article 7 (1).
51 Chemical Weapons (Prohibition) Act 1994, Act no. 26 of 1994 as amended.
52 Compare with the implementation rate within the Commonwealth of other IHL treaties.
53 1980 Convention on Prohibitions or Restrictions on the Use of Certain Conventional Weapons which may be Deemed to be Excessively Injurious or to have Indiscriminate Effects.

14 of amended Protocol II on Prohibitions or Restrictions on the Use of Mines Booby Traps and Other Devices[54] expressly demands that States 'take all appropriate steps, including legislative and other measures, to prevent and suppress violations' of the Protocol and this by persons or on territory under its jurisdiction or control, there is an argument for States to go further than this and implement the Convention and its Protocols in their entirety.

Amended Protocol II necessitates, for example, that States prohibit the use of mines booby-traps and other devices that cause superfluous injury and unnecessary suffering and restrict the use of mines in areas containing a concentration of civilians and that are used in an indiscriminate manner. Such measures are superfluous with regard to anti-personnel mines if the State is a party to the Anti-personnel Mine Ban Convention,[55] however there is still the requirement to legislate for such restrictions with regard to mines other than anti-personnel mines. Implementation of the Protocol also entails restricting the use of booby traps, forbidding their attachment to or association with articles such as children's toys, animals or sick, wounded or dead people. States need to create penalties for breaches of these prohibitions or restrictions. If a State is going to enact implementing legislation to address these subjects, it is not too great a leap to incorporate the prohibitions of blinding laser weapons[56] and undetectable fragments[57] and the restriction on incendiary weapons[58] as set out in the Protocols. The ICRC has recently developed a model law to enable States to implement the CCW.

The Anti-personnel Landmine Ban Convention goes further than the Conventional Weapons Convention and, similar to the Chemical and Biological Weapons Conventions, aims at creating a complete ban of these weapons. The Convention requires States to prohibit the use, development, acquisition, stockpiling, retention and transfer of anti-personnel mines and to provide penalties for violations. It also necessitates the destruction of anti-personnel mines that have been stockpiled within a four-year period and that are emplaced, within a ten-year period. Some States have explicitly provided for these require-ments by empowering the relevant Minister to ensure that this action is undertaken.

Article 9 of the Convention requires States Parties to 'take all appropriate legal, admin-istrative and other measures, including the imposition of penal sanctions, to prevent and suppress any activity prohibited to a State Party under this Convention undertaken by persons or on territory under its jurisdiction or control'. It is clear from the negotiating history that Article 9 does not require extra-territorial jurisdiction for prohibited acts; it is also clear, however, that the use of the term 'appropriate' in 'all appropriate legal, adminis-trative and other measures' leaves States Parties a wide margin of discretion when drafting implementing legislation, and in practice many States Parties have provided for extra-territorial jurisdiction in their domestic implementing legislation. Given the likely cross-border or extra-territorial nature of crimes committed in breach of this Convention, it may be appropriate to provide for extra territorial jurisdiction in domestic Acts.

States then are expected to prohibit the acts under Article I of the Convention and to provide appropriate penalties. There needs, however, to also be exemptions to the prohi-bitions in keeping with the Convention's allowance for retention of mines for purposes of

---

54 Protocol on Prohibitions or Restrictions on the Use of Mines Booby Traps and Other Devices as Amended on 3 May 1996.
55 1997 Convention on the Prohibition of the Use, Stockpiling, Production and Transfer of Anti-personnel Mines and on their Destruction.
56 Protocol on Laser Blinding Weapons (Protocol IV).
57 Protocol on Non-Detectable Fragments (Protocol I).
58 Protocol on the Prohibitions or Restrictions on the Use of Incendiary Weapons (Protocol III).

training in mine detection, mine clearance, or mine destruction techniques but also for possession with regard to the conduct of criminal proceedings, rendering an anti-personnel mine harmless or for future destruction. In countries where anti-personnel mines still pose a problem, provision needs to be made for the marking, monitoring and protection of mined areas. The facilitation of a visit by a fact-finding mission in compliance with Article 8 of the Convention must be provided for, and a number of Commonwealth States have also empowered the appropriate Minister to gather information to conform with the State's reporting requirements under Articles 7 and 8 of the Convention.[59]

Within the Commonwealth, 12 States have implemented the Anti-personnel Mine Ban treaty. Most have done so in a similar way, providing for the prohibition of the acts referred to in Article 1 of the Convention, though some States have added the word 'possession' to the list of prohibitions. This is mainly to facilitate prosecution, as possession is a word common to the criminal law. Some States have also, in their interpretations section, gone further than the definition of 'anti-personnel mine' in the Convention by adding the words 'intended or altered' to the definition to encompass mines that have not only been designed to be exploded by the presence, proximity or contact of a person but that are also intended or altered to do so, widening the scope of mines caught by the definition. Other States have used the phrase 'performs in a manner consistent' with regard to mines, also broadening the scope. Probably the most complete definition is to be found in the Zambian law, which also refers explicitly to trip wires and sensitive fuses.[60] Most States have provided for destruction of mines, visits by a fact-finding mission and information gathering powers in conformity with the Convention. Once again the ICRC has developed a model law to assist States with the implementation of the Anti-personnel Mine Ban Convention.

The list of international IHL instruments requiring implementing measures continues to grow. In May 2008 in Dublin, States adopted the Convention on Cluster Munitions, a further treaty that will require States to enact implementing law.

Commonwealth States have a reasonably good record in the ratification of IHL, however, recent years have shown that the legislation needed to implement the obligations arising under these Conventions is often missing. While not all of the 28 principal treaties relating to IHL require implementation, most do. As shown, this is all the more true in common law States, where treaties are not normally directly applicable in the domestic law of States Parties. The nature of many of the obligations which flow from the treaties requires independent implementation under domestic legislation to give effect to these obligations.

The International Committee of the Red Cross created its Advisory Service on IHL in 1996 with the intention of having a specific body to advise governments on the national measures needed to fulfill their obligations under IHL. The Service's ongoing tasks are to promote the ratification of IHL treaties, to promote national implementation of those treaties and to promote the creation of national committees on IHL within the governments of States to assist in these tasks of ratification and implementation.

It is hoped that efforts to adopt new model legislation for IHL treaties, together with more direct work with States, and the holding of regional and Commonwealth meetings such as the August 2007 Second Commonwealth Red Cross and Red Crescent Conference on IHL in Wellington, New Zealand will help improve domestic implementation by helping make States aware of the technical assistance available to support their consideration of

---

59 Article 7 refers to transparency measures and Article 8 to facilitation and clarification of compliance.
60 Prohibition of Anti-personnel Mines Act 2003, no. 16 of 2003, Article 2.

existing legislation and their adoption of appropriate and effective laws to fulfil their obligations under IHL treaties.

National Red Cross and Red Crescent Societies: Humanitarian Partner of Choice for Commonwealth States

MICHAEL MEYER

Head of International Law, British Red Cross

The International Red Cross and Red Crescent Movement consists of three components, each with its own specific legal status and role. National Societies have a unique position as auxiliaries to the public authorities of their respective countries in the humanitarian field. The Commonwealth and the Movement share common values and concerns. More could be done, both nationally and within the Commonwealth, to strengthen links and co-operation. Commonwealth Governments may find it to their benefit to make greater use of their National Societies.

The Red Cross and Red Crescent—both the organisation and the emblems—are well known throughout most of the world, including in the Commonwealth. What is less well known and understood is the structure of the organisation or, more properly, Movement; the significance and protected status of the emblems used by its components, and the legal position of its different components, in particular, the status and role of National Red Cross and National Red Crescent Societies as auxiliaries to the public authorities of their respective countries in the humanitarian field. This short article will seek to explain these matters, with reference to Commonwealth States. It is hoped to show why the National Society should be considered the humanitarian partner of choice of Commonwealth Governments, deserving of support nationally, regionally and internationally, including within the Commonwealth.

The International Red Cross and Red Crescent Movement

The International Red Cross and Red Crescent Movement consists of three components: the recognised National Red Cross and Red Crescent Societies (presently 186), found in most Commonwealth countries,[1] the International Committee of the Red Cross (ICRC) and the International Federation of Red Cross and Red Crescent Societies (Federation).

---

1   For differing reasons, four Commonwealth States do not yet have recognised National Societies: Cyprus, Maldives, Nauru and Tuvalu. National Societies must fulfil strict conditions in order to achieve recognition by the International Committee of the Red Cross (ICRC) and obtain admission to membership of the International Federation of Red Cross and Red Crescent Societies (Federation). The ten conditions for recognition by the ICRC are set out in Article 4 of the Statutes of the International Red Cross and Red Crescent Movement 1986; the requirements for admission to membership of the Federation are contained in Article 7 of the Constitution of the Federation and Rule 2 of the Federation's Rules of Procedure, both dated 2007. One looks forward to the day when all Commonwealth States have a recognised National Society.

The Movement itself is neither a legal nor an operational entity. It is a group of independent institutions, respecting common Fundamental Principles,[2] which work together to carry out a common humanitarian mission. The Movement may be described as an almost world-wide network of humanitarian organisations, thus, being at the same time both global and local.

Although not a legal entity, the Movement has Statutes, which define the three components and their Movement-level statutory bodies: the International Conference of the Red Cross and Red Crescent (in which the States Parties to the 1949 Geneva Conventions[3]—which include all Commonwealth States—are equal members); the Council of Delegates (a biennial meeting of all components of the Movement); and the Standing Commission (a body composed of representatives of the components which acts as a trustee between the normally quadrennial International Conferences).

The Statutes also define the relationship between the States Parties to the Geneva Conventions (in effect, all countries of the world) and Red Cross and Red Crescent organisations, and the conditions for recognition as a National Society.

The Statutes, adopted by States and Movement components in 1986, are not legally binding, but they do have some binding force for both States and the Movement, depending on the context, particularly for components of the Movement. The Statutes are not articles of association, but rather, may be likened to rules for co-operation between independent institutions.

The ICRC and the International Federation

The two international institutions of the Movement, the ICRC and the International Federation of Red Cross and Red Crescent Societies (Federation), both have headquarters in Geneva, Switzerland.

The International Committee is the successor to the body which initiated both the founding of the Movement in 1863, and the adoption of the original Geneva Convention for the Amelioration of the Condition of the Wounded in Armies in the Field in 1864. Its governing Assembly continues to be composed of Swiss citizens,[4] although many of its staff have different nationalities. It is a private organisation, being an association governed by the Swiss Civil Code, Article 60 et seq. At the same time, the ICRC has functional international legal personality, by virtue of the mandate and roles it has been given by States under the most recent Geneva Conventions of 1949 and their Additional Protocols of 1977.

The ICRC has a special connection with the Geneva Conventions and with international humanitarian law (also called the law of armed conflict or the laws of war) generally, of which the Conventions are an integral part. This involves promotion and development of the law, as well as the provision of protection and assistance to persons affected by situations of armed conflict (with the permission of the relevant authorities, the ICRC also

---

2   The seven Fundamental Principles of the Movement are Humanity, Impartiality, Neutrality, Independence, Voluntary Service, Unity and Universality, each defined in a particular way (for the texts, see the Preamble to the Statutes of the Movement 1986).
3   The four Geneva Conventions for the Protection of War Victims of 12 August 1949. Their texts may be found in 75 UNTS (1950) 31–417 and on the ICRC website: www.icrc.org.
4   Statutes of the ICRC 2003, Articles 7 and 9(2); also see the Movement's Statutes, Article 5(1). The ICRC's website has both texts.

carries out such humanitarian activities in other situations, including internal violence). It directs and co-ordinates Movement relief operations during these circumstances.

The International Federation is the membership body of the recognised National Societies. Founded at the end of World War I in 1919, the Federation's governing organs, its secretariat in Geneva and its staff world-wide are multi-national (the current Secretary-General, Mr. Bekele Gelata, is a Canadian citizen). Like the ICRC, it is a private organisation, governed by the same provisions of the Swiss Civil Code. The Federation has a measure of recognition as an international organisation, as evidenced in part by having concluded status agreements with some 54 States (including Commonwealth Members, e.g. Sri Lanka) in countries in which it operates, as well as a headquarters agreement with Switzerland.

The Federation has long experience in the provision of disaster relief in peacetime situations, such as earthquakes, floods, famines and epidemics. It co-ordinates and directs the Movement's international relief actions in response to such non-conflict disasters. In recent years, it has led work to develop international disaster response laws, rules and principles (IDRL). The Federation also assists National Societies in their development and in their peacetime activities, and serves as the official representative of National Societies at the international level.[5]

Both the ICRC and the Federation have observer status at the United Nations General Assembly. The Federation was granted this largely in recognition of the status and role of National Societies as humanitarian auxiliaries to their respective Governments.[6] This special position and function of National Red Cross and Red Crescent Societies is explained below.

The National Societies

National Red Cross and Red Crescent Societies have a special legal status and role. One of the conditions for recognition is that a National Society must be recognised by the legal government of its country as a voluntary aid society, auxiliary to the public authorities in the humanitarian field. This means that, although it is a private organisation, a National Society has public functions; in Commonwealth countries, it is usually established by legislation referred to as a Red Cross or Red Crescent Act (or Law of Recognition).[7] This Law, in addition to recognising the Society as an auxiliary to the public authorities, frequently recognises it as the sole Red Cross or Red Crescent Society in the country (another requirement for official recognition), and authorises it to use the red cross or red crescent designation (name) and emblem. The Act usually establishes the National Society as 'a body corporate' and sets out its objects (purposes) and powers. It may also refer to its governing bodies, although often there is a separate Constitution (or Statutes) dealing with issues of governance and management. The effect is that the National Society is neither

5   For detail on the Federation's functions, please see the Federation's Constitution 2007, Article 5 (the text can be found on the Federation's website, www.ifrc.org); also see the Movement's Statutes, Article 6(4).
6   UNGA Resolution 49/2 dated 27 October 1994, preambular paragraph 1.
7   Examples are the Brunei Red Crescent Society (Incorporation Act) 1983, Ghana Red Cross Society Act 1958, Jamaica Red Cross Society Act 1964, Kenya Red Cross Society Act 1965, Malta Red Cross Society Act 1992, Singapore Red Cross Society (Incorporation) Act 1973, South African Red Cross Society and Legal Protection of Certain Emblems Act 2007, and the Tonga Red Cross Society Act 1972.

a non-governmental organisation (NGO) nor a part of the State machinery; it has a unique position and function between the two.

The auxiliary relationship between a National Society and its Government has been recognised by the international community as 'a specific and distinctive partnership, entailing mutual responsibilities and benefits, based on international and national laws'.[8] In this partnership, the national public authorities and the National Society agree on the areas in which the Society supplements or substitutes for public humanitarian services. These services depend on the needs of the population in each country. They can and do range from supporting people living with HIV/AIDS to sanitation to first aid to disaster preparedness. In many countries, the National Society's auxiliary activity includes work with its authorities, and on its own initiative, in disseminating and implementing international humanitarian law. Like the ICRC, the 1949 Geneva Conventions give National Societies certain roles in providing assistance to the victims of armed conflict.

An increasing number of National Societies are also becoming involved in IDRL, for example, working with their Governments to help ensure that their legal and administrative arrangements for receiving international disaster assistance reflect guidelines to ensure rapid and effective facilitation of such assistance.[9]

As auxiliaries, National Societies have a duty to give serious consideration to an appropriate request from their respective Governments for their humanitarian services. At the same time, Societies have a duty to decline a request which would put them in contravention of Movement rules, in particular, the Fundamental Principles, such as humanity, impartiality or neutrality, and States have agreed to respect such decisions of the National Societies.

To succeed, the auxiliary relationship must be based on co-operation, mutual support, respect and trust. The Government should be able to view the National Society as a reliable partner, knowing that it can depend upon it to respect certain principles and rules, and that it is the Society's observance of these principles and rules that give it access to those who are most vulnerable.

Moreover, the fact that, if necessary, the National Society can call upon the international network of the Movement to help provide appropriate support is another special and important benefit of having a Society. The fact that such external aid can be delivered through a known local, national organisation can be a particular advantage, i.e. rather than being or being perceived as being entirely foreign.

Red Cross, Red Crescent and Red Crystal Emblems

The original role of National Societies was to provide support to the medical service of their country's army, and many National Societies retain at least a formal commitment in this respect. By virtue of this specific auxiliary function, National Societies adopted the same

---

8   30th International Conference of the Red Cross and Red Crescent (Geneva 2007), Resolution 2: 'The specific nature of the International Red Cross and Red Crescent Movement in action and partnerships and the role of National Societies as auxiliaries to the public authorities in the humanitarian field', operative paragraph 3. A number of the statements which follow are based on this significant resolution; most Commonwealth States participated in its adoption by consensus.

9   These guidelines are annexed to Resolution 4: 'Adoption of the Guidelines for the Domestic Facilitation and Regulation of International Disaster Relief and Initial Recovery Assistance', 30th International Conference of the Red Cross and Red Crescent (Geneva 2007).

emblem as used by their States' military medical service, and this practice—that the National Society uses the emblem of its country's military medical service (or the equivalent)—continues to this day. Over time, regulation of the emblem used by the medical services of armed forces has developed, and it is now the State that controls the emblem and the related designation, e.g. Red Cross or Red Crescent. Most Commonwealth Member States have legislation relating to the emblem. In a number of these, the matter is included in the Geneva Conventions Act which gives effect to certain obligations contained in those treaties and, where applicable, their Additional Protocols, in domestic law.[10] Other Commonwealth countries protect the emblem under trademark or other legislation or include the matter in the Red Cross or Red Crescent Act referred to above.[11] States Parties to the Geneva Conventions have an obligation to control use of the emblem and designation and prevent and repress unauthorised use. This normally requires specific legislation and, when required, prosecution of abuses. As part of the privilege to use a protective emblem and designation, National Societies have a recognised role and responsibility to work with the relevant authorities of their country to uphold the integrity of these special symbols and words.

The red cross and red crescent emblems and designations are intended to signify neutrality and protection. Where they are perceived differently, e.g. as representing a particular religion or other grouping, a new protective device, the red crystal, may be used instead. It too is a treaty-based emblem and designation, being prescribed in 2005 Additional Protocol III to the 1949 Geneva Conventions, and the red crystal emblem and name will also require protection under national law, in the same way as the red cross and red crescent.

The Commonwealth and the Movement: Shared Values and Humanitarian Concerns

The Commonwealth and the Red Cross and Red Crescent Movement share a number of features. Both are committed to dignity, humanity and the rule of law and to acting in a spirit of co-operation and mutual support. Both are locally based but globally effective, working to provide technical and other practical assistance to develop the capacity of Common-wealth Governments and peoples in areas of humanitarian concern. (It is appreciated that the Commonwealth is involved in other fields as well.)

National Societies represent a reliable partner to national and local public authorities, providing service through their diverse volunteer base and their unique capacity to mobilise human and material resources at the community level. The special status and role of National Societies as humanitarian auxiliaries to the public authorities, together with their commit-ment to neutrality and impartial assistance, provide the best available means to gain the confi-dence of all in order to have access to those in need. The co-operation and permanent

---

10 Examples are Australia, India, Kiribati, Malaysia, New Zealand, Nigeria, Papua New Guinea, the Seychelles, Singapore, the United Kingdom, Vanuatu and Zimbabwe.

11 As illustrations, Canada protects the emblem under its Trade Marks Act 1952 (as amended) and Uganda does so through its Penal Code (Exclusive Use of the Red Cross and Red Crescent Emblems) Order 1993. The National Society Acts in, for example, Antigua and Barbuda, Botswana, Brunei Darussalam, Saint Kitts and Nevis, Tonga and Zambia also regulate use of the emblem. It should be noted that the mere existence of emblem legislation does not ensure the fulfilment of a State's obligations, some legis-lation being out-dated or inadequate in other respects. Advice can be obtained from the ICRC's Advi-sory Service on International Humanitarian Law: advisoryservice.gva@icrc.org.

dialogue of National Societies with their respective Governments includes the key role and responsibilities of Societies in the fields of promotion, dissemination and implementation of international humanitarian law (IHL). National Societies also work with their public authorities in the evolving area of international disaster response laws, rules and principles (IDRL).

At the international level, Commonwealth States and National Societies have already begun to develop their Commonwealth link in the fields of IHL and IDRL. Commonwealth Red Cross and Red Crescent Conferences on IHL were held in 2003 (London) and 2007 (Wellington), and it is hoped that a third will be held in 2011 (perhaps in the Caribbean region). A meeting of representatives of Commonwealth National IHL Committees was held in 2005 (Nairobi), and it is hoped that another will be held in 2009 (perhaps in New Delhi). The communiqués of Commonwealth Law Ministers Meetings and of Meetings of Senior Law Officials have made reference to these events and encouraged their follow-up by Member States.[12] The common legal heritage of Commonwealth States, and their shared language, provide a strong basis on which to exchange experience and expertise, and to encourage the adoption of effective national laws and good practice.

Commonwealth States, like all other States, have a commitment to establish and to develop their National Society.[13] Where this does not already happen, more should be done by Commonwealth States to negotiate clearly defined roles and responsibilities with their respective National Societies in risk reduction and disaster management activities, as well as in public health, development, social care and other areas of humanitarian concern according to the specific needs of their country. Commonwealth States should take advantage of the availability of their National Red Cross or Red Crescent Society, seeing them as their partner of choice in meeting their obligations under IHL and, more generally, in providing humanitarian assistance to vulnerable persons on their respective territories. The primary purpose of National Societies as auxiliaries to the public authorities in the humanitarian field is to co-operate with their Governments in the fulfilment of these vital responsibilities.

---

12 The most recent example is the Communiqué of the Commonwealth Law Ministers Meeting held in Edinburgh in July 2008 (numbered paragraph 50(a)).

13 Statutes of the Movement, Article 2(2); United Nations General Assembly Resolution 55 (I) of 19 November 1946, and later resolutions of International Conferences of the Red Cross and Red Crescent.

The International Humanitarian Fact-Finding Commission

CHARLES GARRAWAY
Commissioner, International Humanitarian Fact-Finding Commission

The International Humanitarian Fact-Finding Commission was established in 1977 by Article 90 of Additional Protocol I to the Geneva Conventions of 1949. Unfortunately, it has never been used. This article looks at the Commission, its history and whether it is still relevant in the modern world.

Introduction

'In war, truth is the first casualty.' This well-known saying is as old as the laws of war themselves, being ascribed first to the Greek dramatist Aeschylus. In every conflict, the air has been thick with claim and counter-claim. Who can resolve such issues? The Geneva Conventions of 1949 recognized this difficulty and provided for enquiries to be established 'in a manner to be decided between the interested Parties'. If there was no agreement, an 'umpire' was to be chosen. It was hardly surprising that these provisions were never invoked.

In 1977, two Additional Protocols were drafted to supplement the 1949 Conventions. The First Protocol that dealt with international armed conflict, conflict between States, contained an innovative proposal. It established an independent Commission, now called the International Humanitarian Fact-Finding Commission, which could act as a further option to the enquiries envisaged under the Conventions themselves. In fact, it took some time for the Commission to come formally into existence as the Protocol requires that States not merely ratify the Protocol itself but also submit a specific declaration to sign up to the Commission. It needed 20 such declarations before it could come into existence and that only occurred in 1991.

The purpose of this short article is to outline what the Commission is and what it can do.

What is the International Humanitarian Fact-Finding Commission?

The International Humanitarian Fact-Finding Commission consists of 15 'members of high moral standing and acknowledged impartiality'. States that have signed up to the Commission may each nominate one candidate and elections are then carried out. The Commissioners are elected for a five-year period but they are free to stand again for further terms. The last elections were in December 2006.

Although there are 168 State Parties to Additional Protocol I, only 70 of them have made the declaration to accept the competence of the Commission. Figure 1 shows the geographic spread and it will be noticed that there are many notable absentees and some areas of the world that are under-represented—not least Africa and Asia. Despite this, the Commissioners are designed to reflect the geographic diversity of the Parties and come from all parts of the world, reflecting many different disciplines. There are lawyers, doctors, military experts and others. Only about ten Commonwealth countries appear amongst those States that have recognized the competence of the Commission though there are two Commonwealth Commissioners, myself and Professor Ian Refalo of Malta. Previous Commissioners have included New Zealand's Sir Kenneth Keith, now a Judge at the International Court of Justice.

What is the Commission supposed to do? The answer lies in Article 90 itself. It can investigate grave breaches and other serious violations and can offer its good offices. Between States who have made the Article 90 Declaration, there is a right to inquire but in any other case, it is only by consent. As a matter of practicality, consent would be required in any event as the Commission, like the International Criminal Court, has no enforcement arm. The Commission has promulgated rules, financial regulations and operational guidelines in order to enable it to achieve its mandate.

But what does the Commission actually do? The answer, regrettably, is not very much. In the 16 years that the Commission has been established, it has never been called into action. This is unfortunate for a number of reasons. In the early days, little was known of the Commission but, especially under the current President, Professor Michael Bothe of Germany, a series of promotional activities have been undertaken to raise consciousness amongst States. In the view of the Commission, particularly in the modern world, it has an important role to play and is anxious to fulfil that role.

Does the Commission's inactivity mean that there have been no investigations at all? On the contrary, 'Fact-Finding' has taken off in a big way over the last 15 or so years, starting of course with the Balkans. In recent times, there has been a spate of enquiries. For example, Darfur has had a veritable avalanche of groups looking into alleged breaches of

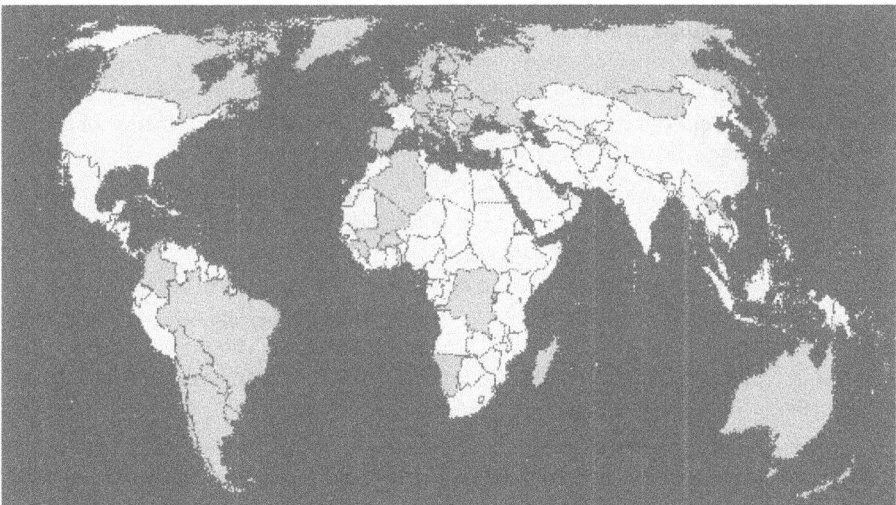

Figure 1.   Countries that have accepted the competence of the Commission (in dark grey).

international humanitarian law and human rights law, with differing results. There has been the Cassese mission, that led to the referral of the Darfur situation to the International Criminal Court, the various initiatives by the Human Rights Commission and Council, missions by numerous NGOs and of course the ongoing assessments carried on confidentially by the ICRC. These have contributed to the public awareness of the situation but there has been comparatively little change on the ground with allegation and counter-allegation. The Government of Sudan has challenged the impartiality of some reports, even by international bodies.

There was a similar situation with the conflict in Lebanon in 2006. The Human Rights Council despatched a mission though its mandate was criticized by some as being 'partial'. The Government of Israel refused to co-operate and thus the mission could only obtain evidence from one side. The United Nations Environment Programme looked at pollution but not specifically at international humanitarian law issues. Amnesty International and Human Rights Watch also conducted enquiries but again suffered from a lack of Israeli co-operation. This can be a serious drawback when seeking to examine targeting issues where it is necessary to balance the 'anticipated' collateral damage against the 'anticipated' military advantage. Results on the ground only present half the picture. The difficulty is that targeting decisions are often based on intelligence reports and States are understandably reluctant to release such reports to outside agencies. Where human intelligence is concerned, such an action could put at risk valuable sources.

Despite the lack of official activity, members of the Commission have been involved in their private capacity in other enquiries. Two of our Commissioners have been involved in separate enquiries in Lebanon and occasionally Commissioners are approached as to our availability for other such missions. However, in such cases, Commissioners are acting within the mandate of the particular organization concerned, not as Commission members.

At the same time, the Commission has offered its services and its good offices in a number of situations and delicate negotiations have taken place with various parties. However, none of these initiatives have come to fruition although they continue.

So is the IHFFC a white elephant, or does it have a role in this complex picture? Does it provide added value?

The Commission would seem to offer two particular advantages. The first is legitimacy. It is a treaty body with an international mandate. It is not an NGO with a duty to its funders. It is States themselves who fund the Commission. As a result, there is a stronger argument for States to co-operate with us. Indeed, in cases where States have made the Article 90 Declaration, the Commission would expect that co-operation both as a matter of law and also one of common sense.

Secondly, the Commission offers a degree of efficiency in that any enquiry carried out must adopt a low key, confidential approach. A report is submitted to the Parties with recommendations and that report will not be made public 'unless all the Parties to the conflict have requested the Commission to do so' [Article 90(5)(c)]. However, 'if the Chamber is unable to secure sufficient evidence for factual and impartial findings, the Commission shall state the reasons for that inability'. The task of the Commission is not to 'blame and shame' but to try to resolve disputes. The intention is to try to take some of the heat out of the propaganda wars that develop at present.

So how does the Commission intend to counter this lack of action? At the moment, it plans to concentrate on the 'good offices' role and to take a proactive approach. Situations where it is possible that the Commission might have a role are monitored and the parties are approached quietly and privately to see if they are prepared to use the services of the

Commission. This has two effects. Firstly, it increases the profile of the Commission with States but also, even if it does not lead to an invitation in, it can lead to an invitation for Commissioners in their private capacity to involve themselves in other initiatives, thus building up experience.

What of the future? The Commission is seeking to expand our capabilities, both as individuals and as a team. This includes more training for Commissioners. However, all of this will be of little use without the support of the international community. There have been references to the Commission in a number of international fora, including a General Assembly Resolution encouraging States to use our services as well as resolutions at the International Conferences of the Red Cross and the Red Crescent. However, the Commission still needs to make itself better known in capitals. Many States do not seem to realize that a separate Declaration is required to accept the competence of the Commission and that ratification of Additional Protocol I is not enough in itself. Each Commissioner now has a regional responsibility to try to raise the profile of the Commission in their area.

Put simply, States created the Commission. Only States can decide whether this child of the 1970s will be allowed to reach adulthood. In 1977, the Diplomatic Conference thought that the Commission had something to offer to the new era of international humanitarian law introduced by the Protocols. They were—and remain—right! However, there is a need for more States to make the Article 90 Declaration and subsequently to use the Commission.

The Contribution of the Special Court for Sierra Leone to the Development of International Humanitarian Law

SUSAN C. BREAU
School of Law, University of Surrey

The Special Court for Sierra Leone has been mandated to try those with the greatest responsibility for serious violations of international humanitarian law, crimes against humanity and Sierra Leonean law committed on the territory of Sierra Leone since 30 November 1996. This article will analyse some of the significant jurisprudence emerging from this tribunal and the contribution these cases make to the clarification and development of international humanitarian law. There may be some disquiet that the Appeals Tribunal in some of the cases has been too restrictive with the requirements of culpability in the recruitment of child soldiers. Ultimately, it is submitted that these cases will provide excellent material for the future work of the International Criminal Court and other hybrid or national tribunals in their consideration of criminal charges resulting from the violation of the laws and customs of war.

1. Introduction

The Special Court for Sierra Leone has been mandated to try those with the greatest responsibility for serious violations of international humanitarian law, crimes against humanity and Sierra Leonean law committed on the territory of Sierra Leone since 30 November 1996. The charges arise out of a long and bloody civil war that tore the country apart and resulted in international intervention by the European Community of West Africa forces (ECOMOG), the United Nations (UNOMSIL and UNAMSIL) and finally by British Forces.[1]

There were three main groups involved in this war, the Armed Forces Revolutionary Council (AFRC), the Civil Defence Forces (CDF) and the Revolutionary United Front (RUF). The Court has been mandated to try those with the greatest responsibility. The trials of three former leaders of the AFRC and of two members of CDF have been completed, including appeals. Testimony has ended in the trial of three former RUF leaders and a Trial Judgment is expected later this year. There have been a total of 13 indictments issued but two were withdrawn due to the deaths of the accused. The former President of Liberia, Charles Taylor, was charged for his role in initiating and supporting the conflict and his trial is in the prosecution phase at The Hague.

This article will analyse some of the significant jurisprudence emerging from this tribunal and the contribution these cases make to the clarification and development of international humanitarian law. The focus will be on two areas of special significance; the considerations in the rulings and judgments of the threshold of armed conflict and the

---

[1] For the background of the conflict see Akinrinade, B. (2001) International humanitarian law and the conflict in Sierra Leone, *Notre Dame Journal of Law, Ethics & Public Policy*, 15(391), pp. 392–405 and the two Judgments discussed in this article.

recruitment of child soldiers. The recruitment of child soldiers has been the subject of a very important jurisdictional appeal which is discussed initially. The judgments in the AFRC and CDF trials are the first that have considered this pervasive problem of child recruitment and these decisions will do much to clarify the jurisdiction and elements of this offence. In an article written prior to the first judgments, Morss and Bagaric predicted that unlike the ICTR, where the dual charges of crimes against humanity and war crimes tended to produce convictions in the category of the former, in the case of the Special Court it was likely that prosecutions for war crimes would be more successful.[2] That prediction has turned out to be correct as the jurisprudence of this tribunal focuses to a far greater degree on the violations of the laws and customs of war.

2. Crimes Included in the Statute that Relate to Violations of International Humanitarian Law

There are two sections in the Statute for the Special Court for Sierra Leone dealing with crimes under international humanitarian law. Article 3 encompasses violations of both Common Article 3 to the four Geneva Conventions and Additional Protocol II as Sierra Leone had ratified both Conventions. It states:

> The Special Court shall have the power to prosecute persons who committed or ordered the commission of serious violations of article 3 common to the Geneva Conventions of 12 August 1949 for the Protection of War Victims, and of Additional Protocol II thereto of 8 June 1977. These violations shall include:
>
> a. Violence to life, health and physical or mental well-being of persons, in particular murder as well as cruel treatment such as torture, mutilation or any form of corporal punishment;
>
> b. Collective punishments;
>
> c. Taking of hostages;
>
> d. Acts of terrorism;
>
> e. Outrages upon personal dignity, in particular humiliating and degrading treatment, rape, enforced prostitution and any form of indecent assault;
>
> f. Pillage;
>
> g. The passing of sentences and the carrying out of executions without previous judgment pronounced by a regularly constituted court, affording all the judicial guarantees which are recognized as indispensable by civilized peoples;
>
> h. Threats to commit any of the foregoing acts.

The Statute also contains Article 4 which criminalizes other serious violation of international humanitarian law. This article specifies:

> The Special Court shall have the power to prosecute persons who committed the following serious violations of international humanitarian law:
>
> a. Intentionally directing attacks against the civilian population as such or against individual civilians not taking direct part in hostilities;

---

2 Morss, J.R. and Bagaric, M. (2006) The banality of justice: reflections on Sierra Leone's Special Court, *Oregon Review of International Law*, 8(1), p. 13.

b. Intentionally directing attacks against personnel, installations, material, units or vehicles involved in a humanitarian assistance or peacekeeping mission in accordance with the Charter of the United Nations, as long as they are entitled to the protection given to civilians or civilian objects under the international law of armed conflict;

c. Conscripting or enlisting children under the age of 15 years into armed forces or groups or using them to participate actively in hostilities.[3]

Although it was confirmed in the *Tadic* decision that there can be criminal responsibility for violations of Common Article 3,[4] the serious violations provisions in this Statute contain customary provisions that have not been criminalized in the past, including the recruitment of child soldiers.[5] The tribunal has considered both the jurisdiction of the tribunal over these offences and the material elements of the crimes.

3. The Jurisprudence of the Tribunal

A. Sam Hinga Norman (deceased)

Perhaps the most significant ruling from the Special Court for Sierra Leone was on a preliminary motion by the accused Sam Hinga Norman arguing that the Court did not have jurisdiction to try him for Count 8 of the indictment, which was a charge that he recruited child soldiers. This was an important debate as in 2002 children were fighting in 37 of the world's 55 ongoing or recently concluded conflicts and they numbered around 300,000.[6]

Norman's defence team argued that the crime was not part of customary international law. The defence also argued in the alternative that while Protocol II Additional to the Geneva Conventions of 1977 and the Convention of the Rights of the Child of 1990 may have created an obligation on the part of States to refrain from recruiting child soldiers, these instruments did not criminalize such activity. Furthermore, while the Rome Statute of the International Criminal Court criminalizes child recruitment it did not codify customary international law.[7]

The prosecution argued that the crime of child recruitment was part of customary international law at the time of these offences. The Geneva Conventions established the protection of children under 15 as an undisputed norm of international humanitarian law. They also argued that a number of states had made the practice illegal under their domestic law and the subsequent international conventions addressing child recruitment demonstrated the existence of the customary international norm. The next submission was that the ICC Statute codified existing customary international law. In any event, the prosecution

---

3   Statute of the Special Court for Sierra Leone, established by an Agreement between the United Nations and the Government of Sierra Leone pursuant to Security Council resolution 1315 (2000) of 14 August 2000.

4   *Prosecutor v. Dusko Tadic* (a/k/a Dule), No. It-94-1-AR72, para. 102 (2 October 1995) (Decision on the Defence Motion for Interlocutory Appeal on Jurisdiction).

5   For a detailed discussion of this topic see Happold, M. (2005) *Child Soldiers in International Law* (Manchester: Manchester University Press).

6   Bald, S. (2002–2003) Searching for a lost childhood: will the Special Court of Sierra Leone find justice for its children?, *American University International Review*, 18(537), p. 540.

7   *Prosecutor v. Sam Hinga Norman*, Special Court for Sierra Leone, Decision on Preliminary Motion based on lack of Jurisdiction, 31 May 2005, SCSL-2004-14-AR72 (E) p. 3.

relied on the *Tadić* case that individual criminal responsibility can exist notwithstanding lack of treaty provisions referring to criminal liability. Finally, the prosecution argued that the principle of *nullem crimen sine lege* should not be rigidly applied to an act universally regarded as abhorrent. The question is whether it was foreseeable and accessible to a possible perpetrator that the conduct was punishable.[8]

In their significant decision the Appeals Chamber accepted that that there was a norm prohibiting child recruitment as the widespread recognition and acceptance of Additional Protocol II and the Convention on the Rights of the Child (hereafter CRC) was compelling evidence that the norm entered customary international law well before 1996. The fact that there was not a single reservation to lower the legal obligation under Article 38 of the CRC (prohibiting child recruitment under 15) underlines this, particularly since Article 38 is one of the very few conventional provisions which can claim universal acceptance.[9]

The court significantly extended these obligations to non-state actors by stating:

> Customary international law represents the common standard of behaviour within the international community, thus even armed groups hostile to a particular government have to abide by these laws. It has also been pointed out that non-state entities are bound by necessity by the rules embodied in international humanitarian law instruments, that they are 'responsible for the conduct of their members' and may be 'held so responsible by opposing parties or by the outside world'. Therefore all parties to the conflict in Sierra Leone were bound by the prohibition of child recruitment that exists in international humanitarian law.

The second part of the decision focused on whether the prohibition had been criminalized. In a well reasoned decision the court held that by 1996 the recruitment of child soldiers was indeed a criminal offence and thus did not violate the principle of *nullem crimen sine lege*. The Court specifically referred to the criminalization of the offence in Article 8 of the Rome Statute and the Convention of the Rights of the Child Optional Protocol II which had been ratified by 74 States. Most persuasive might be the reliance on the statement in *Tadic* that the clear and unequivocal recognition of the rules of warfare in international and State practice indicate an intention to criminalize the prohibition.[10] This court concluded there need not be a clear indication in the prohibition that there would be individual criminal responsibility.

There was some unease about this decision as there was a dissenting opinion from Judge Robertson. He found that the crime of non-forcible enlistment did not enter international criminal law until the Rome Statute of 1998.[11] It can be argued that Robertson failed to consider the historical background and development of this offence, or the important criteria of *Tadic* of State practice indicating an intention to criminalize the prohibition which in this case is extensive.[12]

Although this issue of jurisdiction may be resolved in the International Criminal Court it is significant for those countries not party to the Statute or for those situations that pre-date the ambit of the Rome Statute's temporal jurisdiction.

---

8 *Ibid.*, pp. 3–4.
9 *Convention on the Rights of the Child*, New York, 1577 UNTS 3, Article 38.
10 *Prosecutor v. Dusko Tadic* (a/k/a Dule), No. It-94-1-AR72, para. 102 (2 October 1995) (Decision on the Defence Motion for Interlocutory Appeal on Jurisdiction), para. 70.
11 *Prosecutor v. Sam Hinga Norman*, Special Court for Sierra Leone, Decision on Preliminary Motion based on lack of Jurisdiction, 31 May 2005, SCSL-2004-14-AR72 (E) Dissenting Opinion of Judge Robertson, p. 35.
12 *Ibid.*, in the main opinion, p. 23, where it was argued that 108 states explicitly prohibited child recruitment.

B. The AFRC trial

The next significant ruling also considered child recruitment and the threshold of armed conflict. This was the judgment in the AFRC trial. It was the first time that an international tribunal had ruled on the charge of recruitment of child soldiers into an armed force, and on the crime of forced marriage in an armed conflict.

The Armed Forces Revolutionary Council was the group that seized power from the elected Government of President Kabbah on 25 May 1997.[13] Johnny Paul Koroma was the Chairman of the ruling council. From that time until the Lome Peace accords in July 1999, the AFRC engaged in a number of military operations resulting in atrocities against the civilian populations.[14] As a result of these activities three of the leaders of the council were charged with crimes against humanity and war crimes. On 20 June 2007, in the AFRC trial, Alex Tamba Brima, Brima Bazzy Kamara and Santigie Borbor Kanu were each found guilty on Count 1 (acts of terrorism), Count 2 (collective punishments), Count 3 (extermination), Count 4 (murder, a crime against humanity), Count 5 (murder, a war crime), Count 6 (rape), Count 9 (outrages upon personal dignity), Count 10 (physical violence, a war crime), Count 12 (conscripting or enlisting children under the age of 15 years into armed forces or groups, or using them to participate actively in hostilities), Count 13 (enslavement), and Count 14 (pillage). All three defendants appealed their convictions but the Appeals Chamber dismissed all of the defendants' Appeals.

In the context of the contribution to international humanitarian law perhaps the most significant development is the convictions of the three leaders of Count 12, conscripting or enlisting children under the age of 15 years into armed forces or groups. The Trial Chamber did not review again the jurisdictional issue as it had been canvassed in Norman. In this case, the significant contribution to international humanitarian law was that the trial chamber in this case, guided by the Rome Statute, adopted the elements of the crime which were:

1. The perpetrator conscripted or enlisted one or more persons into an armed force or group or used one of more persons to participate actively in hostilities;
2. Such person or persons were under the age of 15 years;
3. The perpetrator knew or should have known that such person or persons were under the age of 15 years;
4. The conduct took place in the context of and was associated with an armed conflict;
5. The perpetrator was aware of factual circumstances that established the existence of an armed conflict.[15]

Based on the evidence of expert witnesses, for both the prosecution and defence, former child soldiers, and other civilians, the court was satisfied that children were routinely recruited and used for military purposes by the AFRC. The Chamber found that the AFRC fighting forces conscripted children under the age of 15 years old and used them as combatants as they were easy to manipulate and programme and resilient in battle. The evidence was held to be conclusive that most, if not all, of the children in question were abducted

---

13 *Prosecutor v. Brima, Kamara and Kanu*, Special Court for Sierra Leone SCSL-04-16-T, Judgment, 20 June 1997, p. 67.
14 *Ibid.*, pp. 65–79, 85–91 and 351–363.
15 *Ibid.*, p. 225.

from their families.[16] In this case, as the accused were members of the Supreme Council of the AFRC and they were present when many of these incidents occurred, they were criminally responsible.[17] The case is noteworthy and will no doubt be used as precedent for its detailed consideration of the elements of the crime.

This case is also significant for its ruling on the existence of an armed conflict. The Court found that at all times relevant to the indictment, there was an armed conflict in Sierra Leone, which lasted from March 1991 to January 2002, and involved the RUF, AFRC and CDF, and that the crimes involved were closely related to the conflict. The Judgment firstly quoted the *Tadic* Jurisdiction case that the distinction between internal and international armed conflicts was no longer of great relevance in relation to the crimes articulated in Article 3 of the Statute even though Common Article 3 was to apply to non-international armed conflicts. However, the Court did declare this conflict to be a non-international armed conflict.[18] The interesting part of this issue is the consideration by the Court of the criteria for the existence of an armed conflict as being the intensity of the conflict and the degree of organization of the warring factions. Although it is the case that criteria for conflict often included some degree of control over territory, this was not considered. Again this case may be support for the idea that control over territory is not necessary.[19]

4. The CDF Trial

The Judgment and Appeal in the CDF trial also discussed the issue of recruitment of child soldiers. The Civil Defence Forces organized themselves due to the fact that that armed forces could not protect the entire territory from the Revolutionary United Front; these forces included the popular Kamajo militia. Regrettably these forces also liberally violated the laws and customs of war.[20] The Trial Chamber in their Judgment on 2 August 2007 convicted Moinina Fofana, the National Director of War of the CDF and Allieu Kondewa, the High Priest of the CDF on four counts for murder, cruel treatment, pillage and collective punishments. Kondewa was convicted on an additional count for the recruitment of child combatants under the age of 15. The case against a third accused, Sam Hinga Norman, was halted after his death in February. The three-judge panel found the two not guilty on two counts of crimes against humanity and one count of war crimes. In addition, Fofana was found not guilty on the charge of recruitment of child combatants.[21]

In the judgment the court at this stage took judicial notice of the fact that there was an armed conflict in Sierra Leone from March 1991 and January 2002. For the serious violations of international humanitarian law they also took judicial notice of the nexus between the alleged offences and the armed conflict.[22] Although these individuals were convicted of many of the charges, Fofana was not convicted of Count 8, enlisting children under the age of 15 into armed forces or groups or using them to participate actively in hostilities. Although Kondewa was convicted of that charge it was overturned on Appeal. For the purposes of

---

16 *Ibid.*, p. 361.
17 *Ibid.*, pp. 102–166 for detailed consideration of the role of the accused persons in the AFRC structure.
18 *Ibid.*, p. 95.
19 *Ibid.*, pp. 92–96.
20 Akinrinade, *op. cit.*, n 1, p. 402.
21 *Prosecutor v. Moinina Fofana and Allieu Kondewa*, Special Court for Sierra Leone, SCSL-04-14-T, Judgment, 2 August 2007.
22 *Ibid.*, pp. 210–211.

the contribution to international humanitarian law it is the Appeals judgment discussing this aspect of child recruitment that is of interest. The allegation had been that as senior leaders in the CDF they knew and approved of the use of children to participate actively in hostilities.[23]

Unlike the Appeals in the AFRC trials there were major changes in convictions registered in the Appeal. The Appeals Chamber, in a majority Judgment, on 28 May 2008 overturned convictions against Moinina Fofana and Allieu Kondewa for collective punishments and against Kondewa for recruiting of child soldiers.[24] With respect to the recruitment of child soldiers the Appeals Chamber expressed the view that the crime of enlisting children under the age of 15 years may be committed irrespective of the number of children enlisted by the accused person.[25]

The issue in this case was whether an initiation ceremony was equivalent to recruitment. The Appeal Chamber acknowledged that there was a paucity of jurisprudence on how direct an act must be to constitute 'enlistment' under the statute as well as possible means. In an important ruling, the Appeals Chamber held that for enlistment there must be a nexus between the act of the accused and the child joining the armed force or group. There must also be knowledge on the part of the accused that the child is under the age of 15 and, importantly, that he or she may be trained for combat.[26] In this case the child witness had been captured by the CDF in 1997 and was forced to carry looted property. This act in itself constituted enlistment. For this finding they relied upon paragraph 4557 of the ICRC Commentary to Article 43 (c) of Additional Protocol II which stated:

> The principle of non-recruitment also prohibits accepting voluntary enlistment. Not only can a child not be recruited, or enlist himself, but furthermore he will not be 'allowed to take part in hostilities', i.e. to participate in military operations such as gathering information, transmitting orders, transporting ammunition and foodstuffs, or acts of sabotage.[27]

This was useful to the Appeal Chamber as in the case of an armed group which is not a conventional army, enlistment cannot be defined narrowly as a formal process.[28] As this witness had been initiated before Kondewa's involvement with him, he was acquitted of this charge on Appeal. The Appeals Court also upheld Fofana's acquittal but interestingly there was a dissent on this point which could be significant in later rulings.

In her dissent, Judge King stated that no reasonable trier of fact could have come to any conclusion other than that Fofana was aware that children were both enlisted in the CDF and used to participate in hostilities. She based this opinion on the fact that Fofana was present at the parade in early January 1998, where children involved in operations were present. He was also present at a commanders' meeting later that day when the late accused person Norman commented that 'adult fighters were doing less than children, just eating and looting'. Children were also present at this meeting. Fofana was also one of the architects of the Black December Operation where children were present in the frontlines. He was also present at Base Zero and at that base Kondewa also initiated children into the CDF and child initiates were trained at that base. Furthermore, according to Judge King, children were present throughout CDF operations and children who appeared to be under the age

---

23 *Prosecutor v. Moinina Fofana and Allieu Kondewa*, Special Court for Sierra Leone, SCSL-04-14-A, Appeals Judgment, 28 May 2008, p. 8.

24 *Ibid.*, pp. 187–192.

25 *Ibid.*, p. 45.

26 *Ibid.*, p. 50.

27 ICRC Commentary to Additional Protocol II, para. 4557.

28 *Prosecutor v. Moinina Fofana and Allieu Kondewa*, Special Court for Sierra Leone, SCSL-04-14-A, Appeals Judgment, 28 May 2008, p. 50.

of 15 were conscripted, enlisted, or used to participate actively in hostilities in various loca-tions. They participated directly in combat, often leading the Kamajors into combat and served at checkpoints. King argues that the only conclusion available to any reasonable Trial Chamber is that Fofana knew that children under the age of 15 were being enlisted and used to participate actively in hostilities because Fofana was the 'Director of War' for the CDF. He was part of the High Command and actually made many decisions along with Norman and Kondewa and was the overall boss of the Commanders at Base Zero. He was also the one responsible for the receipt and provision of logistics to the frontline, including the provi-sion of manpower. Given that he had to have known that the CDF was enlisting and 'using' children in active military service, his provision of logistics, manpower, and strategic direc-tions provided practical assistance and had a substantial effect on the commission of the crime of enlisting and using children under the age of 15 to participate actively in hostilities. King would find on Appeal that Fofana aided and abetted the commission of this crime.[29]

She also supported the view that Fofana, as a leader in the High Command of the CDF, did not take a stand in public or at any commanders' meeting against the enlistment of children. Although King found that Fofana did not enlist the child soldiers personally, he held a high position within the CDF command structure and his physical presence at meetings where child soldiers were either present or were discussed constituted tacit approval, encouragement and moral support to the commanders and Kamajors to continue to enlist and use children under the age of 15 to participate actively in hostilities. Therefore, King would find criminal culpability on tacit approval and his conduct would have a substantial effect on the commission of this crime.

This division of opinion in the Appeals Court on this issue does cause concern as it seems to contradict the earlier finding in the AFRC trial of culpability based on overall control and approval of recruitment. The distinguishing factor may be the lack of direct evidence against the accused CDF leaders. However, Judge King's dissent seems to accord with the view of criminal responsibility for those who are in overall command of operations.

5. Conclusion

There may be some disquiet that the Appeals Tribunal in the CDF trial is being too restric-tive with the requirements of culpability in the recruitment of child soldiers but that ruling can be contrasted with the AFRC trial. It remains to be seen how the RUF trial will deal with this issue. Nevertheless, the jurisdictional ruling in *Norman* and the specification of the elements of child recruitment in the AFRC trial will be a significant contribution to the development of international humanitarian law as it signifies that in customary international law the recruitment of child soldiers is a criminal offence.

Finally the jurisprudence of the tribunal illustrates detailed judicial consideration of international humanitarian law both in the aspect of the threshold of armed conflict and the elements of various offences. These cases will provide excellent material for the future work of the International Criminal Court and other hybrid or national tribunals in their consid-eration of criminal charges resulting from the violation of the laws and customs of war.

---

29 *Ibid.*, Dissenting Judgment of Renate King, pp. 10–12.

Samoa's Experience with the International Criminal Court

MING LEUNG WAI
Attorney General of Samoa

This presentation was originally delivered by the Attorney General of Samoa at the International Criminal Court Regional Advocacy Seminar, held in Canberra, Australia, on 6 August 2007. It provides rare insights into the negotiations leading up to the Rome Statute of the International Criminal Court (ICC) from the perspective of a small State. The presentation, moreover, describes the successful lobbying which preceded the election of a Samoan judge onto the ICC and the challenges in implementing domestic legislation.

Introduction

It gives me great pleasure to present at this Seminar.

Samoa is a strong supporter of the International Criminal Court (ICC) because it believes that such an institution has the potential to contribute to peace and stability and the rule of law, not only around the world, but also within our Asia–Pacific region.

My presentation will focus on Samoa's experience with the ICC, particularly in negotiating and becoming a party to the Rome Statute of the ICC, passing of domestic legislation implementing the Rome Statute, addressing concerns with the ICC and sharing the lessons learnt by Samoa from its association with the ICC.

It is my hope that Samoa being represented at this Seminar and sharing its experience, will encourage other countries that have not signed or ratified the Rome Statute to reconsider their position.

But before I elaborate on Samoa's experience I want to share briefly with you Samoa's background because I know some here may not be familiar with my country. I do not blame you and I have grown accustomed to being stopped at various international airports for up to half an hour at times whilst officials there check the existence of my country.

Background

Samoa was the first country in the South Pacific region to gain independence. Before independence in 1962, Samoa was a United Nations Trust Territory administered by New Zealand. Samoa comprises of nine volcanic islands and is located around the middle of the South Pacific ocean just east of the international dateline and south of the equator. The distance between Canberra, Australia and Samoa is about 4,600 miles. Samoa's population is about 180,000 people.

It is generally accepted that Samoa was settled more than 3,000 years ago. Samoans belong to the Polynesian race which is theorized to have originated from somewhere in

South East Asia. Some of my grand uncles dispute that when they recount myths that we originated from the very grounds of Samoa itself since Samoa means the 'sacred centre' of the world.

Whilst Samoa is relatively small, it is well known for producing strong, skilful and hard tackling sports people. You only have to look at the national rugby team of Australia's neighbour, the famous All Blacks, and you will find that about half are Samoans or of Samoan origin—now you know the secret of the All Blacks' success. Or if you want an example closer to here then there was that player that saved the Soccerroos in the game against Japan at the last Soccer World Cup Tournament—Tim Cahill, who of course is a Samoan.

Visitors to Samoa always comment upon the peaceful nature of my country, and I urge you all to pay us a visit if life becomes too stressful. Our entire society is based upon a strong commitment to the rule of law and we have no general law and order problems, such as those that pose such a great challenge to many of our neighbours. But just as our young Samoan warriors do battle nowadays on the sports fields of the world, we have a long history of warfare and of major battles fought in our islands. In fact some hundreds of years ago Samoa was invaded by our neighbours from Tonga (we Samoans never quite understood why they were later to become known as the 'friendly islands'). My mother's ancestors, being members of the warriors of the great district of Falealili, engaged the Tongan invaders in battle. I am happy to say that no war crimes were reported from these running battles. In fact the departing Tongan King paid tribute to the victorious leaders of the Samoan warriors (twin brothers named Tuna and Fata) with the words 'Ua malie toa, ua malie tau' (Brave warrior, you have fought a good fight) which have been retained by their family as their name ('Malietoa') and is amongst the highest chiefly titles in Samoa.

In the mid- and late-1800s colonial wars were fought in Samoa. It is not widely known that the most decisive battle ever fought in the Pacific took place in Apia harbour. It was after this naval engagement, which was finally determined by the intervention of an act of God in the form of a cyclone, that the entire Pacific area was divided up amongst the colonial powers of England, Germany and America. The great writer Robert Louis Stevenson settled in Apia not long after this period and wrote a magnificent historical account of these conflicts. In his book *Seven Turbulent Years in Samoa*, no lesser authority than Mr Stevenson records certain war crimes committed by Samoan villagers against a party of German marines. He recounts the observations of an early trader, Mr Moors, who was astounded to be greeted by a group of villagers from Fagalii Village in the most friendly terms of 'Good Morning Mr Moors' whilst they held the severed heads of the German soldiers. Prosecutions are not likely in any court though as these young men are the ancestors of our current Police Commissioner!

Negotiating the Rome Statute

Samoa, through its Permanent Mission to the United Nations in New York led by H. E. Ambassador Tuiloma Neroni Slade (as he was then known), was actively involved in negotiating and drafting the Rome Statute of the ICC ('Statute'). Ambassador Tuiloma was ably assisted by Professor Roger Clark, a New Zealander who is a Professor of Law at Rutgers University in Camden, New Jersey. With limited resources, Samoa's participation in establishing the ICC was greatly dependent upon funding from other organizations such as DePaul University, Chicago. Samoa's active participation in the lead up discussions was rewarded when Ambassador Tuiloma was elected as one of the Vice Presidents of the Conference at the United Nations Diplomatic Conference of Plenipotentiaries on the

Establishment of the ICC which was held in Rome, Italy from 15 June to 17 July 1998. This Conference was mandated to negotiate and finalize the Statute to establish a permanent international criminal court.

The idea of an international criminal court is not a new idea and probably emerged after the First World War with the unsuccessful attempt to establish an international tribunal. Following the Second World War, the Nuremburg and Tokyo war tribunals set the stage for efforts to create a permanent Court. It was first considered in the United Nations context which had aimed to create an international penal tribunal to hear crimes relating to genocide pursuant to Article VI of the Convention on the Prevention of the Crime of Genocide 1948. At this time, Samoa played no role at all, being a former German colony and later placed under the administrative authority of New Zealand from 1914.

Further development of the notion was probably forestalled by differences of opinions over the years and the environment of the Cold War. It was not until 1992 that the United Nations General Assembly directed the International Law Commission ('ILC') to elaborate a draft statute for an international criminal court. Further public interest in the notion was fuelled by the Security Council's establishment of the International Criminal Tribunals for the former Yugoslavia in 1993 and for Rwanda in 1994. It was around this time that Samoa committed itself to playing its role as a member of the community of nations.

In the ensuing years, the General Assembly created a Preparatory Committee to discuss the draft Statute prepared by ILC with a view to provide a widely accepted convention for an ICC for consideration by a conference of plenipotentiaries. After sessions of the Preparatory Committee between 1996 and early 1998, which Samoa took part in, the Committee submitted for consideration by the Conference a draft Statute for the ICC.

At the Conference in Rome in 1998, Samoa chaired two working group negotiations which looked at the Preamble and the final clauses (i.e. Part 13, Articles 119–128) of the Statute.

There were many difficult issues that were negotiated at the Conference but only a few important ones involving Samoa will be highlighted in this presentation.

During the negotiations of the Statute, Samoa had, with other countries, strongly argued for the specific inclusion of the use or threat of use of nuclear weapons under the ICC's definition of war crimes, as they were methods of warfare that caused unnecessary suffering or were inherently indiscriminate. Their inclusion in the Statute was strongly opposed by others. It was believed that if the issue was pushed it was clear that powerful countries would not sign up on the Statute and could result in wrecking the Conference. In the end, Samoa had to accept that nuclear issues could not be resolved within the ICC negotiations, and that it would need to be continued to be fought elsewhere, such as in the United Nations General Assembly or the Disarmament Conference.

Be that as it may, Samoa successfully argued with other countries for the Prosecutor to be independent. The Prosecutor must have the power to initiate investigations on his or her own volition and that no political body, Security Council or State could stop or delay an investigation or prosecution.

In relation to funding, Samoa had argued with other developing countries for the expenses of the Court to be paid from the assessed contributions in accordance with the United Nations scale. Other countries argued that it was more appropriate for the Court to be independent from the United Nations and tried to introduce other funding proposals. In the end it was decided that the expenses of the Court and the Assembly of the Parties shall be paid (in addition to any funds provided by the United Nations as approved by the

General Assembly) from contributions of States Parties 'assessed in accordance with an agreed scale of assessments, based on the scale adopted by the United Nations for its regular budget and adjusted in accordance with the principles on which the scale is based'.

The relationship of the Court and the role of the Security Council in relation to its special responsibility for international peace and security under Chapter VII of the United Nations Charter was also the focus of much heated debate. Many countries, including Samoa, were concerned that the unfettered control by the Security Council will, especially with the veto, subject the Court to undue political pressure. The resulting compromise in Rome is reflected in Article 13 (reference by the Prosecutor to the Security Council) and Article 16 which provides that 'No investigation or prosecution may be commenced or proceeded with ... for ... 12 months after the Security Council, in a resolution adopted under Chapter VII ..., has requested the Court to that effect; that request may be renewed by the Council under the same conditions'.

Another matter of importance negotiated at the Conference was the concept of 'complementarity'. The need for the Court to be complementary to, and not in place of, national Courts, was an issue of fundamental importance for many States, including Samoa, at the Conference. The ICC is not superior to and not intended in any way to take the place of national Courts. This was one of many thorny issues which took a great deal of time over several years leading up the Conference to resolve. At heart were the concerns about State sovereignty, and the fear of being overwhelmed by a supra-national institution and jurisdiction. As a result, the need for 'complementarity' is stressed in the Statute's Preamble, Article 2, etc.

Aside from the said specific matters that Samoa had argued to be included in the Statute, there was broad agreement that the Court should be an independent, fair, impartial, effective and broadly representative international criminal judiciary, and that it should be free from political and other influences. It was also emphasized at the Conference that the Court should not become a tool of political struggles or a means of interfering in other countries' internal affairs.

After the adoption of the text by the Conference, the text of the Statute, as well as the Final Act of the Conference, were opened for signature in Rome. Some 127 delegations, including Samoa, signed the Final Act; and 26 delegations, again including Samoa, signed the Statute on 17 July 1998. So on that historic day, the Conference adopted the Statute by a vote of 120 in favour to 7 against, with 21 abstentions. The non-recorded vote was requested by the United States of America.

Samoa's signing of the Final Act and Statute on 17 July 1998 was a public indication of Samoa's participation at the Conference and of its general concurrence with the principles contained in the Statute. Of course the act of signing has no binding force in the legal sense. Ratification was to come later once Samoa's Cabinet had the chance to fully consider the Statute, its value and implications.

Ratifying the Rome Statute

It was not until several years later that Samoa's Prime Minister Honourable Tuilaepa Lupesoliai Sailele Malielegaoi lodged, during the United Nations General Assembly session, the formal instrument of ratification of the Rome Statute on 16 September 2002.

In the year before, the Honourable Prime Minister's address to the Fifty-Sixth Session of the United Nations General Assembly had expressed Samoa's support for the establishment of the ICC, especially with Samoa being one of the first countries to sign the Statute. In his address he also stated that, 'We consider it essential to renew efforts to promote the rapid entry into force of the Rome Statute of the International Criminal Court'.

Following his address, Samoa's Cabinet considered in detail plans to ratify the Rome Statute. The two main issues of concern to Samoa related to the immunity of Samoa's Head of State and sovereignty. The Head of State Act 1965 guarantees the office holder immunity from criminal and civil liability. However, this would be inconsistent with the Rome Statute which could subject Heads of State to the jurisdiction of the ICC if implicated in crimes of genocide, crimes against humanity and war crimes. Samoa is a stable and peaceful country and it is unlikely that our Head of State, whose position is more of a ceremonial position far removed from the administration of Government, will ever be implicated in any such heinous crimes.

The second concern was the assumption that the ICC will take away the sovereign rights of Samoa. This is clearly incorrect as the State is given priority and authority to act in the usual manner when a crime is committed and that it is only where they are unable or unwilling to do so that the jurisdiction of the ICC can be activated. The Rome Statute preserves the sovereign rights of the countries but provides access to an international forum and body where serious international crimes of genocide, crimes against humanity and war crimes can be brought and prosecuted.

On 21 August 2002 Samoa's Cabinet agreed for Samoa to ratify the Rome Statute.

Samoan Judge in the ICC

Following Samoa's ratification of the Rome Statute, Samoa began to lobby for Ambassador Tuiloma to be elected a judge of the ICC as a Category A judge (Criminal Law). With very limited resources and very tough competition from other developed countries, the task was indeed a very challenging one. But Samoa is not a country that gives up easily and so the lobbying began.

Both Samoa's Ministry of Foreign Affairs and Permanent Mission to the United Nations in New York wrote to their respective counterparts in all State Parties. Attached to the letter asking for support was Ambassador Tuiloma's Curriculum Vitae—a very impressive one since he was the Attorney General of Samoa, the Deputy Director Legal and Constitutional Affairs Division of the Commonwealth Secretariat and Ambassador and Permanent Representative for Samoa to the United Nations, USA and Canada.

Aside from the letters, bilateral meetings with every State Parties at the time also took place. My predecessor also travelled to New York to help with the campaign. Because Samoa was not able to afford hosting receptions or cocktails, Samoa's campaign party would attend other countries' cocktail parties to promote its candidate. The telephone was also extensively used to contact every person at every level that mattered.

Samoa's hard fought effort was rewarded at the elections in 2003. There were 35 rounds of voting and Ambassador Tuiloma was elected after the 33rd round. When all 18 judges were elected, lots were drawn to determine the term of office. The terms were for three years, six years or nine years. Although it was unfortunate that Judge Tuiloma ended up with a three-year term, Samoa's efforts to have him elected were successful. Judge Tuiloma's term expired last year and he was not re-elected.

Enacting Domestic Legislation

An obligation following ratification of the Rome Statute that proved to be a challenge to Samoa was the enactment of domestic legislation to implement the Rome Statute.

The first draft domestic legislation was rejected by experts in the field in 2002 when it was circulated for comments. It appeared that the first draft was not clear in addressing the criminality of offences under the Rome Statute since offences under Articles 6, 7 and 8 committed in Samoa had to be caught statutorily. There was also the need to address the applicability of jurisdiction over such offences wherever they may be committed.

Samoa's attempt at drafting domestic legislation did not really go anywhere until it received a model legislation from the Commonwealth Secretariat. This was followed by the assistance provided by the University of Nottingham when it sent Dr Olympia Bekou, a specialist in the area of the ICC. Dr Bekou worked with local Parliamentary Counsel in 2006 and produced a proper draft of the legislation. The draft legislation was forwarded towards the end of last year to Samoa's Cabinet, which endorsed and referred it to Samoa's Parliament. Following its second reading a few months ago the ICC Bill is now with the Bills Select Committee to hear submissions from the public before it is considered in detail by Parliament and if approved, for its third reading in October 2007. To date, no view against the ICC Bill has been expressed and so it will likely be passed by Parliament.[1]

Lessons Learnt

So what has Samoa learnt from its experience with the ICC and was it all worth it?

The first lesson learnt is that Samoa, even though small and with limited resources, can contribute to issues that are of global concern such as world peace and stability. Samoa was able to make use of whatever resources were available, such as grants and donor funding, to actively take part in the discussions that led up to the presentation to the United Nations of a convention to establish the ICC. Samoa's determination was rewarded with the election of Judge Tuiloma as a judge of the ICC.

The second lesson learnt is that even though Samoa may not be a place where heinous crimes will ever be committed, by being a member of the Rome Statute, Samoa will never be a safe haven for international criminals. Samoa has also recognized the danger that if it is outside the jurisdiction of the ICC, then it potentially becomes a repository for evidence, criminals, profits and the instrumentalities of international crime.

The third lesson learnt is that by ratifying the Rome Statute Samoa has not signed away its sovereignty. Samoa can investigate and prosecute any international crime committed within Samoa or it can refer the matter to the ICC. If sovereignty was eroded by the ICC, then Samoa, and I believe the other 104 countries, would not have ratified or acceded to the Statute.

With limited resources the fourth lesson learnt by Samoa was that it being a party was not expensive. Samoa's annual financial contribution to the ICC is ST$3,343—which in Australian dollars is about $1,671.

---

1 The ICC Act 2007 was assented to by the Head of State of Samoa on 21 November 2007 and came into force on 1 July 2008.

The fifth lesson learnt is that small countries like Samoa heavily depend upon the assistance and expertise offered by the developed countries and international organizations. Even though Samoa ratified the Statute in 2002, it took Samoa several years before it was able to come up with a suitable domestic implementing legislation. With Australia showing strong support for the ICC, it is hoped that Australia and New Zealand and relevant international organizations like those represented at this Seminar will provide the necessary assistance to the countries within the Asia–Pacific region to enable ratification and enactment of legislation implementing the Rome Statute.

The final lesson learnt is that by supporting the ICC, Samoa is honouring its obligations as a responsible member of the international community. Supporting an institution such as the ICC helps guard against extreme political and military behaviour. Such support complements Samoa's civilian police officers that are presently sent to various United Nations peacekeeping operations in countries around the world such as East Timor, Solomon Islands, Liberia, Sudan etc. Whilst the ICC will not solve all of our world's conflicts, such an institution has the potential to contribute towards world peace and security.

Conclusion

The intention behind the ICC is noble and has been described by Amnesty International to be 'the twentieth century's most important creation in the struggle against impunity for the worst crimes known to humanity' (September 2004).

The ICC may not be perfect and is still in its infancy. It is therefore vital that the international community guides and directs its development in accordance with the principles under which it was created. This can be better achieved by every country, big and small, developed or developing, to become party to the Statute. By becoming a party to the Statute, Samoa believes that it has sent out the following messages:

(a) it has no tolerance for international crimes;

(b) it has adopted the noble purposes for which the Statute is founded; and

(c) it is resolved to strengthening ties between countries and regions through participation in this global endeavour requiring development and cooperation.

The same message can be sent out by your country if it decides to become a party to the Statute. If most, if not all, of our countries in our region can become parties to the Statute, then we in the Asia–Pacific region will in effect be issuing a joint statement that we care about world peace, stability and the rule of law.

The Laws of War and Traditional Cultures: A Case Study of the Pacific Region*

HELEN DURHAM

Senior Research Fellow and Program Director, Research and Development, Asia Pacific Centre for Military Law, Melbourne Law School

This article reflects upon the process of ascertaining whether there is any traction between modern principles of international humanitarian law (IHL) codified in specific treaties and customary law, and traditional, cultural practices in warfare. Exploring the dangers and benefits of research of this nature, the article highlights some of the findings from a study based in the Pacific region.

> Norms attract compliance if they take root in the hearts and minds of those called to apply them. Without cultural legitimacy, there is danger that humanitarian law aspires to self-defeating universalism.[1]

The modern codification of international humanitarian law (IHL) is found pre-dominantly in the Geneva Conventions[2] and their 1977 Additional Protocols,[3] documents which are relatively new and European in name. However the core concepts embedded in these treaties (distinction, proportionality and limitation)[4] and the notion that 'Even Wars Have Limits'[5] are not recent. Throughout the ages there have been countless instances of limitations during armed conflict. Deemed the oldest area of international relations and international law, law relating to warfare can be found in every culture in some form or other.[6] Indeed from the ancient Greek myths[7] to sixth century BC Chinese writings[8]

---

* The author would like to acknowledge the many people involved in this project and in particular to thank Letitia Anderson and Nicole Hogg. This piece is based on a paper given by the author on behalf of the ICRC at the Commonwealth Red Cross/Crescent International Humanitarian Law Conference held in Wellington in August 2007.

1 Provost, R. (2006) The international committee of the red widget? The diversity debate and international humanitarian law, *Israel Law Review*, 1318, p. 39.

2 *Geneva Convention for the Amelioration of the Condition of the Wounded and the Sick in Armed Forces in the Field*, 12 August 1949, 75 UNTS 31 (*First Geneva Convention*); *Geneva Convention for the Amelioration of the Condition of Wounded, Sick and Shipwrecked Members of the Armed Forces at Sea*, 12 August 1949, 75 UNTS 85 (*Second Geneva Convention*); *Geneva Convention Relative to the Treatment of Prisoners of War*, 12 August 1949, 75 UNTS 135 (*Third Geneva Convention*); *Geneva Convention Relative to the Protection of Civilian Persons in Time of War*, 12 August 1949, 75 UNTS 287 (*Fourth Geneva Convention*). All entered into force 21 October 1950.

3 *Additional Protocols to the Geneva Conventions of 12 August 1949*, entered into force 7 December 1978.

4 The fundamental principle of distinction can be found throughout international humanitarian law. In particular, *Additional Protocol I, op. cit.*, n 3, Article 48 states: 'the Parties to the conflict shall at all times distinguish between the civilian population and combatants and between civilian objects and military objectives'. Proportionality is found in many articles including *Additional Protocol I, op. cit.*, n 3, Article 51(5)(b) which prohibits attacks that cause damage 'excessive in relation to the concrete and direct military advantage anticipated'. See also Article 51(4). *Additional Protocol I, op. cit.*, n 3, Article 35(1) states: 'In any armed conflict, the right of the Parties to the conflict to choose methods or means of warfare is not unlimited'.

5 This slogan was coined by the International Committee of the Red Cross as a tool for communicating international humanitarian law.

there are references to the benefits, both humane and pragmatic, in placing restrictions on violence during armed conflict.

In this context, when the former Deputy Prime Minister of Tonga, Dr Langi Kavaliku, challenged the International Committee of the Red Cross (ICRC) to identify some connections between IHL principles and traditional warring practices in the Pacific region, the concept of finding such correlations was not without precedent. Despite the perceived need for such a project, however, the conceptualisation and implementation of research in this area inherently raised a range of difficulties. Whilst fighting strategies involving the avoidance of unnecessary bloodshed and destruction during armed conflict are neither Western nor new, the history of Pacific warfare, as told by early missionaries and anthropologists, is inundated with examples to the contrary. Further, there were risks associated in compounding the exotic and 'other' view of this complex region of the world by a European-based international institution such as the ICRC. There were also perils involved in placing the universal and secular norms of the modern codification of IHL into local, transient and, in many instances, contrary contexts. International law has always struggled with the tension of claiming to be both global and local—wanting to have a transformative role on some 'contrary' traditional practices whilst concurrently seeking to have universal value and strong connections within specific communities and histories. As Sally Engle Merry observes:

> Rights need to be presented in local cultural terms in order to be persuasive, but they must challenge existing relations of power in order to be effective.[9]

This article reflects upon the process of ascertaining whether there is any traction between the modern principles of IHL and traditional, cultural practices in warfare. It also provides an insight into the findings of the ICRC study entitled 'Protected by the Palm: Wars of Dignity in the Pacific'.

The Pacific

The Pacific is a region which has long been of interest to those studying culture. Over the decades, anthropologists working in this large geographical area have generated some of the discipline's most provocative theories—from notions of sexuality, power and social conditioning,[10] to debates over cannibalism,[11] sorcery and ritual.[12] As a region made up of 14 independent countries with a population of approximately eight million spread over

---

6   For an account of various ancient laws of war see: McCormack, T. (1997) From Sun Tzu to the Sixth Committee: The Evolution of International Criminal Law Regime, in T. McCormack and G. Simpson (Eds) The Law of War Crimes (Kluwer Law International), p. 33.

7   See Durham, H. (2007) IHL and the Gods of war: the story of Athena versus Ares, Melbourne University Journal of International Law, 8(2), pp. 148–158.

8   Writings by the Chinese warrior Sun Tzu prescribe a number of humanitarian limitations on the conduct of hostilities. See McCormack, op. cit., n 6, p. 32.

9   Engel Merry, S. (2006) Human Rights and Gender Violence: Translating International Law Into Local Justice (Chicago: University of Chicago Press), p. 5.

10 See Mead, M. (1961) Coming of Age in Samoa (Penguin); and Mead, M. (1963) Sex and Temperament in Three Primitive Societies (New York: William Morrow).

11 See Degusta, D. (199) Fijian cannibalism: osteological evidence for Natau, American Journal of Physical Anthropology, 110, pp. 215–241.

12 Hogbin, I. (1978) The Leaders and the Led: Social Control in Wogeo, New Guinea (Melbourne University Press), pp. 54–67; see also Schieffelin, E. (1977) The Sorrow of the Lonely and the Burning of the Dancers (University of Queensland Press); Hogbin, I. (Ed.) (1973) Anthropology in Papua New Guinea (Melbourne University Press).

three million square kilometres, the development of stereotypical cultural attributes in the Pacific is difficult. Early writings by missionaries and explorers traditionally tended to empha- sise the 'exotic' elements of cultural practices located in the three major racial groupings of Melanesia, Micronesia and Polynesia.[13]

To further complicate attempted analysis of the region, in many of the Pacific island cultures written historical sources were scarce and for many years those outside the societies lacked the capacity to gain access to indigenous oral traditions.

Current researchers on the Pacific have expressed their determination to be 'island- centred' in their approach, to avoid the past practices where:

> [T]he Pacific was treated as solely the site where nineteenth and twentieth century Western nations vied for hegemony, as they sought in the islands of this vast ocean imperial aggrandis- ement or souls for Christ, precious resources or strategic bases.[14]

As well as an increased attention by academics to the approach of studies on the Pacific, the identification of shared characteristics of the region's islands is becoming important in political negotiations. In the 1970s, regional leaders coined the term 'Pacific Way' to deal with perceived insensitivities of the colonial powers that initially controlled institutions such as the South Pacific Commission.[15]

Culture and IHL

The 'universal' versus 'relative' nature of the international legal framework, in particular international human rights norms, has been a constant source of debate since the inception of international law.[16] IHL in comparison to the international human rights law dialogue has not been actively caught up in the 'cultural relativism' debate to the same degree. A review of the literature indicates that most writing in this area relates to attempts to give IHL cultural legitimacy and develop linkages between laws of war and traditional practices rather than critique the relevance of such laws to all countries.

There is a plethora of articles written about the linkages between IHL and various cultures.[17] Thus rather than examine whether this process has been undertaken, a more pertinent question relates to the value and perceived need to draw such connections between IHL and traditional practices/cultures. Indeed, the term 'culture' itself has evaded a universally-agreed, precise definition. Rather, anthropologists in this area have highlighted a few fundamental principles relating to culture. The first is that culture is learned rather than a biological feature; second, that the various elements which construct 'culture' (i.e. language, rituals, behaviours) must be taken as an integrated whole, and finally that culture

---

13 See Miller, C. (1986) *Missions and Missionaries in the Pacific* (Edwin Meller Press).

14 Grimshaw, P. (1999) The covenant makers: islander missionaries in the Pacific—review, *Journal of Social History*, Spring.

15 Rolfe, J. (2001) The Pacific Way: where 'non-traditional' is the norm, *International Negotiations*, 5 (Kluwer Law International), p. 434.

16 For an overview of this debate see Steiner, H. and Alston, P. (2000) *International Human Rights in Context: Law, Politics, Morals* (Oxford University Press), pp. 366–401, in particular the article by Pannikar, 'Is the notion of Human Rights a Western concept', pp. 383–389.

17 See Sornarajah, M. (1981) An overview of Asian approaches to international humanitarian law, *Australian Year Book International Law*, 9, pp. 238–239; Viljoen, F. (2001) Africa's contribution to the development of international human rights and humanitarian law, *African Human Rights Law Journal*, 18; see also McCormack, *op. cit.*, n 6.

is not static and can evolve over time. Many of the definitions stress the important role symbolism plays within cultural practices. As Haviland writes, 'culture comprises the ideals, values, and beliefs members of a society share to interpret experience and generate behaviour'.[18] From this definition it appears culture is located not only within the actions and deeds of a community (explicit indicators) but within the ways these actions are understood, interpreted and given meaning (implicit indicators).

Even taking into account the complex nature of 'culture', perhaps part of the answer as to why it is deemed of use to search for connections between the philosophical principles of IHL and culture/traditional practices lies in the collective human desire for stories and interpretations. Studies by scholars such as Karen Armstrong point out that the creation of myths is part of a universal language, the yearning to find meaning and order in the chaos of experience.[19] Everyone loves a story—we learn and understand extremely complex concepts from a quality narrative. Narratives and stories (be they fairytales or 'historical' accounts of great events) build on what is known and infuse events and actions with meaning. As psychologist Jonathan Haidt writes:

> Human thinking depends on metaphor. We understand new or complex things in relation to the things we already know.[20]

The notion that even when social structures break down and there is a resort to violence, there are still principles to adhere to, is a concept that lends itself to parallels and symbols. The idea of the spirit of humanity prevailing in circumstances of great horror is appealing and can be seen as a tenet of important narratives throughout the world. In significant Western literature, IHL has been examined in the famous works of Shakespeare and an eminent academic in the IHL field has noted that:

> Shakespeare's plays convey a message about international humanitarian law and our code of civilized behaviour, in civil society as well as in war that is more poignant, more powerful and more memorable than anything we can read in the language of international treaties or even customary law.[21]

Such reflection has also been taken up by Sir Kenneth Keith who writes about Shakespeare making numerous references to limitations during warfare 'forcefully and elegantly' in Henry V.[22]

Over the years, the ICRC has completed a number of studies which link cultural behaviour with the application of limitations during armed conflict. In Spared from the Spear: Traditional Somali Behaviour in Warfare,[23] experts in Somali oral history and literature were involved in researching traditional war-time practices of Somalis which continue to be used today in some parts of the country. Despite modern day images of Somalia being a country lacking codes pertaining to warfare, the results of the study demonstrated that many traditional and long-standing practices not only had general consistency with modern IHL, but had existed long before the adoption of the Geneva Conventions. In Arabian Epics,[24] folk-tales from the Middle East were compiled to assess the impact of oral literature on the

---

18 Haviland, W. (1999) Cultural Anthropology (Harcourt Brace College Publishers).

19 Armstrong, K. (2005) A Short History of Myth (New York: Canongate).

20 Haidt, J. (2006) The Happiness Hypothesis: Putting Ancient Wisdom and Philosophy to the Test of Modern Science (Arrow Books), p. 2.

21 Meron, T. (1998) War Crimes Law Comes of Age: Essays (Oxford University Press), p. 120.

22 Keith, K. (1999) Rights and responsibilities: protecting the victims of armed conflict, Duke Law Journal, 48, p. 1084.

23 Spared from the Spear: Traditional Somali Behaviour in Warfare (ICRC, February 1997).

24 Arabian Epics (ICRC, 1997).

development and consolidation of chivalric ideals and the principles of IHL. *Arabian Epics* contains numerous tales and poetry about warfare which demonstrate limitations inherent in much of the fighting:

In the battlefield, when men fight,

It must be man to man and that is right

But women and children, kept out of sight

Should not become victims of the battle's plight.[25]

Across the globe in Latin America, the ICRC has engaged in similar studies in countries such as Guatemala[26] and many other examples of this 'linking' between IHL and local knowledge can be found.

However, this process of story-telling and connection to traditional practices can be dangerous if it takes the universally positioned and secular sensibilities of IHL and reduces them to local and, in particular, transient elements. For every story, poem or traditional practice which highlights compatibility with the legal norms found in the Geneva Conventions and their Additional Protocols, there are examples which digress from the concept of limitations in warfare. Maintaining the connection at a conceptual and philosophical level, as has been done with the projects mentioned above, and using 'case studies' to demonstrate the existence of elements of linkage is essential to ensure IHL is not negatively impacted upon. It is neither intellectually rigorous nor useful to attempt to squeeze inconsistent examples together or 'cut and paste' cultural practices to suit themes. An honest approach, which makes comparisons with traditional cultures as a way of understanding principles found in an area of international law within a local framework, can be powerful. Such an approach can also assist in avoiding criticisms when the legal norms and cultural practices clash. The aim is not to falsely claim perfect alignment in all instances. Rather, the focus should be to highlight stories and practices which demonstrate that a minimum of humanity can be maintained in the worst of circumstances.

Protected by the Palm: Wars of Dignity in the Pacific

As noted previously, in 2004 the ICRC Regional Delegation for the Pacific was asked to reflect upon the local context when disseminating IHL and working with authorities on matters of treaty ratification and implementation. After carefully considering the difficulties involved in the task, a methodology was developed which would enable people from Pacific nations to take 'ownership' of the project. In this sense, the project, whilst involving academic writings and literature on the region, also aimed to be 'bottom-up' and to allow 'implicit indicators' of the diverse regional cultures to be explored by students from Pacific islands, rather than to be analysed exclusively from the outside.

The project in no way aimed to alter the institutional message of the ICRC nor erode or challenge any elements of IHL. The focus was rather to consider the delivery of information relating to the basic principles found in this area of international law. With the assistance of academics at the University of the South Pacific (USP) Port Vila campus, nine

---

25 *Ibid.*, p. 16.
26 *El Derecho Internacional Humanitario Y El orden Juridico Maya: Una Perspectiva historico-Cultural* (ICRC, 1997).

law students with research skills were identified from a range of Pacific countries and provided with a basic brief of the fundamental norms found in the modern codification of IHL. An Australian researcher was also engaged. After undertaking a literature review, these students returned to their communities and spoke to community leaders, chiefs, politicians, historians, museum curators and tribal elders about historical examples of limitations during times of armed conflict. The information uncovered by the students was provided to the ICRC in a range of sources—as stories, songs, pictures, poems, tapes of interviews and in written format. The full findings of this project can be found in 'Protected by the Palm: Wars of Dignity in the Pacific' and this article will highlight some of the broad outcomes of the study.

The results of the research demonstrated that within Pacific islands there are numerous historical instances of conflict being fought with norms and standards to avoid sheer arbitrariness.[27] In general, matters of pride and honour were strong sources of social control and limitations placed on warfare, and served humanitarian purposes as well as broader social functions. In looking at many of the general principles of IHL, correlations can be found in the histories and stories of the Pacific.

IHL requires that certain categories of people shall be protected during times of conflict and in particular civilians may not be attacked. In many traditional Pacific cultures, issues of pride and honour among warriors were strong deterrents against unrestrained warfare. In the Solomon Islands, during temporary wars known as *surumae*, nobody found in the branches of a nut-tree or fruit-tree collecting fruit could be attacked, nor anyone fishing for bonito in a canoe. War was restricted to people 'on the ground'.[28] In Tuvalu, to kill women and children was considered a shameful thing to do. It was strongly believed that a man must only attack another man of equal strength. To do otherwise was considered a disgrace that tainted one's family line permanently.[29]

In a one-on-one fight, sneaking in knives, spears or other weapons was considered *taagata* (not manly) and fighters were considered lesser men. Similarly, introducing a disproportionate number of fighters into the attack was labelled 'cowardly'. Only when conflict was fought in an honourable way could rivals eventually become enduring friends and allies. Many traditional wars in Samoa were said to have been 'wars of dignity'.[30] This phrase refers to the fact that they were regulated by codes. They did not occur out of a thirst for blood, but out of the responsibility the reigning paramount chief felt he had in upholding his duties to the *Malo* (State). During traditional conflict in the Solomon Islands the researcher wrote: 'men were too proud to kill women or generally the innocent', and to do so diminished the standing and status of the warrior.[31]

The norms found in current treaty law relating to the specific protection of women during times of armed conflict can also be identified in some Pacific traditions. In Vanuatu, battles were located in a limited space away from the huts. Women and children were either left on their own during tribal wars or protected by some form of agreement between the chiefs.[32] Women were immune from attack in some islands, such as *Malekula*, where they were never touched in war and free to go where they pleased. Protective measures also

27 For a full account of the project and the results see ICRC project entitled 'Protected by the Palm: Wars of Dignity in the Pacific'.
28 Seremaia Waqainabete, USP research student.
29 'The Story of the Two Great Warriors of Funafuti Island', Simon Kofe, USP research student.
30 Gatoloai Tillanamua Afamasage, Dean of Education, National University of Samoa.
31 Waqainabete, n 28.
32 Daisy Rowaro, USP research student.

existed in favour of women and children on the island of *Aneityum* and there is evidence that in *Shefa* province, women were perceived as too valuable to be killed for a cannibal feast. If a woman was offered to the enemy as a peace token, the offering would be refused.[33] Similarly, in the matrilineal society of the Marshall Islands, when warriors conquered a village or island, women and children were not harmed.[34] Women were also spared in Tuvalu. The Tuvaluan *Story of the Five Palagis* tells of warriors snaring five Europeans who violated a cultural taboo:

> One of the group was a woman and so was spared while the rest of the intruders were bound and thrown into the sea to drown.[35]

In the Papua New Guinean Highlands, communities were able to prepare for the outbreak of fighting and all wards of the belligerent villages were evacuated once battle began. The community would move their women, children, pigs and valuables from houses near the border to safer positions inside the clan domain or allow them to take refuge with friendly neighbours.[36] Further, after evacuation, warriors were not supposed to seek them out:

> A decent man should not try to kill the wives and children of the 'brothers' who oppose them; in particular, they should not set fire to women's houses in order to incinerate the occupants.[37]

The general principles found in IHL relating to the use of child soldiers also have some resonance with traditional Pacific cultures. In provinces in Vanuatu, boys were not permitted to participate in hostilities and were immune from attack until they wore the 'penis-wrapper' which signified initiation into manhood.[38] In the Solomon Islands, small children of the enemy were generally spared and adopted by the conqueror's village. Social norms also regulated when it was acceptable for members of the community to take up arms. Boys aged between four and five years were taken from their homes and commenced their education concerning traditional duties such as 'warriorship' and how to become good men, as well as learning the general rules of society. However it was not until the growth of body hair— a symbol of puberty—and having proved themselves to be men through initiation at the age of 14 or 15, that boys were allowed to fight. Even then, they could only participate in fighting to a limited degree.[39]

IHL obliges those who capture prisoners of war and detained civilians to ensure they are treated in all circumstances with respect for their persons and their honour. Despite many tales to the contrary, and an emphasis on cannibalism, there is evidence that there were traditional practices within the Pacific of humane treatment of captives.

In Fiji, ancient oral legends indicate that there were a number of examples of mercy shown to enemies.[40] In Samoan armed conflict, according to the codes of war, when warriors took over enemy territory, women, children and the infirm could be captured, but it was prohibited to kill them.[41] In the Solomon Islands, prisoners were generally incorpo-

---

33 Beverleigh Kanas, USP research student.
34 Nemani Tuifagalele, USP research student.
35 Kofe, n 29.
36 Meggitt, M. (1977) *Blood is their Argument: Warfare among the Mae Enga Tribesmen of the New Guinea Highland* (Mayfield), p. 10.
37 *Ibid.*, p. 31.
38 Kofe, n 29.
39 Waqainabete, n 28.
40 Jaynen Mangal—example of the warrior Tui Wainunu.
41 Interview with Mr Tamaseses (former Prime Minister of Western Samoa).

rated into the victorious tribe. They were required to be restored to health and treated with basic respect, as dictated by the Fata'abu, chief priest or spiritual leader.[42] The aim was to assimilate prisoners into the tribe, to help build its strength in terms of food gardens or to assist in other battles.

The IHL principle of proportionality can be found throughout the Pacific region. In Melanesia, traditional warfare was usually light. The number of military casualties allowed was a matter of military protocol and was kept in proportion to the original grievance.[43] There are also examples of rules to protect cultural property, another requirement under modern IHL, where in places such as the Highlands of Papua New Guinea it was regarded as wrong for an attacking force to destroy the cult-houses of their 'brothers' or to 'ring bark the old trees shading the ceremonial ground'.[44]

A fundamental tenet of IHL involving obligations of precautions in attack was found in the practice in some islands of giving advance warning of attacks which may affect the civilian population. Stories of local warfare in the Solomon Islands refer to warnings being sounded to mark the commencement of fighting:

> When they came down they blew pipes which they call kuvili (conch shell) so that the village may be ready or run away.[45]

In order to ensure the protection of civilians, the principles of IHL deem it necessary for combatants to distinguish themselves from those not engaged in hostilities. In Fiji, warriors bore arms openly and painted themselves for war.[46] In the Solomon Islands, war canoes from different islands were readily identifiable by virtue of their distinguishing features and markings. Furthermore warriors inserted sprigs of fern known as *amaame* into their hair when going out to fight and donned leaves which were a sign of war.[47] There are also examples of protective emblems, as found in IHL treaties today. In Vanuatu, on particular islands, the frond of the lycas palm served as an emblem of protection and immunity in times of traditional warfare. As the researcher Kanas wrote:

> A man may walk anywhere in war as long as he holds up the frond of the lycas palm and carries no weapons.[48]

Conclusion

The study indicates that there are many instances in the practices, myths, stories and history of armed conflict in the Pacific where humanitarian limitations exist. Traditional examples of some of the fundamental principles of IHL can be found in the protection of civilians during times of armed conflict as well as the existence of notions of proportionality, distinction, and the protection of cultural property. It cannot be claimed that a random collection of examples where traditional warring practices correlate with the principles found in the modern codification of IHL is a comprehensive and complete picture of the history of the Pacific. In the research undertaken by students from Pacific islands and the review of the

---

42 Alasia, S. (2003) *Fata'abu: the Voice of God* (University of the South Pacific, Honiara), p. 68.
43 S. Fischer.
44 Meggitt, *op. cit.*, n 36, p. 31.
45 Interview Mr S. Alasia, Daisy Rowaro.
46 Clunie, F. (2003) *Fijian Weapons and Warfare* (Fiji Museum).
47 Waqainabete, n 28.
48 Kanas, n 33.

literature, there are many cases of instances which are contrary to the principles found in the Geneva Conventions and their 1977 Additional Protocols. As previously noted, much has been written on these 'breaches' of humanity in Pacific conflicts in anthropological and early missionary literature. Every culture has occasions of great savagery and examples of inconsistency with the concept of limitations during armed conflict. Whilst there is much to divide humanity, the instances of connection (even if fragmented and incomplete) also need to be underscored and reflected upon. The study 'Protected by the Palm: Wars of Dignity in the Pacific' provides one starting point for such examination.

It is impossible to generalise about behaviour in any one country or region, and it is even more difficult in the Pacific where any one state can contain numerous ethnic groups, each with unique identities and established norms. To overstate the results of the project and its implications is dangerous, however to underestimate their potential use is imprudent. 'Even Wars Have Limits' is a statement which belongs to everyone.

International Disaster Response Law and the Commonwealth: Answering the Call to Action

VICTORIA BANNON

International Federation of Red Cross and Red Crescent Societies

In 2005, the Commonwealth Heads of Government Meeting issued a 'call to action' for improving disaster management, ensuring effective and timely humanitarian assistance and strengthening the international response system. With weather and climate-related hazards on the rise, coupled with their increasing impact on vulnerable people and economies, it has become critical to answer this call. Significant progress can be made through the elimination or reduction of the many legal and bureaucratic barriers that continue to plague international relief. This article explores how the Commonwealth, and indeed the international community as a whole, can learn from recent research in this area and take steps to implement the Guidelines for the Domestic Facilitation and Regulation of International Disaster Relief and Initial Recovery Assistance ('IDRL Guidelines') and improve legal preparedness for disaster response.

Natural Disasters: A Time for Concern

The Commonwealth has every reason to be concerned about natural disaster. Weather and climate-related natural hazards account for a great majority of disaster-related economic and human losses[1] and in 2007 three of the top five most affected countries were Commonwealth Member States.[2] Six of the ten most deadly disasters also occurred in Commonwealth Member States,[3] including the top three.[4] The United Kingdom ranked second in the world for the highest economic damage incurred by natural disaster, a rank equalled by Dominica which faced the second highest economic damage per capita.[5]

---

1   United Nations International Strategy for Disaster Risk Reduction (2008) *Links Between Disaster Risk Reduction, Development and Climate Change* (Geneva: Commission of Climate Change and Development), p. 1.

2   India, Bangladesh and Zimbabwe ranked second, third and fourth respectively, based on numbers of persons affected. See International Federation of Red Cross and Red Crescent Societies (2008) *World Disasters Report 2008* (Geneva: International Federation of Red Cross and Red Crescent Societies), Table 13, pp. 212–218.

3   Bangladesh (Cyclone Sidr, November 2007 and Floods, July–August 2007); India (Floods, July 2007 and Floods July–August 2007); Pakistan (Cyclone Yemyin, June 2007 and Floods and Landslides, June 2007). Scheuren, J-M. *et al.* (2008) *Annual Disaster Statistical Review—The Numbers and Trends 2007* (Brussels: Center of Research on the Epidemiology of Disasters, Department of Public Health, Universitè Catholique de Louvain), p. 8.

4   In Bangladesh, Cyclone Sidr in November 2007 killed 4,234 people and flooding in July–August 2007 killed 1,110 people. In India, flooding in July–August 2007 killed 1,103 people. *Ibid.*, p. 8.

5   The United Kingdom suffered US$9,648,000 damage as a result of flooding in June and July 2007, behind the July earthquake in Japan which cost US$13,810,000. Dominica suffered a 7.46% loss of GDP from Hurricane Dean in August 2007 behind Oman with 9.62%. *Ibid.*, p. 7.

The alarming trend is that, far from having reached their peak, the overall number of recorded disasters has doubled in just ten years, characterised by an increased frequency in storms, droughts and intense rainfall.[6] The Commonwealth Heads of Government have collectively recognised this phenomenon and its destructive impact on the world's economy, in particular for least developed countries and small States.[7] In 2005, following the unprecedented devastation caused by the Indian Ocean Tsunami, they

> called for action at the national, regional and international levels to strengthen disaster management through increased capacity for disaster preparedness, early warning systems, risk mitigation and post-disaster recovery and reconstruction ... emphasised the critical importance of effective, timely and equitable humanitarian action in support of disaster affected populations ... [and] called on member countries to support efforts to further strengthen the international humanitarian response system.[8]

With international commitment to the key priorities of disaster risk reduction, embodied in the Hyogo Framework for Action,[9] there can be some confidence that the international community is on the right path. However, one frequently overlooked aspect of disaster preparedness is the role of legal frameworks and their impact on facilitating, or conversely hindering, the conduct of international humanitarian relief and recovery activities. Although much is known about the international and domestic legal environment in conflict situations, comparatively little attention has been devoted to the laws and principles applicable in non-conflict disasters.

A prominent contribution to this area is the recent work initiated by the International Federation of Red Cross and Red Crescent Societies (International Federation), which itself has a long history of response and coordination in disaster relief.[10] Over the past few years, the International Federation's International Disaster Response Laws, Rules and Principles (IDRL) Programme has been leading and conducting research on the international legal framework for international disaster response and collecting data on the various domestic legal issues faced by governments and relief providers during large scale operations.[11] The findings from this work, captured in a recent Desk Study,[12] provide some sobering facts

---

6   United Nations International Strategy for Disaster Risk Reduction, op. cit., n 1, p. 1.

7   Communiqué of the Commonwealth Heads of Government Meeting, Auckland New Zealand, 10–13 November 1995, para 30 states: '[...] improved performance was not shared by several least developed countries and particularly small states, which are vulnerable to natural disasters and external shocks'; Communiqué of the Commonwealth Heads of Government Meeting, Uganda, 23–25 November 2007, para 59 states: 'They expressed concern at the recent increase in frequency and intensity of natural disasters and their often devastating social, economic and environmental impact, particularly on small island developing states'.

8   Communiqué of the Commonwealth Heads of Government Meeting, Malta, 25–27 November 2005, paras 75–76.

9   Hyogo Framework for Action 2005–2015: Building the Resilience of Nations and Communities to Disasters, World Conference on Disaster Reduction, 18–22 January 2005, Kobe, Japan.

10 The International Federation of Red Cross and Red Crescent Societies is the world's largest humanitarian organisation, whose mission is to improve the lives of vulnerable people by mobilising the power of humanity, including through the coordination and direction of international assistance to victims of natural and technological disasters, to refugees and in health emergencies. Founded in 1919, the International Federation comprises 186 member Red Cross and Red Crescent societies—with an additional number in formation. It is a component of the International Red Cross and Red Crescent Movement, which also comprises the International Committee of the Red Cross and National Red Cross and Red Crescent Societies.

11 The IDRL Programme seeks to reduce human vulnerability by promoting legal preparedness for disasters through advocacy, technical assistance, training and research. See website: www.ifrc.org/idrl.

12 Fisher, D. (2007) Law and Legal Issues in International Disaster Response: A Desk Study (Geneva: International Federation of Red Cross and Red Crescent Societies).

about the challenges that lie ahead for ensuring that international disaster response is timely and effective.

Making Sense of the International Legal Framework

Unlike international humanitarian law, which benefits from the flagship Geneva Conventions and Additional Protocols,[13] the laws and rules for international disaster response are spread throughout a bewildering array of international, regional and bilateral treaties, resolutions, declarations, codes, guidelines, protocols and procedures. They are found in many different areas of international law including: privileges and immunities; customs; transport; telecommunications; donations; civil defence; human rights; refugee law; health; environment; and space.[14]

The majority of instruments are bilateral treaties between States or between States and international humanitarian organisations. These variously take the form of mutual assistance agreements between States on specific cooperation measures in times of disaster, agreements relating to militaries such as Status of Forces and Visiting Forces Agreements which can include emergency assistance arrangements, as well as agreements between States and inter-governmental or international organisations, such as the United Nations International Federation regarding legal status, privileges and immunities during their presence in-country.[15]

Global treaties are less prevalent and tend to target specific issues rather than address a comprehensive range of topics. Notable examples include: the Tampere Convention of 1998[16] which commits parties to reducing regulatory barriers and restrictions on the use, import and export of various telecommunications equipment for disaster relief and mitigation activities; the Kyoto Customs Convention of 1973[17] which contains specific annexes relating to the exemption of relief goods sent by charitable organisations and the expedited clearance of relief consignments; and the Framework Convention on Civil Defence Assistance of 2000[18] which provides a mechanism for States to offer and accept the deployment

---

13   Geneva Convention for the Amelioration of the Condition of the Wounded and Sick in Armed Forces in the Field, opened for signature 12 August 1949, 75 UNTS 31 (entered into force 21 October 1950); Geneva Convention for the Amelioration of the Condition of Wounded, Sick and Shipwrecked Members of Armed Forces at Sea, opened for signature 12 August 1949, 75 UNTS 85 (entered into force 21 October 1950); Geneva Convention Relative to the Treatment of Prisoners of War, opened for signature 12 August 1949, 75 UNTS 135 (entered into force 21 October 1950); Geneva Convention Relative to the Protection of Civilian Persons in Time of War, opened for signature 12 August 1949, 75 UNTS 287 (entered into force 21 October 1950); Protocol I Additional to the Geneva Conventions of 12 August 1949, and relating to the Protection of Victims of International Armed Conflicts, opened for signature 8 June 1977, 1125 UNTS 17512 (entered into force 7 December 1978); Protocol Additional II to the Geneva Conventions of 12 August 1949, and relating to the Protection of Victims of Non-international Armed Conflicts, opened for signature 8 June 1977, 1125 UNTS 17513 (entered into force 7 December 1978).

14   For an overview of these instruments, see Fisher, *op. cit.*, n 12, Chapters 3–5.

15   See Fischer, H. (2003) International Disaster Law Treaties: Trends, Patterns and Lacunae, in V. Bannon (Ed.) *International Disaster Response Laws, Principles and Practice: Reflections, Prospects and Challenges* (Geneva: International Federation of Red Cross and Red Crescent Societies).

16   Tampere Convention on the Provision of Telecommunication Resources for Disaster Mitigation and Relief Operations, 18 June 1998, United Nations depositary notification C.N.608.1998.TREATIES-8 of 4 December 1998 (entered into force 8 January 2005) ('Tampere Convention').

17   International Convention on the Simplification and Harmonization of Customs Procedures, 18 May, 1973, TIAS 6633, Annexes B.3 and J.5 ('Kyoto Customs Convention').

18   Framework Convention on Civil Defence Assistance, 2 May 2000, 2172 UNTS 231 (2000).

of civil defence units that then enjoy certain facilities such as reduced customs and administrative barriers, 'necessary' privileges and immunities and transit facilitation. However, in addition to their narrow scope, these instruments are also limited by their low level of ratification, posing a further barrier to their effective use in many disaster relief operations.

There are some relevant global treaties which have enjoyed wide ratification. The Nuclear Assistance Convention of 1986,[19] Industrial Accidents Convention[20] and Chemical Weapons Convention[21] are three such examples, all of which cover arrangements for the sending, receiving and facilitation of international assistance, including the movement of goods and equipment. However their exclusivity to specific types of disaster is, again, a limiting factor.

More comprehensive treaties tend to find favour at regional, rather than global, levels. From the Americas[22] to Africa,[23] from Europe[24] to Asia[25] and the Middle East[26] many regional and sub-regional groupings of States have developed some form of agreement or mechanism to encourage cooperation in cross-border disaster response. Some, such as the Arab Agreement,[27] the Inter-American Convention[28] and the Association of Caribbean States Agreement[29] have suffered from limited ratification and implementation. Others

---

19 Convention on Assistance in the Case of Nuclear Accident or Radiological Emergency, 26 September 1986, 1439 UNTS 275.

20 International Labour Organisation Convention 147 on Prevention of Major Industrial Accidents of 1993, available at: http://www.ilo.org/ilolex/english.

21 Convention on the Prohibition of the Development, Production, Stockpiling and Use of Chemical Weapons and on their Destruction, 13 January 1993, 32 ILM 804.

22 See for example: Inter-American Convention to Facilitate Assistance in Cases of Disaster, 7 June 1991, available at: http://www.oas.org/legal/intro.htm; Organization of American States Office of International Law, A-54 Inter-American Convention to Facilitate Disaster Assistance, available at: http://www.oas.org/juridico/english/Sigs/a-54.html; Agreement Establishing the Caribbean Disaster Emergency Response Agency, 26 February 1991, available at: http://www.ifrc.org/what/disasters/idrl/publication.asp; Centro de Coordinación para la prevención de los Desastres Naturales en América Central, Antecedentes, available at: http://www.cepredenac.org/antecedentes.htm; Agreement between Member States and Associate Members of the Association of Caribbean States for Regional Cooperation on Natural Disasters, 17 April 1999 (not yet in force), available at: http://www.acs-aec.org/Summits/Sum mit/English/AgrmtNatDesas_eng.htm; and Consejo Andino de Ministros de Relaciones Exteriores, Decisión 529, Creación del Comité Andino para la Prevención y Atención de Desastres (CAPRADE), 7 July 2002, available at: http://www.comunidadandina.org/normativa/dec/D529.htm.

23 See for example the Dar es Salaam Declaration on Feeding Infants and Young Children in Emergency Situations in Africa, adopted in 1999, available at: http://www.ifrc.org/Docs/idrl/I303EN.pdf; and Field, T. (2007) Regional (Africa) Survey of Disaster Response Laws, Policies and Principles, available at: www.ifrc.org/idrl.

24 See for example: Council Regulation (EC) 1257/96 of 20 June 1996, Official Journal L 163, 2 July 1996; Partnership Agreement between the Members of the African, Caribbean and Pacific Group of States, of the One Part, and the European Community and its Member States, of the Other Part, Signed in Cotonou, Benin on 23 June 2000 (hereinafter, 'Cotonou Agreement'); Agreement Amending the Partnership Agreement between the Members of the African, Caribbean and Pacific Group of States, of the One Part, and the European Community and its Member States, of the Other Part, Signed in Cotonou, Benin on 23 June 2000, both available at: http://www.acpsec.org/en/treaties.htm.

25 ASEAN Agreement on Disaster Management and Emergency Response, 26 July 2005, available at: http://www.aseansec.org; Agreement on Establishing the SAARC Food Bank, 4 April 2007, available at: http://www.ifrc.org/Docs/idrl/I646EN.pdf.

26 See for example, Arab Cooperation Agreement on Regulating and Facilitating Relief Operation, League of Arab States Decision No. 39, 3 September 1987.

27 Ibid.

28 Inter-American Convention to Facilitate Assistance in Cases of Disaster, 7 June 1991 (hereinafter 'the Inter-American Convention'), available at: http://www.oas.org/legal/intro.htm.

29 Agreement between Member States and Associate Members of the Association of Caribbean States for Regional Cooperation on Natural Disasters, 17 April 1999 (not yet in force), available at: http://www.acs-aec.org/Summits/Summit/English/AgrmtNatDesas_eng.htm.

however, have played a key role in response operations. The ASEAN Agreement on Disaster Management and Emergency Response ('ASEAN Agreement')[30] is one such example which recently came to prominence following Cyclone Nargis when it struck Myanmar in May 2008. Although this agreement has not yet entered into force, it provided an important platform for the ASEAN Secretariat and Member States to send a joint assessment team and to play a key role, together with the Government of Myanmar and the United Nations, in the coordination of humanitarian assistance.[31]

In addition to treaty law, there are numerous soft law instruments, such as resolutions and declarations, covering a wide variety of topics relevant to non-conflict disasters and related assistance. Key among these are resolutions of the United Nations General Assembly, the Economic and Social Council (ECOSOC) and the International Conference of the Red Cross and Red Crescent. In the case of the International Conference, a unique forum composed of representatives of each component of the Red Cross and Red Crescent Movement[32] and all State Parties to the Geneva Conventions, a number of resolutions have been adopted to tackle specific issues frequently encountered during international disaster relief operations, covering both the legal challenges of access and issues of humanitarian accountability. These include the adoption of the Principles and Rules for Red Cross and Red Crescent Disaster Relief ('Principles and Rules'),[33] the welcoming of the Code of Conduct for the International Red Cross and Red Crescent Movement and NGOs in Disaster Relief ('Code of Conduct')[34] and resolutions on the standards for medical personnel and supplies,[35] emergency radio communication,[36] visas[37] and air transport.[38] In a collaborative effort between the International Federation (then the League of Red Cross Societies) and the Office of the United Nations Disaster Relief Coordinator (UNDRO) in 1977, a series of specific legal measures for facilitating international relief were developed and adopted both by the International Conference of the Red Cross and Red Crescent and ECOSOC

---

30 ASEAN Agreement on Disaster Management and Emergency Response, 26 July 2005 (hereinafter, 'ASEAN Agreement'), available at: http://www.aseansec.org.

31 See 'ASEAN to Lead International Coalition of Mercy for Myanmar, Secretary-General of ASEAN Surin Pitsuwan to Meet World Bank President Robert Zoellick in Washington DC', Media Release, ASEAN Secretariat, Indonesia, 13 May 2005, available at: http://www.aseansec.org/21536.htm; and 'Chair of ASEAN Humanitarian Task Force Meets International Organisations and Groups to Coordinate Humanitarian Operations for the Victims of Cyclone Nargis', Media Release, ASEAN Secretariat, Indonesia, 27 May 2008, available at: http://www.aseansec.org/21585.htm.

32 The International Red Cross and Red Crescent Movement comprises the International Committee of the Red Cross, the International Federation of Red Cross and Red Crescent Societies and National Red Cross and Red Crescent Societies.

33 Principles and Rules for Red Cross and Red Crescent Disaster Relief, adopted by the 21st International Conference of the Red Cross, Istanbul, 1969—revised by the 22nd, 23rd, 24th, 25th and 26th International Conferences—Tehran, 1973; Bucharest, 1977; Manila, 1981; Geneva, 1986; and Geneva, 1995.

34 See Resolution 4, Principles and values in international humanitarian assistance and protection, para. E(1), 26th International Conference of the Red Cross and Red Crescent, Geneva, 1995.

35 Resolution 26, The role of medical personnel in the preparation and execution of Red Cross emergency medical actions, 24th International Conference of the Red Cross and Red Crescent, Manila, 1981 and Resolution 19, Medical supplies in Red Cross and Red Crescent emergency operations, 25th International Conference of the Red Cross and Red Crescent, Geneva, 1986.

36 Resolution 9, Red Cross emergency radio communications, 23rd International Conference of the Red Cross and Red Crescent, Bucharest, 1977.

37 Resolution 5, Issue of visas to delegates appointed in connection with appeals for assistance in time of disaster, 23rd International Conference of the Red Cross and Red Crescent, Bucharest, 1977.

38 Resolution 23, Air transport in international relief actions, 21st International Conference of the Red Cross, Istanbul, 1969.

and later endorsed by the United Nations General Assembly.[39] These covered issues such as reducing customs formalities for relief goods, facilitating visas and transport and allowing access to communications facilities.

The United Nations has tended towards more generalised resolutions covering coordination and facilitation issues.[40] One of those most frequently referred to is the 1991 United Nations General Assembly resolution 46/182 on 'Strengthening of the coordination of humanitarian emergency assistance of the United Nations'.[41] This resolution establishes the conditions upon which international assistance should be provided, namely 'with the consent of the affected country and in principle on the basis of an appeal by the affected country',[42] and calls on States to facilitate the activities of inter-governmental and non-governmental organisations working 'impartially and with strictly humanitarian motives' particularly in the supply of food, medicines, shelter and healthcare.[43] It also establishes the position of the 'Emergency Relief Coordinator' which, together with its secretariat (now the United Nations Office for the Coordination of Humanitarian Affairs), is tasked with leadership and coordination, including the negotiation of humanitarian access in disaster and conflict emergencies.[44]

A number of other bodies have adopted resolutions and declarations on various aspects of international disaster relief, including the International Parliamentary Union, the International Telecommunications Union and the World Customs Organisation.[45] Additionally, a number of academic institutes and associations such as the International Law Association, the United Nations Institute for Training and Research and the Max Planck Institute for Comparative Public Law and International Law have developed various models and guidelines recommending legal arrangements for the delivery of humanitarian assistance in disaster situations.[46]

Finally, an activity which has recently been flourishing is the development of standards, codes and mechanisms to improve the quality, accountability and coordination of humanitarian assistance.[47] Many of these have been developed by the humanitarian community itself in an effort to increase the effectiveness of relief, encourage the integration of longer-term risk reduction and development objectives in emergency operations, and to maintain public confidence in humanitarian activities. In addition to the 'Principles and Rules' and 'Code of Conduct' mentioned above, these initiatives include the Sphere Project Humanitarian Charter and Minimum Standards in Disaster Relief,[48] the Principles of Accountability

---

39 See Resolution 6, Measures to expedite international relief, 23rd International Conference of the Red Cross and Red Crescent, Bucharest, 1977; ECOSOC Res. 2012 (LXIII) (1977); UN GA Res 32/56, UN Doc. No. A/RES/32/56 (1977).

40 See for example Assistance in Cases of Natural Disaster, GA Res 2034(XX), UN GAOR, session, UN Doc A/Res/2034(XX) (1965); Humanitarian Assistance to Victims of Natural Disasters and Similar Emergencies, GA Res 43/131, UN GAOR, 43rd sess, 75th plen mtg, UN Doc A/Res/43/131 (1988); and International Cooperation on Humanitarian Assistance in the Field of Natural Disasters from Relief to Development, GA Res 56/103, UN GAOR, 56th sess, 87th plen mtg, UN Doc A/Res/56/103 (2002). For an overview see Katoch, A. (2003) International Natural Disaster Response and the United Nations, in Bannon (Ed.), op. cit., n 15.

41 UN General Assembly Res. 46/182, UN Doc. A/RES/46/182 (1991).

42 Ibid., at annex para 3.

43 Ibid., at annex paras 5–6.

44 Ibid., at annex paras 12, 33 and 35.

45 These are described in Fisher, op. cit., n 12, pp. 40–45 and 57.

46 For an analysis of these, see Ibid., pp. 60–61.

47 For an overview see Ibid., pp. 58–60.

48 Sphere Project, Humanitarian Charter and Minimum Standards in Disaster Response (2004 edition), available at: http://www.sphereproject.org.

and Standards in Humanitarian Quality and Management developed by the Humanitarian Accountability Partnership International,[49] the International Non-Governmental Organizations Accountability Charter,[50] the People in Aid Code of Good Practice in the Management and Support of Personnel[51] and the 'PVO Standards' developed by InterAction.[52] Additionally, the Inter-Agency Standing Committee, another body established by UN General Assembly resolution 46/182, has also been active in developing frameworks and guidance on the coordination of humanitarian assistance, including a 'Guidance Note' on the newly established Cluster Approach.[53]

It is clear from the overview above that, although this field of research is yet to be formally recognised as a body of international law in its own right, international disaster relief does not suffer from a lack of international laws and rules. However, until recently, little attempt has been made to map and analyse the compatibility of these instruments and assess their application during specific disaster operations. Indeed, making sense of the various rules applicable to different parties, organisations, types of disaster and issues poses a great challenge, as illustrated in the International Federation's Desk Study using the hypothetical disaster scenario of an earthquake-induced leak of radioactive materials from a nuclear plant in Bulgaria.[54] The large, confusing, and at times contradictory array of applicable instruments would be almost comic if the implications on the delivery of humanitarian assistance were not so serious.

Moreover, as will be discussed further below, States and humanitarian organisations have not proactively availed themselves of many of these instruments to facilitate relief activities in the field and they suffer from poor implementation at the domestic level. Nor do the various rules cover every type of legal challenge, or address issues to the level of detail necessary. Thus, the legal framework for international disaster response is not as accessible, comprehensive and coherent as it should be.

Views from the Field on the Impact of Law on Relief Operations

Looking through the lens of those in the field working in disaster relief operations, the existence of such a large body of international laws and rules has not helped to solve many day-to-day legal challenges. A global survey conducted by the International Federation during 2006–2007 ('IDRL Global Survey')[55] involving recipient and donor governments, National Red Cross and Red Crescent Societies, NGOs, UN and other entities, revealed a number of common issues, many of which have been addressed in some form or other by

---

49 Available at: http://www.hapinternational.org.

50 Available at: http://www.ingoaccountabilitycharter.org.

51 People in Aid Code of Good Practice in the Management and Support of Personnel (2003), available at: http://www.peopleinaid.org/pool/files/code/codeen.pdf.

52 'Private Voluntary Organisation' Standards, see the overview provided by InterAction available at: http://www.interaction.org/pvostandards/ index.html.

53 See for example: Inter-Agency Standing Committee (2004), *Implementing the Collaborative Response to Situations of Internal Displacement: Guidance for UN Humanitarian and/or Resident Coordinators and Country Teams*; Inter-Agency Standing Committee (2003), *Terms of Reference for the Humanitarian Coordinator*; and Inter-Agency Standing Committee (2006), *Guidance Note on Using the Cluster Approach to Strengthen Humanitarian Response*. The above are available at: http://www.humanitarianinfo.org/iasc.

54 See Fisher, *op. cit.*, n 12, Box 5, pp. 86–87.

55 See *Ibid.*, Appendix 3: Report of the IDRL Questionnaire of 2006, pp. 196–211.

the international legal and regulatory framework, but which nevertheless continue to impact the timeliness and effectiveness of relief. These same issues, and many others, were also identified in the findings of a series of pre and post-disaster studies undertaken at regional and country level,[56] including in a number of Commonwealth countries.[57] The issues fall into three main categories: the initiation and entry of international disaster relief; the facilitation of international disaster relief once in-country; and the coordination, quality and accountability of disaster relief and recovery activities.

Turning to the first of these areas, it is apparent that the process of initiating international assistance in times of disaster is at best confused and at worst obstructive. While the provision of international relief depends on the request or consent of the country concerned, some governments have been reluctant or slow to issue any formal request for international assistance, as is usually required by the United Nations and others in order to mobilise resources.[58] More frequently, States prefer to express a willingness to accept offers of international assistance rather than request it, but even this can be fraught with difficulty when, as in Indonesia following the tsunami, this message is not effectively communicated at the relevant time,[59] or, as in the case of the United States following Hurricane Katrina, mixed messages are conveyed by different official sources as to whether foreign offers of assistance will be accepted.[60]

Once international assistance is accepted, a number of stumbling blocks remain. The most widely reported among these are customs formalities, with reports of relief goods being held for months, or even years, awaiting clearance. As reported following the tsunami in Indonesia, 'perishable items rotted, medicines expired, and emergency relief items like clothes, tents, blankets and surgical equipment, which were essential at the start of the relief effort, were redundant by the time they were cleared months later'.[61] Additionally, complications with the receipt of exemptions from import duties and charges can also cause delays. In Eritrea hundreds of tonnes of UN food aid was held up as a result of government tax demands and were not released for drought victims for over a month.[62] Vehicles have also caused particular problems as they are often subject to enormous import fees. In one

---

56 A full of list studies conducted between 2002 and 2007 can be found in *Ibid.*, Appendix 2, pp. 194–195.

57 See in particular: Calvi-Parisetti, P. (2003) *International Disaster Response Law Project: Report on Findings from South Asia, Southern Africa and Central America* (Geneva: International Federation of Red Cross and Red Crescent Societies); Bannon, V. *et al.* (2006) *Legal Issues from the International Response to the Tsunami in Sri Lanka* (Geneva: International Federation of Red Cross and Red Crescent Societies); Rochester, C. (2007) *Legal Challenges to International Response to Natural Disasters in Jamaica: Context of Hurricanes Ivan, Dennis and Emily*, available at: www.ifrc.org/idrl; Field, *op. cit.*, n 23; and De Windt, C. (2007) *Law of Disasters: Toward a Normative Framework in the Americas*, Discussion Paper prepared by the Department of Sustainable Development of the Organization of American States prepared for the Americas Regional Forum on International Disaster Response Laws, Rules and Principles, Panama, 23–24 April 2007, available at: www.ifrc.org/idrl.

58 See for example Fiji and Turkey described in Bannon, V. *et al.* (2005) *Fiji—Laws, Policies, Planning and Practices on International Disaster Response* (Geneva: International Federation of Red Cross and Red Crescent Societies), p. 30; and Turkish Red Crescent Society (2006) *International Disaster Response Law: 1999 Marmara Earthquake Case Study*, available at: www.ifrc.org/idrl, p. 38.

59 See Telford, J., Cosgrave, J. and Houghton, R. (2006) *Joint Evaluation of the International Response to the Indian Ocean Tsunami: Synthesis Report* (London: Tsunami Evaluation Coalition), p. 43, describing how the decision to open the affected Aceh province to the international community was not widely known for two days.

60 See Fisher, *op. cit.*, n 12, pp. 89–90.

61 Bannon, V. *et al.* (2007) *Legal Issues from the International Response to the Tsunami in Indonesia* (Geneva: International Federation of Red Cross and Red Crescent Societies), p. 22. See also examples from Sri Lanka, South Africa, Bolivia, Mozambique, Angola and Dominican Republic described in Fisher, *op. cit.*, n 12, p. 99.

62 IRIN, *Food Aid Held for Taxes to be Released Says Gov't Official* (16 August 2005).

instance in Sri Lanka, Oxfam was required to pay over US$1 million to import 25 vehicles for use in the tsunami relief effort.[63] The IDRL Global Survey also identified medications, telecommunications equipment and food as being particularly challenging for rapid entry.[64]

Additionally, restrictions on transport have hindered the rapid delivery of aid. Goods brought across borders by land have faced the imposition of tolls, fees and charges, as well as more unusual requirements, such as the unloading and reloading of trucks so that Chadian drivers could have exclusive driving rights over an 80 km stretch of road during the 1974 Sahel famine.[65] Air transport has also suffered from a general lack of coordination, delays in the issuing of landing permits and the imposition of hefty fees and charges.[66] Similarly shipments by sea can also be hampered by delays in obtaining 'flag waivers' for international vessels and high or even deliberately inflated berthing, wharfage and storage fees.[67]

More than two thirds of international humanitarian organisations responding to the IDRL Global Survey reported difficulties in obtaining visas and work permits.[68] While many countries are initially willing to allow prompt access for humanitarian personnel,[69] problems generally arise a few weeks or months into the operation when temporary entry permits and more commonly, tourist visas, expire requiring frequent renewal in neighbouring countries, adding additional time and funding burdens.[70] Internal movement of relief personnel can also be delayed as a result of cumbersome procedures, such as those initially imposed on tsunami relief workers in Aceh and Nias requiring their identity cards to be renewed in Banda Aceh City every two weeks, which for some personnel required several days travel.[71] Additionally, relief agencies have reported difficulties obtaining recognition for certain professional qualifications, in particular for medical personnel, forcing them to either limit the scope of their medical activities despite urgent needs[72] or take the risk of providing services anyway.[73]

Once in-country, there are a number of facilities required by disaster relief providers to effectively carry out their activities. Of central importance is having recognised domestic legal personality in the affected country, which allows the organisation to enter into contracts, initiate judicial proceedings and potentially benefit from a number of tax and other exemptions.[74] In the case of inter-governmental organisations, such as the United Nations and its agencies, domestic legal personality is granted through the various laws on privileges and immunities. For governments this often occurs through diplomatic channels, and for international organisations such as the International Federation, through the conclusion of legal status agreements, described above.

---

63 Bannon, *op. cit.*, n 57.

64 In Fisher, *op. cit.*, n 12, Appendix 3: Report of the IDRL Questionnaire of 2006, p. 200.

65 See *Ibid.*, pp. 122–123.

66 See *Ibid.*, p. 123.

67 *Ibid.*, pp. 123–124.

68 In *Ibid.*, Appendix 3: Report of the IDRL Questionnaire of 2006, pp. 196–211.

69 An exception to this was following the immediate aftermath of Cyclone Nargis in Myanmar where it was reported that visas were not initially being granted to aid agencies: Bowley, G., Newman, A. *et al.* (2008) Myanmar faces pressure to allow major aid effort, *New York Times*, 5 May, available at: http://www.nytimes.com/2008/05/08/world/asia/08myanmar.html?ref=world.

70 See instances reported from Indonesia, Sri Lank and Thailand following the Indian Ocean Tsunami and the Bam Earthquake in Iran, in Fisher, *op. cit.*, n 12, pp. 116–117.

71 Bannon *et al.*, *op. cit.*, n 61, p. 16.

72 See for example *Ibid.*, p. 19.

73 See for example Bannon, V. *et al.* (2006) *Legal Issues from the International Response to the Tsunami in Thailand* (Geneva: International Federation of Red Cross and Red Crescent Societies), p. 17.

74 See Fisher, *op. cit.*, n 12, p. 125.

For foreign NGOs there may be several options to acquire legal status, such as the conclusion of a specific MOU with the government or by completing a formal registration process similar to that of local NGOs, however these procedures are often time consuming and complex, making them notoriously difficult to complete during the emergency phase of an operation.[75] In Thailand for example, foreign NGO registration was discouraged by some authorities because many organisations would have already wound up their tsunami operations by the time the formalities were completed.[76] Some NGOs are able to avoid the issue by working through a pre-existing local organisation but for those unable or unwilling to do so, the operating environment is difficult. Essential tasks such as opening bank accounts, leasing office space, obtaining tax exemptions, procuring goods and services and hiring local staff can be made unduly complicated or even impossible without the necessary paperwork.[77]

The final category of challenges relates to the regulatory aspects of the coordination, quality and accountability of international relief. In spite of the numerous standards, codes and principles described above, there are many examples of transgression by the international humanitarian community. The most prevalent of these is the delivery of inappropriate, poor quality or unnecessary relief items, often in staggering quantities.[78] Food and medicine close to or past their expiry date, warm clothing for tropical climates, used underwear, high heeled shoes and food items which contravene cultural or religious practices or local import regulations have all occupied valuable space in transport containers and warehouses, clogging logistics pipelines and delaying the delivery of essential, life-saving equipment and supplies.[79] Cases of proselytising by faith-based organisations, the deployment of untrained or unqualified personnel and culturally inappropriate conduct have also been noted as a significant concern, for example in the case of teams of Scientologists arriving in India, Thailand and Indonesia to practice faith healing on people affected by the tsunami.[80] Other issues have included a lack of respect for humanitarian principles, interference in domestic political affairs, the undermining of national and local disaster management and coordination structures, corruption and bribery, and duplication and/or neglect in provision of humanitarian services.[81] Although organisations engaging in this conduct are considered to be in the minority, it must be recognised that these actions can undermine public confidence in humanitarian assistance as a whole.[82] Additionally, perceptions about the motives and methods of relief organisations can cause reservations by governments when considering the removal of some of the legal restrictions and barriers to freer access in times of disaster, suggesting that the issues of initiation, access and facilitation are in fact inextricably linked to the quality and accountability of humanitarian assistance.[83]

---

75 Ibid., p. 125.

76 Bannon, et al., op. cit., n 73, p. 14.

77 See Fisher, op. cit., n 12, pp. 125–129.

78 In Ibid., Appendix 3: Report of the IDRL Questionnaire of 2006, p. 203.

79 See Ibid., pp. 99–101.

80 Goodman, P. (2005) For tsunami survivors, a touch of Scientology, Washington Post, 28 January. See also International Federation of Red Cross and Red Crescent Societies (2005) World Disasters Report 2005 (Geneva: International Federation of Red Cross and Red Crescent Societies), p. 93.

81 For details and other examples see Fisher, op. cit., n 12, pp. 133–149.

82 See Jacobs, A. (2003) Regulating Humanitarian Intervention (UK: Mango), p. 7; and NGO Impact Initiative (2006) An Assessment by the International Humanitarian NGO Community (USA: NGO Impact Initiative), p. 11.

83 Fisher, op. cit., n 12, p. 133.

Finding a Balanced Approach: The IDRL Guidelines and National Legislation

Considering the limitations of the existing international legal framework and the ongoing challenges facing international disaster relief operations, it is apparent that some sort of guidance is needed to support governments navigating the legal complexities of international assistance and to reduce unnecessary red tape. At the same time, greater incentives and monitoring are also required to ensure that incoming assistance is meeting basic humanitarian principles and quality standards.

In considering these challenges, States and the International Red Cross and Red Crescent Movement called on the International Federation to 'lead collaborative efforts' in addressing these challenges, including through the development of 'guidelines for practical use in international disaster response activities'.[84] Following a series of high level consultations and regional forums conducted by the International Federation involving over 140 governments, 140 National Societies, 40 international organisations and a range of NGOs, academics and other experts, the Guidelines for the Domestic Facilitation and Regulation of International Disaster Response and Initial Recovery Assistance ('IDRL Guidelines') were developed and adopted by the 30th International Conference of the Red Cross and Red Crescent in November 2007.[85]

The IDRL Guidelines are a non-binding set of recommendations to governments for preparing their domestic laws and systems to manage international assistance during the relief and initial recovery phases of a disaster. Their substance is derived primarily from the body of international laws and rules and principles, and where there are gaps or insufficient detail, from lessons and good practices from the field. They reinforce the primary responsibility of governments to address the humanitarian needs caused by disasters within their territory, as well as the role of international relief to support and supplement, not undermine or replace, national and community response efforts. In this regard, the IDRL Guidelines encourage affected States to nominate a national focal point to liaise between international and government actors and highlight the key role played by National Red Cross and Red Crescent Societies as auxiliaries to public authorities in the humanitarian field and the central role of the United Nations Emergency Relief Coordinator concerning UN emergency relief operations.

Specifically, the IDRL Guidelines encourage the development of a process whereby international humanitarian organisations are granted a number of exemptions and facilities including visa, customs and transport facilitation, tax exemptions and a simplified process for acquiring temporary domestic legal personality. These facilities however, are conditional upon ongoing compliance by relief providers with core humanitarian principles and minimum standards drawn from widely recognised sources such as the Code of Conduct and the Sphere Humanitarian Charter and Minimum Standards. They also cover issues such as the initiation and termination of international assistance, the conduct of needs assessments and the need for clarity on the specific types of assistance needed, the role of military actors,

---

84 Final Goal 3.2, Agenda for Humanitarian Action adopted by the 28th International Conference of the Red Cross and Red Crescent, Geneva, 2003.

85 'Resolution 4 on the Adoption of the Guidelines for the Domestic Facilitation and Regulation of International Disaster Relief and Initial Recovery Assistance', 30th International Conference of the Red Cross and Red Crescent Movement, Geneva, 2007, available at: www.ifrc.org/idrl.

responsibilities of States as donors, unlawful diversion and misappropriation of relief, and the security of humanitarian organisations.

Importantly, the IDRL Guidelines encourage the implementation of these recommendations in advance of disasters as part of risk reduction and preparedness activities. Indeed, the United Nations Secretariat of the International Strategy for Disaster Reduction has identified the IDRL Guidelines as an important tool for implementing Priority 5 of the Hyogo Framework for Action on disaster preparedness for effective response.[86]

As a non-binding instrument, the effectiveness of the IDRL Guidelines will ultimately depend on the level of implementation by States. Encouragingly, a number of States have recently developed or updated national disaster management legislation, including a number of Commonwealth countries such as New Zealand, South Africa, Fiji, India, Pakistan, Sri Lanka and Kenya.[87] Indeed, reviewing disaster management legislation presents an ideal opportunity to assess procedures relating to international disaster response. Unfortunately, with only a few exceptions, international assistance is given only cursory attention, suggesting more advocacy is needed to raise awareness of the importance of legal preparedness.

The Role of Inter-governmental Bodies in Strengthening Legal Preparedness

Inter-governmental bodies also have an important role to play in strengthening systems for international disaster response, in particular through encouraging their members to implement key strategies and legal measures. The United Nations Secretary-General in his report on humanitarian assistance, highlighted the adoption of the IDRL Guidelines and noted that '[c]ontinued cooperation between the Federation and the United Nations system in promoting the use of the Guidelines and bringing them into the mainstream is important'.[88]

Similarly, the United Nations Economic and Social Council (ECOSOC) encouraged

> Member States and, where applicable, regional organizations to strengthen operational and legal frameworks for international disaster relief, taking into account, as appropriate, the Guidelines for the Domestic Facilitation and Regulation of International Disaster Relief and Initial Recovery Assistance, adopted at the thirtieth International Conference of the Red Cross and Red Crescent in November 2007.[89]

The International Law Commission (ILC) has also demonstrated its willingness to contribute to the substance of IDRL by including the 'Protection of Persons in the Event of Disaster' as a topic in its long term work plan.[90] The original proposal prepared by the Codification Division of the Office of Legal Affairs of the United Nations Secretariat was titled 'International Disaster Relief Law' and advocated the 'elaboration of a set of provisions which would serve as a legal framework for the conduct of international disaster relief

---

86 *Hyogo Framework for Action 2005–2015: Building the Resilience of Nations and Communities to Disasters*, World Conference on Disaster Reduction, 18–22 January 2005, Kobe, Japan.

87 See the collection of national legislation in the IDRL Online Database, found at: www.ifrc.org/idrl.

88 International cooperation on humanitarian assistance in the field of natural disasters, from relief to development, Report of the Secretary General, UNGA, 13 August 2008, UN Doc. A/63/277, paras 41–42.

89 Strengthening of the coordination of emergency humanitarian assistance of the United Nations, ECOSOC Res, 25 July 2008, UN Doc. E/2008/L.28, OP 5.

90 See Report of the International Law Commission, 58th Sess. (1 May–9 June and 3 July–11 August 2006), UN Doc. No. A/61/10 (2006), at 464.

activities'.[91] At its 59th session in 2007, the ILC appointed Mr Eduardo Valencia-Ospina as Special Rapporteur for this work[92] and during its 60th session was presented with a preliminary report outlining the background, potential issues and scope for this initiative.[93]

Regional inter-governmental organisations have been particularly active in generating not only political will to improve international disaster response, but also the development of regional legal instruments and cooperation mechanisms. A number of these initiatives have involved collaboration with the International Federation in the application of aspects of the IDRL Guidelines, such as the development of Standby Arrangements and Standard Operating Procedures (SASOP) as called for by the ASEAN ADMER[94] and the development of a new handbook for mutual disaster assistance between Andean governments in a joint initiative between the International Federation, Committee for Disaster Prevention and Relief (CAPRADE) and the Pan American Health Organisation.[95] Additionally, the Common Market of the South (MERCOSUR) has recently contacted the International Federation for collaboration in the development of its own regional disaster committee.[96]

The IDRL Guidelines were also welcomed at a meeting of the Arab Supreme Relief Committee in February 2008, which is currently considering updating the Arab Cooperation Agreement Regulating and Facilitating Disaster Operations in an effort to encourage its wider ratification and implementation across the region.[97] Similarly, the Communiqué of the SOPAC-led Inaugural Pacific Regional Disaster Risk Management Meeting for CEOs of Finance, Planning and Disaster Management noted the challenges for Pacific island countries in implementing the IDRL Guidelines but welcomed the International Federation's support through the appointment of a dedicated regional post to support that process.[98]

These and a number of other inter-governmental forums, have contributed to keeping the issue of legal preparedness high on international and national agendas and encouraging or making direct use of the IDRL Guidelines, but more support is needed.

Answering the Call to Strengthen International Disaster Response

Significant opportunities exist for the Commonwealth Secretariat and its member countries to deliver on its 'call to action' for strengthening international disaster response. Given the

---

91 See Valencia-Ospina, E. (2008) *Preliminary Report of the Special Rapporteur on the Protection of Persons in the Event of Disasters*, International Law Commission, 60th Sess. (5 May–6 June and 7 July–8 August 2008), UN Doc. A/CN.4/598, paras 1–2.

92 Official Records of the General Assembly, Sixty-second Session, Supplement No. 10 (A/62/10), para. 375.

93 Valencia-Ospina, *op. cit.*, n 91.

94 See International Federation of Red Cross and Red Crescent Societies (2008), ASEAN Forges Ahead with its Agreement on Disaster Management, *IDRL E-Newsletter* No. 10, March, available at: http://www.ifrc.org/Docs/pubs/idrl/idrl-enews-10-p3.pdf.

95 See International Federation of Red Cross and Red Crescent Societies (2008), CAPRADE Reaches Out to the Red Cross, *IDRL E-Newsletter* No. 11, April, available at: http://www.ifrc.org/Docs/pubs/idrl/idrl-enews-11-p5.pdf.

96 See *Ibid*.

97 See International Federation of Red Cross and Red Crescent Societies (2008) Arab League Group Considers IDRL Guidelines, *IDRL E-Newsletter* No. 11, April, available at: http://www.ifrc.org/Docs/pubs/idrl/idrl-enews-11.pdf.

98 See 'Communiqué: A Call for Action', Inaugural Pacific Regional Disaster Risk Management Meeting for CEOs of Finance/Planning and Disaster Management, 24–25 July 2008, Nadi, Fiji Islands.

commitment of the Commonwealth to promoting good government, human rights, the rule of law and sustainable economic and social development,[99] it seems natural that the promotion of legal preparedness for international disaster response should resonate strongly among Commonwealth members.

In this regard, much can be learned from the important role the Commonwealth has taken on in furthering the promotion and implementation of international humanitarian law. This has included, for example, the adoption of a Declaration on Strengthening Cooperation in International Humanitarian Law at the Meeting of National Commonwealth National Committees on International Humanitarian Law in 2005,[100] consideration by the Commonwealth Law Ministers Meeting[101] and support for the Commonwealth Red Cross and Red Crescent International Humanitarian Law Conference.

Some progress has already been made in introducing the subject of IDRL to these last two forums. In 2007, the Second Commonwealth Red Cross and Red Crescent International Humanitarian Law Conference agreed 'to encourage Commonwealth States and National Societies to work together in support of further work on International Disaster Response Laws, Rules and Principles (IDRL)'[102] and in July 2008 the Commonwealth Law Ministers Meeting received an initial briefing on the issue.[103] The task is now to build on these initial advances and encourage further discussion among members and the International Red Cross and Red Crescent Movement on the specific issues facing Commonwealth countries, sharing good practices and encouraging the implementation of the IDRL Guidelines in the national contexts.

The Commonwealth Secretariat and its related associations are also well placed to provide resources and expertise for other initiatives relating to legal preparedness, such as the series of technical assistance projects being conducted by the International Federation in selected countries to provide advice and support on the implementation of the IDRL Guidelines and other key regional and international instruments relating to disaster response. There are also plans in place to develop model legislation and a handbook for policymakers, for which the International Federation will be seeking support and expertise from a number of organisations. This work will also be complimented by the development and delivery of training programmes for policy makers and the humanitarian community to encourage greater understanding of legal issues in disaster management, and strategies for the effective implementation of the IDRL Guidelines.[104]

It is hoped that the Commonwealth will take up the challenge of improving the legal environment for international disaster response as a means to strengthen the international system as a whole. Given the threats that disasters continue to pose to the people and economies of the Commonwealth and to vulnerable communities everywhere, this is a call to action which cannot be ignored.

---

99 See the Harare Declaration, issued by the Commonwealth Heads of Government in Harare, Zimbabwe, on 20 October 1991.

100 Meeting of Commonwealth National Committees on International Humanitarian Law, Nairobi, 21 July 2005.

101 See for example Communiqué of the Commonwealth Law Ministers Meeting, Edinburgh, 7–10 July 2008.

102 The Second Commonwealth Red Cross and Red Crescent International Humanitarian Law Conference, Wellington, New Zealand, 29–31 August 2007.

103 Communiqué of the Commonwealth Law Ministers Meeting, Edinburgh, 7–10 July 2008.

104 For the full work plan of the International Federation's IDRL Programme see www.ifrc.org/idrl.

Legislation

Commonwealth Countries Legislation 2005–2008

The following is a cross-section of legislative initiatives related to international humanitarian law taken by Commonwealth States in the period 2005–2008.

Canada

Canadian Red Cross Society Act[1]

This Act amends the Geneva Conventions Act to approve the adoption of an additional distinctive emblem and to include the Third Protocol Emblem (Red Crystal) along the emblems mentioned in Article 85, paragraph 3(f) of Schedule V, thus affording it the same protection currently enjoyed by the Red Cross, Red Crescent and, Red Lion and Sun emblems. The Act also amends the Act to incorporate the Canadian Red Cross Society adding a provision which prohibits the unlawful use of Red Cross, Red Crescent and Red Crystal names and emblems and establishes penal and administrative sanctions for this offence. Finally, the Act amends the Trade-marks act by adding the Red Crystal emblem to those marks whose unauthorized use is prohibited.

Cyprus

Law 23 (III)/2006,[2]

This Act amends the Rome Statute of the International Criminal Court (ratification) law of 2002, entered into force on 28 July 2006, following its publication in the Official Gazette.

This law defines genocide, crimes against humanity and war crimes as criminal offences punishable by life imprisonment. It deems certain ancillary acts punishable as well: participating in the commission of any of the core crimes under the Rome Statute; inciting, inducing or procuring another to commit such offences; and attempting or conspiring to commit such offences. The Assize Court is given jurisdiction over the crimes defined in the law, irrespective of the place of commission and the nationality of the perpetrator. The court may take into consideration the International Criminal Court's Elements of Crimes when interpreting and applying the provisions of the law. Criminal prosecution for these

---

1   Bill C-61, An Act to Amend the Geneva Conventions Act, An Act to Incorporate the Canadian Red Cross Society and the Trade-marks Act. Assented to on 22 June 2007, officially published on 20 February 2008 in the *Canada Gazette*, 142(4). Entered into force on 31 January 2008.
2   Law 23 (III)/2006 amending the Rome Statute of the International Criminal Court (ratification) law of 2002.

crimes may be conducted only by the attorney-general, or initiated upon his written approval.

The Additional Protocol (Protocol III) to the Geneva Conventions (Ratification) Law, 2007[3]

The Law gives effect to the Additional Protocol III to the Geneva Conventions. The Law also prohibits the use for any purpose, without permission in the Republic of Cyprus of any distinctive emblem or sign which pursuant to the provisions of the Protocol is prohibited. The Law provides that such permission may be granted by the Council of Ministers generally or for any specific purpose and must be published in the Official Gazette. The Law provides for administrative fines for persons who misuse the emblem or sign as established in the Protocol.

Fiji

Geneva Conventions Promulgation 2007[4]

The Law gives effect to the four Geneva Conventions as well as to the Additional Protocols I, II and III. The law establishes sanctions for persons, regardless of their nationality, in the territory of the Fiji Islands or elsewhere, commits grave breaches of any of the Conventions or of Protocol I. For cases where the grave breach is committed outside the territory of the Fiji Islands, the law establishes that those persons can be tried and punished in any place in the Fiji Islands as if the offence had been committed in that place. The law also provides punishment for persons who commit any other breaches of the Conventions or Protocols whether in or outside the Fiji Islands. The law also prohibits the use or display without permission by the Minister of Home Affairs of the Red Cross, Red Crescent, Red Lion and Sun, Red Crystal and the emblem of the Swiss Confederation and other distinctive signs as well as the wording of these signs. The law establishes administrative sanctions or imprisonment for those who commit these offences and the prohibition is extended to the use of them in or outside the Fiji Islands.

3　Law No. 39(III) of 2007. A Law to Ratify the Additional Protocol to the Geneva Conventions of 12 August 1949 and Relating to the Adoption of an Additional Distinctive Emblem (Protocol III) and Providing for Related Matters. Published in the *Cyprus Official Gazette*, Supplement I(III) on 2 November 2007. Entered into force on 2 November 2007.

4　Promulgation No. 52 of 2007. To Enable Effect to be Given to Certain Conventions done at Geneva on 12 August 1949 and to the Protocols Additional to those Conventions done at Geneva on 8 June 1977, and 8 December 2005, and for Related Purposes. Adopted on 13 December 2007 and officially published on 29 December 2007 in the *Republic of Fiji Islands Government Gazette*, 7(100). Entered into force on 1 January 2008.

Lesotho

Chemical Weapons Act 2005[5]

The Lesotho *Chemical Weapons' Act 2005* was published in the Official Gazette on 9 June 2005. The purpose of the Act is to make provision for giving effect to certain obligations of the Kingdom of Lesotho as a party to the Convention on the Prohibition of the Development, Production, Stockpiling, and Use of Chemical Weapons and on Their Destruction, and for related matters. It establishes a legal framework for inspection and for the seizure and forfeiture of goods controlled and prohibited under that Convention, and provides for penalties for violators. The Chemical Weapons' Act authorizes the Minister to designate a National Authority on Chemical Weapons within a department, organ or unit of Lesotho's security establishment. The Act also grants the Minister the authority to adopt regulations giving effect to the provisions of the Act and of the said Convention.

Samoa

International Criminal Court Act, 2007[6]

The Law establishes that any person, who in Samoa or elsewhere commits genocide as defined in the Rome Statute, shall be punishable to life imprisonment. For crimes against humanity and war crimes, as defined in the Rome Statute, the punishment provided for is a maximum period of life imprisonment. The Law also provides for command responsibility and rules out the possibility of superior orders as a defence. In addition, the Law defines and provides punishment for crimes in connection with the International Criminal Court. The Law also allows for universal jurisdiction and rules out official capacity as a bar to arrest and surrender to the ICC, allowing for the charging, prosecution and arrest of Head of State where he or she is suspected of or charged with a crime under the jurisdiction of the ICC. The Law includes rules on cooperation with the ICC and rules on the enforcement of sentences, specifying that Samoa may act as a State of enforcement.

Singapore

Biological Agents and Toxins Act 2005[7]

The *Biological Agents and Toxins Act* No. 36 of 2005 was passed by the Parliament of Singapore on 18 October and entered into force on 3 January 2006. The Act implements

---

5   Chemical Weapons' Act 2005, published in *Lesotho Government Gazette (Extraordinary)*, L.(62) of 9 June 2005, p. 583.
6   Act No. 26, International Criminal Court Act. Adopted on 9 November 2007. Entered into force 1 July 2008.
7   Biological Agents and Toxins Act 2005, No. 36 of 2005. An Act to prohibit or otherwise regulate the possession, use, import, transhipment, transfer, and transportation of biological agents, inactivated biological agents and toxins, to provide for safe practices in the handling of such biological agents and toxins, and to make a related amendment to the Infectious Diseases Act (Revised Edition, Chapter 137).

the Convention on the Prohibition of the Development, Production and Stockpiling of Bacteriological (Biological) and Toxin Weapons and on their Destruction and provides for prohibitions relating to biological agents and toxins as defined in that Convention. Any person who contravenes the prohibitions contained in the Act commits a criminal offence and is liable to a fine or imprisonment, or both. Moreover, the Act stipulates that a District Court shall have jurisdiction to try offences under the Act other than the offences under Sections 5, 16 and 30, and to impose appropriate penalties under the Act.

Geneva Conventions (Amendment) Act, 2007[8]

The Act amends the Geneva Conventions Act, by adding the definitions of the Red Cross, Red Crescent, Red Crystal and Red Lion and Sun Emblems. It also repeals and re-enacts Section 8 of the Geneva Conventions Act 1973, substituting it with a section prohibiting the use of all the Emblems without authority, including the Red Crystal emblem and the words 'Red Cross' or 'Geneva Cross'. Sections 9 and 10 are also amended and a new Section 10A on Inspectors is created. This new section provides for the appointment of public officers as inspectors to investigate the commission of offences under Section 10. Finally, the principal Act is amended by inserting two new schedules, namely, the Fifth Schedule which includes the Third Protocol to the Geneva Conventions and the Sixth Schedule containing the distinctive emblems of the Geneva Conventions,[9] including the Red Crystal emblem.

Terrorism (Suppression of Bombings) Act 2007[10]

The purpose of this Act is to give effect to the International Convention for the Suppression of Terrorist Bombings, adopted by the General Assembly of the United Nations on 15 December 1997, and for matters connected therewith. The Act defines terrorist bombing and provides that anyone who is found guilty of committing such offence shall be punished with death if the intention was to cause death or serious bodily harm and death is cause; or with life imprisonment in any other case. The law also establishes both administrative and penal sanctions for anyone who fails to disclose information which may assist in preventing others from committing terrorist bombings or in securing the apprehension, persecution or conviction for a terrorist bombing. The law adds terrorist bombing to the list of extradition crimes of the Extradition Act, it provides that acts committed outside Singapore which in Singapore would amount to a terrorist bombing offence, may be proceeded against, charged, tried and punished. The Act also amends Part II of the Schedule of the Terrorism (Suppression of Financing) Act, 2003 by adding that any act or omission constituting an offence under Section 3 of the Terrorism (Suppression of Bombings) Act 2007 are also actions which constitute terrorist acts with effect from 20 February 2008.

---

8   Act No. 55/2007. Adopted on 12 November 2007 and officially published in GN No.S6/2008. Entered into force on 15 January 2008.
9   Protocol Additional to the Geneva Conventions of 12 August 1949, and Relating to the Adoption of and Additional Distinctive Emblem.
10 Act No. 50/2007. Adopted on 23 October 2007 and officially published in the Government Gazette Acts Supplement No. 54 on 21 December 2007. Entered into force on 30 January 2008.

Penal Code Amendment, 2007[11]

This Act amends the Penal Code of 1985 in order to criminalize genocide in domestic penal law. It defines genocide as established in Article 2 of the 1948 Convention on the Prevention and Punishment of the Crime of Genocide and provides for the death penalty if the offence consists of the killing of any person, or imprisonment for life or for a term which may extend to 20 years, in any other case.

Sri Lanka

Geneva Conventions Act 2006

The *Geneva Conventions Act*, No. 4 of 2006, was adopted on 26 February 2006 and published in the Official Gazette on 3 March 2006. The Act gives effect to the Geneva Conventions of 1949. It contains provisions on the punishment of grave breaches of the four Geneva Conventions and establishes universal jurisdiction over these crimes.

The Act sets out the obligation to serve notice of trial of protected prisoners of war and internees on the protecting power or on the prisoner's representative. It contains provisions on the legal representation of any person brought for trial for a breach of the Act, on appeals by protected prisoners of war and internees, and on reduction of sentence and custody. The Act also establishes the jurisdiction of the High Court of Sri Lanka for the purpose of determining whether persons who have taken part in hostilities should be granted prisoner-of-war status in accordance with Article 5 of the Third Geneva Convention. The Act provides for the prevention and sanction of misuse of the Red Cross emblem and other distinctive emblems.

Chemical Weapons Convention Act No. 58 of 2007[12]

This Act is divided into six parts and three schedules which contain of a list of toxic chemicals and their precursors. Part Two provides for the establishment of a National Authority for the Implementation of the Chemical Weapons Convention the Chair of which shall be the Secretary to the Minister of the Ministry in charge of Industries. Part Three establishes the prohibition to use, develop, produce, acquire, stockpile or retain, or transfer chemical weapons, engage in military preparations to use such weapons, knowingly assist, encourage or induce any prohibited activity or, use riot control agents as a method of warfare. Whoever is found guilty of an offence under the Act will be punished with imprisonment for a period not exceeding 20 years and a fine not exceeding one million rupees. For certain offences under the Act, defences such as not knowing or suspecting that the object was a chemical weapon or riot control agent or, if upon knowing or suspecting, he took all

11 Penal Code 1985, Amendment No. 51 of 2007. Adopted on 23 October 2007. Entered into force in January 2008.
12 An Act to Provide for the Implementation of the Convention on the Prohibition of the Development, Production, Stockpiling and use of Chemical Weapons and their Destruction and to Provide for Matters Connected Therewith or Incidental Thereto. Published on 23 November 2007 as a Supplement to Part II of the Gazette of the Democratic Socialist Republic of Sri Lanka. Adopted [certified] on 20 November 2007, entered into force on 15 April 2008.

reasonable steps to inform the authorities, may be accepted. The Act details the procedure for registration or persons engaged in production, etc. of toxic chemicals or precursor and for providing information regarding their activities and establishes a punishment of imprisonment for no longer than six months or a fine not exceeding 100,000 rupees to anyone who fails to provide such information or who gives false information. The Act also punishes the disclosure of confidential information supplied to or obtained by an inspector with imprisonment not exceeding two years or a fine not exceeding 100,000 rupees or both. In the final part of the Act, it is specified that those who attempt to commit or abet the commission of an offence under the Act will also be guilty of such offence and also that anyone who is found guilty of an offence under the Act shall be liable on conviction for each such offence, to a fine not exceeding 500,000 rupees or to imprisonment for a period not exceeding two years or both.

South Africa

South African Red Cross Society and Legal Protection of Certain Emblems Act, 2007[13]

The Act provides statutory recognition to the South African Red Cross Society, which existed previously, as the National Red Cross Society for the Republic of South Africa. The Act also provides protection for the emblems of the Red Cross and Red Crescent and limits their use to those authorized by the Geneva Conventions and Additional Protocols. The Act establishes both criminal and administrative penalties for the misuse of the emblems by persons or by corporate bodies.

Uganda

The Penal Code (Amendment) Act, 2007[14]

This act amends the Penal Code Act, making provision for the abolition of corporal punishment, substituting the section on defilement with offences ranging from death to imprisonment for committing or attempting to defile a person below 18 and 14 years of age under various circumstances. The Act also provides for payment of compensation to victims of defilement. Furthermore, the Act makes a provision for the definition of a deadly weapon and its use during robbery.

---

13 Act No. 10/2007 South African Red Cross Society and Legal Protection of Certain Emblems Act, 2007. Adopted 9 August 2007. Published 16 August 2007, *Government Gazette* 506(30178). Entered into force 16 August 2007.

14 Act 8/2007 The Penal Code (Amendment) Act, 2007. Published in the Acts Supplement No. 4 to *The Uganda Gazette* C(43) on 17 August 2007. Date of adoption 20 July 2007. Date of entry into force 17 August 2007.

United Kingdom (Gibraltar)

Weapons of Mass Destruction (Amendment) Ordinance 2005

The *Weapons of Mass Destruction (Amendment) Ordinance 2005 [Gibraltar]*[15] was enacted by the Gibraltar House of Assembly on 23 May 2005. The Ordinance provides new definitions for and clarifications of the Weapons of Mass Destruction Ordinance 2004 [Gibraltar].[16]

---

15 Weapons of Mass Destruction (Amendment) Ordinance 2005 [No. 38 of 2005], First Supplement to the *Gibraltar Gazette*, (3471) of 26 May 2005.

16 The Weapons of Mass Destruction Ordinance 2004 [Gibraltar]. An Ordinance to make provision for the purpose of prohibiting the development, production, acquisition and possession of certain weapons of mass destruction; implementing in Gibraltar the Convention on the Prohibition of the Development, Production and Stockpiling of Bacteriological (Biological) and Toxin Weapons and on their Destruction, signed at Washington, London and Moscow on 10 April 1972, and the Convention on the Prohibition of the Development, Production, Stockpiling and Use of Chemical Weapons and on Their Destruction, signed at Paris on 13 January 1993; and for connected purposes, Second Supplement to the *Gibraltar Gazette*, (3437) of 4 November 2004 [Legal Notice No. 105 of 2004].

IHL Treaty Accession

IHL Treaty Accession

Country	GC I-IV 1949	Protection of victims of armed conflicts				CRC 1989	Opt Prot. CRC 2000	International Criminal Court	Protection of Cultural Property		
		AP I 1977	AP I Declaration art. 90	AP II 1977	AP III 2005			ICC Statute 1998	Hague Conv. 1954	Hague Prot. 1954	Hague Prot. 1999
Antigua and Barbuda	06/10/1986	06/10/1986		06/10/1986		05/10/1993		18/06/2001			
Australia	14/10/1958	21/06/1991	23/09/1992	21/06/1991		17/12/1990	26/09/2006	01/07/2002	19/09/1984		
Bahamas	11/07/1975	10/04/1980		10/04/1980		20/02/1991					
Bangladesh	04/04/1972	08/09/1980		08/09/1980		03/08/1990	06/09/2000		23/06/2006	23/06/2006	
Barbados	10/09/1968	19/02/1990		19/02/1990		09/10/1990		10/12/2002	09/04/2002	02/10/2008	02/10/2008
Belize	29/06/1984	29/06/1984		29/06/1984	03/04/2007	02/05/1990	01/12/2003	05/04/2000			
Botswana	29/03/1968	23/05/1979		23/05/1979		14/03/1995	04/10/2004	08/09/2000	03/01/2002		
Brunei Darussalam	14/10/1991	14/10/1991		14/10/1991		27/12/1995					
Cameroon	16/09/1963	16/03/1984		16/03/1984		11/01/1993			12/10/1961	12/10/1961	
Canada	14/05/1965	20/11/1990	20/11/1990	20/11/1990	26/11/2007	13/12/1991	07/07/2000	07/07/2000	11/12/1998	29/11/2005	29/11/2005
Cyprus	23/05/1962	01/06/1979	14/10/2002	18/03/1996	27/11/2007	07/02/1991		07/03/2002	09/09/1964	09/09/1964	16/05/2001
Dominica	28/09/1981	25/04/1996		25/04/1996		13/03/1991	20/09/2002	12/02/2001			
Fiji	09/08/1971	30/07/2008		30/07/2008	30/07/2008	13/08/1993		29/11/1999			
Gambia	20/10/1966	12/01/1989		12/01/1989		08/08/1990		28/06/2002			
Ghana	02/08/1958	28/02/1978		28/02/1978		05/02/1990		20/12/1999	25/07/1960	25/07/1960	
Grenada	13/04/1981	23/09/1998		23/09/1998		05/11/1990					
Guyana	22/07/1968	18/01/1988		18/01/1988		14/01/1991		24/09/2004			
India	09/11/1950					11/12/1992	30/11/2005		16/06/1958	16/06/1958	
Jamaica	20/07/1964	29/07/1986		29/07/1986		14/05/1991	09/05/2002				
Kenya	20/09/1966	23/02/1999		23/02/1999		30/07/1990	28/01/2002	15/03/2005			
Kiribati	05/01/1989					11/12/1995					
Lesotho	20/05/1968	20/05/1994		20/05/1994		10/03/1992	24/09/2003	06/09/2000			
Malawi	05/01/1968	07/10/1991		07/10/1991		02/01/1991		19/09/2002			
Malaysia	24/08/1962					17/02/1995			12/12/1960	12/12/1960	
Maldives	18/06/1991	03/09/1991		03/09/1991		11/02/1991	29/12/2004				
Malta	22/08/1968	17/04/1989	17/04/1989	17/04/1989		30/09/1990	09/05/2002	29/11/2002			
Mauritius	18/08/1970	22/03/1982		22/03/1982		26/07/1990	09/05/2002	05/03/2002	22/09/2006		
Mozambique	14/03/1983	14/03/1983		12/11/2002		26/04/1994	19/10/2004				
Namibia	22/08/1991	17/06/1994	21/07/1994	17/06/1994		30/09/1990	16/04/2002	26/06/2002			
Nauru	27/06/2006	27/06/2006		27/06/2006		27/07/1994		12/11/2001			
New Zealand	02/05/1959	08/02/1988	08/02/1988	08/02/1988		06/04/1993	12/11/2001	07/09/2000	24/07/2008		
Nigeria	20/06/1961	10/10/1988		10/10/1988		19/04/1991		27/09/2001	05/06/1961	05/06/1961	21/10/2005
Pakistan	12/06/1951					12/11/1990			27/03/1959	27/03/1959	

Country	Protection of victims of armed conflicts							International Criminal Court	Protection of Cultural Property		
	GC I-IV 1949	AP I 1977	AP I Declaration art. 90	AP II 1977	AP III 2005	CRC 1989	Opt Prot. CRC 2000	ICC Statute 1998	Hague Conv. 1954	Hague Prot. 1954	Hague Prot. 1999
Papua New Guinea	26/05/1976					02/03/1993					
Saint Kitts and Nevis	14/02/1986	14/02/1986		14/02/1986		24/07/1990		22/08/2006			
Saint Lucia	18/09/1981	07/10/1982		07/10/1982		16/06/1993					
Saint Vincent & Grenadine	01/04/1981	08/04/1983		08/04/1983		26/10/1993		03/12/2002			
Samoa	23/08/1984	23/08/1984		23/08/1984		29/11/1994		16/09/2002			
Seychelles	08/11/1984	08/11/1984	22/05/1992	08/11/1984		07/09/1990			08/10/2003		
Sierra Leone	10/06/1965	21/10/1986		21/10/1986		18/06/1990	15/05/2002	15/09/2000			
Singapore	27/04/1973				07/07/2008	05/10/1995					
Solomon Islands	06/07/1981	19/09/1988		19/09/1988		10/04/1995					
South Africa	31/03/1952	21/11/1995		21/11/1995		16/06/1995		27/11/2000	18/12/2003		
Sri Lanka	28/02/1959					12/07/1991	08/09/2000		11/05/2004		
Swaziland	28/06/1973	02/11/1995		02/11/1995		07/09/1995					
Tanzania (United Rep.of)	12/12/1962	15/02/1983		15/02/1983		10/06/1991	11/11/2004	20/08/2002	23/09/1971		
Tonga	13/04/1978	20/01/2003	20/01/2003	20/01/2003		06/11/1995					
Trinidad and Tobago	24/09/1963	20/07/2001	20/07/2001	20/07/2001		05/12/1991		06/04/1999			
Tuvalu	19/02/1981					22/09/1995					
Uganda	18/05/1964	13/03/1991		13/03/1991		17/08/1990	06/05/2002	14/06/2002			
United Kingdom	23/09/1957	28/01/1998	17/05/1999	28/01/1998		16/12/1991	24/06/2003	04/10/2001			
Vanuatu	27/10/1982	28/02/1985		28/02/1985		07/07/1993	26/09/2007				
Zambia	19/10/1966	04/05/1995		04/05/1995		06/12/1991		13/11/2002			

Environment columns: ENMOD Conv. 1976, Geneva Gas Prot. 1925, BWC 1972. Weapons columns: CCW 1980 through Ottawa Treaty 1997.

Country	ENMOD Conv. 1976	Geneva Gas Prot. 1925	BWC 1972	CCW 1980	CCW Prot. I 1980	CCW Prot. II 1980	CCW Prot. III 1980	CCW Prot. IV 1995	CCW Prot. II a 1996	CCW Amdt 2001	CCW Prot. V 2003	CWC 1993	Ottawa Treaty 1997
Antigua and Barbuda	25/10/1988	27/04/1989	29/01/2003									29/08/2005	03/05/1999
Australia	07/09/1984	24/05/1930	05/10/1977	29/09/1983	29/09/1983	29/09/1983	29/09/1983	22/08/1997	22/08/1997	03/12/2002	04/01/2007	06/05/1994	14/01/1999
Bahamas			26/11/1986										31/07/1998
Bangladesh	03/10/1979	20/05/1989	13/03/1985	06/09/2000	06/09/2000	06/09/2000	06/09/2000	06/09/2000	06/09/2000			25/04/1997	06/09/2000
Barbados		16/07/1976	16/02/1973									03/07/2007	26/01/1999
Belize			20/10/1986									01/12/2003	23/04/1998
Botswana			05/02/1992									31/08/1998	01/03/2000
Brunei Darussalam			31/01/1991									28/07/1997	24/04/2006
Cameroon		20/07/1989		07/12/2006	07/12/2006	07/12/2006	07/12/2006	07/12/2006	07/12/2006			16/09/1996	19/09/2002
Canada	11/06/1981	06/05/1930	18/09/1972	24/06/1994	24/06/1994	24/06/1994	24/06/1994	05/01/1998	05/01/1998	22/07/2002		26/09/1995	03/12/1997
Cyprus	12/04/1978	12/12/1966	06/11/1973	12/12/1988	12/12/1988	12/12/1988	12/12/1988	22/07/2003	22/07/2003			28/08/1998	17/01/2003
Dominica	09/11/1992		08/11/1978									12/02/2001	26/03/1999
Fiji		21/03/1973	01/10/1973									20/01/1993	10/06/1998
Gambia		05/11/1966	21/11/1991									19/05/1998	23/09/2002
Ghana	22/06/1978	03/05/1967	06/06/1975									09/07/1997	30/06/2000
Grenada		03/01/1989	22/10/1986									03/06/2005	19/08/1998
Guyana												12/09/1997	05/08/2003
India	15/12/1978	09/04/1930	15/07/1974	01/03/1984	01/03/1984	01/03/1984	01/03/1984	02/09/1999	02/09/1999	18/05/2005	18/05/2005	03/09/1996	17/07/1998
Jamaica		28/07/1970	13/08/1975	25/09/2008	25/09/2008			25/09/2008	25/09/2008	25/09/2008	25/09/2008	08/09/2000	17/07/1998
Kenya		06/07/1970	07/01/1976									25/04/1997	23/01/2001
Kiribati												07/09/2000	07/09/2000
Lesotho		10/03/1972	06/09/1977	06/09/2000	06/09/2000	06/09/2000	06/09/2000					07/12/1994	02/12/1998
Malawi	05/10/1978	14/09/1970										11/06/1998	13/08/1998
Malaysia		10/12/1970	06/06/1991									20/04/2000	22/04/1999
Maldives		27/12/1966	02/08/1993									31/05/1994	07/09/2000
Malta		21/09/1964	07/04/1975	26/06/1995	26/06/1995	26/06/1995	26/06/1995	24/09/2004	24/09/2004	24/09/2004	22/09/2006	28/04/1997	07/05/2001
Mauritius	09/12/1992	12/03/1968	11/01/1973	06/05/1996	06/05/1996	06/05/1996	06/05/1996	24/12/2002				09/02/1993	03/12/1997
Mozambique												15/08/2000	25/08/1998
Namibia												24/11/1995	21/09/1998
Nauru												12/11/2001	07/08/2000
New Zealand	07/09/1984	24/05/1930	18/12/1972	18/10/1993	18/10/1993	18/10/1993	18/10/1993	08/01/1998	08/01/1998		02/10/2007	15/07/1996	27/01/1999
Nigeria		15/10/1968	09/07/1973									20/05/1999	27/09/2001
Pakistan	27/02/1986	15/04/1960	03/10/1974	01/04/1985	01/04/1985	01/04/1985	01/04/1985	05/12/2000	09/03/1999			28/10/1997	

Country	Environment			Weapons									
	ENMOD Conv. 1976	Geneva Gas Prot. 1925	BWC 1972	CCW 1980	CCW Prot. I 1980	CCW Prot. II 1980	CCW Prot. III 1980	CCW Prot. IV 1995	CCW Prot. II a 1996	CCW Amdt 2001	CCW Prot. V 2003	CWC 1993	Ottawa Treaty 1997
Papua New Guinea	28/10/1980	02/09/1980	27/10/1980									17/04/1996	28/06/2004
Saint Kitts and Nevis		27/04/1989	02/04/1991									21/05/2004	02/12/1998
Saint Lucia	27/05/1993	21/12/1988	26/11/1986									09/04/1997	13/04/1999
Saint Vincent & Grenadine	27/04/1999	24/03/1999	13/05/1999									18/09/2002	01/08/2001
Samoa												27/09/2002	23/07/1998
Seychelles			11/10/1979	08/06/2000	08/06/2000	08/06/2000	08/06/2000	08/06/2000	08/06/2000			07/04/1993	02/06/2000
Sierra Leone		20/03/1967	29/06/1976	30/09/2004	30/09/2004	30/09/2004	30/09/2004	30/09/2004	30/09/2004	30/09/2004	30/09/2004	30/09/2004	25/04/2001
Singapore		02/12/1975	02/12/1975									21/05/1997	
Solomon Islands	19/06/1981	01/06/1981	17/06/1981									23/09/2004	26/01/1999
South Africa		24/05/1930	03/11/1975	13/09/1995	13/09/1995	13/09/1995	13/09/1995	26/06/1998	26/06/1998			13/09/1995	26/06/1998
Sri Lanka	25/04/1978	20/01/1954	18/11/1986	24/09/2004	24/09/2004	24/09/2004	24/09/2004	24/09/2004	24/09/2004	24/09/2004		19/08/1994	22/12/1998
Swaziland		23/07/1991	18/06/1991									20/09/1996	13/11/2000
Tanzania (United Rep.of)		22/04/1963	28/07/2008									25/06/1998	
Tonga		19/07/1971	28/09/1976									29/05/2003	
Trinidad and Tobago		31/08/1962	19/07/2007									24/06/1997	27/04/1998
Tuvalu												19/01/2004	
Uganda	16/05/1978	24/05/1965	12/05/1992	14/11/1995	14/11/1995	14/11/1995	14/11/1995					30/11/2001	25/02/1999
United Kingdom		09/04/1930	26/03/1975	13/02/1995	13/02/1995	13/02/1995	13/02/1995	11/02/1999	11/02/1999	25/07/2002		13/05/1996	31/07/1998
Vanuatu			12/10/1990									16/09/2005	16/09/2005
Zambia			15/01/2008									09/02/2001	23/02/2001

Model Laws

Model Law: Geneva Conventions (Consolidation) Act

Legislation for Common Law States on the 1949 Geneva Conventions and their 1977 and 2005 Additional Protocols

Model Geneva Conventions Act (for Common Law States)

Using the Geneva Conventions Acts adopted by different States, and following discussions held with common law experts, the ICRC Advisory Service on IHL has drawn up this model Geneva Conventions Act. This Model Act gives effect to the provisions of the four Geneva Conventions of 12 August 1949, their Additional Protocols I and II of 8 June 1977, and their Additional Protocol III of 8 December 2005.

Model Geneva Conventions (Consolidation) Act [200X]

An Act to enable effect to be given to certain Conventions done at Geneva on 12 August 1949, to the Protocols additional I and II to those Conventions done at Geneva on 8 June 1977, and to Protocol additional III to those Conventions of 8 December 2005, and for related purposes

BE it enacted by [the Parliament of INSERT COUNTRY NAME] as follows:

PART I—PRELIMINARY

Short title and commencement

1. (1) This Act may be cited as the *Geneva Conventions Act [INSERT YEAR]*.
   (2) This Act shall come into force on [INSERT DATE].

Interpretation

2. (1) In this Act, unless the contrary intention appears:

      'court' does not include a court-martial or other military court;

      'the First Convention' means the Geneva Convention for the Amelioration of the Condition of the Wounded and Sick in Armed Forces in the Field, adopted at Geneva on 12 August 1949, a copy of which Convention (not including the annexes to that Convention) is set out in Schedule 1;

'the Second Convention' means the Geneva Convention for the Amelioration of the Condition of Wounded, Sick and Shipwrecked Members of Armed Forces at Sea, adopted at Geneva on 12 August 1949, a copy of which Convention (not including the annex to that Convention) is set out in Schedule 2;

'the Third Convention' means the Geneva Convention relative to the Treatment of Prisoners of War, adopted at Geneva on 12 August 1949, a copy of which Convention (not including the annexes to that Convention) is set out in Schedule 3;

'the Fourth Convention' means the Geneva Convention relative to the Protection of Civilian Persons in Time of War, adopted at Geneva on 12 August 1949, a copy of which Convention (not including the annexes to that Convention) is set out in Schedule 4;

'the Conventions' means the First Convention, the Second Convention, the Third Convention and the Fourth Convention;

'prisoners' representative', in relation to a particular protected prisoner of war at a particular time, means the person by whom the functions of prisoners' representative within the meaning of Article 79 of the Third Convention were exercisable in relation to that prisoner at the camp or place at which that prisoner was, at or last before that time, detained as a protected prisoner of war;

'protected internee' means a person protected by the Fourth Convention or Protocol I, and interned in [INSERT COUNTRY NAME];

'protected prisoner of war' means a person protected by the Third Convention or a person who is protected as a prisoner of war under Protocol I;

'the protecting power', in relation to a protected prisoner of war or a protected internee, means the power or organization which is carrying out, in the interests of the power of which he or she is a national, or of whose forces he or she is, or was at any material time, a member, the duties assigned to protecting powers under the Third Convention, the Fourth Convention or Protocol I, as the case may be;

'Protocol I' means the Protocol Additional to the Geneva Conventions of 12 August 1949, and relating to the Protection of Victims of International Armed Conflicts (Protocol I), done at Geneva on 8 June 1977, a copy of which Protocol (including Annex I to that Protocol) is set out in Schedule 5;

'Protocol II' means the Protocol Additional to the Geneva Conventions of 12 August 1949, and relating to the Protection of Victims of Non-International Armed Conflicts (Protocol II), done at Geneva on 8 June 1977, a copy of which Protocol is set out in Schedule 6;

'Protocol III' means the Protocol Additional to the Geneva Conventions of 12 August 1949, and relating to the Adoption of an Additional Distinctive Emblem (Protocol III), done at Geneva on 8 December 2005, a copy of which Protocol is set out in Schedule 7;

'the Protocols' means Protocol I, Protocol II and Protocol III.

(2) If the ratification on behalf of [INSERT COUNTRY NAME] of any of the Conventions or of either of the Protocols is subject to a reservation or is accompanied by a declaration, that Convention or that Protocol shall, for the purposes of this Act, have effect and be construed subject to and in accordance with that reservation or declaration.

PART II—PUNISHMENT OF OFFENDERS AGAINST THE CONVENTIONS AND PROTOCOL I

Punishment of grave breaches of the Conventions and Protocol I

3. (1) Any person, whatever his or her nationality, who, in [INSERT COUNTRY NAME] or elsewhere, commits, or aids, abets or procures any other person to commit, a grave breach of any of the Conventions, of Protocol I or of Protocol III, is guilty of an indictable offence.

    (2) For the purposes of this section:

    (a) a grave breach of the First Convention is a breach of that Convention involving an act referred to in Article 50 of that Convention committed against persons or property protected by that Convention;

    (b) a grave breach of the Second Convention is a breach of that Convention involving an act referred to in Article 51 of that Convention committed against persons or property protected by that Convention;

    (c) a grave breach of the Third Convention is a breach of that Convention involving an act referred to in Article 130 of that Convention committed against persons or property protected by that Convention;

    (d) a grave breach of the Fourth Convention is a breach of that Convention involving an act referred to in Article 147 of that Convention committed against persons or property protected by that Convention;

    (e) a grave breach of Protocol I is anything referred to as a grave breach of the Protocol in paragraph 4 of Article 11, or paragraph 2, 3 or 4 of Article 85, of the Protocol; and

    (f) a grave breach of Protocol III is any misuse of the third Protocol emblem amounting to perfidious use in the meaning of Article 85 paragraph 3 (f) of Protocol I.

    (3) In the case of an offence against this section committed outside [INSERT COUNTRY NAME], a person may be proceeded against, indicted, tried and punished therefore in any place in [INSERT COUNTRY NAME] as if the offence had been committed in that place, and the offence shall, for all purposes incidental to or consequential on the trial or punishment thereof, be deemed to have been committed in that place.

Punishment of other breaches of the Conventions and Protocols

4. (1) Any person, whatever his or her nationality, who, in [INSERT COUNTRY NAME], commits, or aids, abets or procures any other person to commit, a breach of any of the Conventions or Protocols not covered by section 3, is guilty of an indictable offence.

    (2) Any national of [INSERT COUNTRY NAME] who, outside [INSERT COUNTRY NAME], commits, or aids, abets or procures the commission by another person of a breach of any of the Conventions or Protocols not covered by section 3 is guilty of an indictable offence.

Penalties and procedure

5. (1) The punishment for an offence against section 3 or section 4 is:

    (a) where the offence involves the wilful killing of a person protected by the relevant Convention or by Protocol I—imprisonment for life or for any lesser term; and

    (b) in any other case—imprisonment for a term not exceeding 14 years.

   (2) An offence against section 3 or section 4 shall not be prosecuted in a court except by indictment by or on behalf of the [Attorney-General/Director of Public Prosecutions].

Proof of application of the Conventions or Protocols

6.   If, in proceedings under this Part in respect of a breach of any of the Conventions or of either of the Protocols, a question arises under:

    (a) Article 2 or Article 3 of that Convention (which relate to the circumstances in which the Convention applies);

    (b) Article 1 or Article 3 of Protocol I (which relate to the circumstances in which that Protocol applies); or

    (c) Article 1 of Protocol II (which relates to the circumstances in which that Protocol applies);

    (d) Article 1 of Protocol III (which relates to the circumstances in which that Protocol applies);

    a certificate under the hand of the [Minister of State for Foreign Affairs] certifying to any matter relevant to that question is prima facie evidence of the matter so certified.

Jurisdiction of courts

7. (1) A person shall not be tried for an offence against section 3 or section 4 by a court other than the [INSERT NAME OF COURT].

   (2) The enactments relating to the trial by court-martial of persons who commit civil offences shall have effect for the purposes of the jurisdiction of courts-martial convened in [INSERT NAME OF COUNTRY] as if this Part had not been passed.

PART III—LEGAL PROCEEDINGS IN RESPECT OF PROTECTED PERSONS

Notice of trial of protected persons to be served on protecting power, etc.

8. (1) The court before which:

    (a) a protected prisoner of war is brought up for trial for an offence; or

(b) a protected internee is brought up for trial for an offence for which that court has power to sentence him or her to imprisonment for a term of two years or more;

shall not proceed with the trial until it is proved to the satisfaction of the court that a notice containing the particulars mentioned in subsection (2), so far as they are known to the prosecutor, has been served not less than three weeks previously on the protecting power (if there is a protecting power) and, if the accused is a protected prisoner of war, on the accused and the prisoners' representative.

(2) The particulars referred to in subsection (1) are:

(a) the full name, date of birth and description of the accused, including his or her profession or trade; and where the accused is a protected prisoner of war, the accused's rank and his or her army, regimental, personal and serial number;

(b) the accused's place of detention, internment or residence;

(c) the offence with which the accused is charged; and

(d) the court before which the trial is to take place and the time and place appointed for the trial.

(3) For the purposes of this section, a document purporting:

(a) to be signed on behalf of the protecting power or by the prisoners' representative or by the person accused, as the case may be; and

(b) to be an acknowledgement of the receipt by that power, representative or person on a specified day of a notice described in the document as a notice under this section;

shall, unless the contrary is shown, be sufficient evidence that the notice required by subsection (1) was served on that power, representative or person on that day.

(4) A court which adjourns a trial for the purpose of enabling the requirements of this section to be complied with may, notwithstanding anything in any other law, remand the accused for the period of the adjournment.

Legal representation of certain persons

9. (1) The court before which:

(a) any person is brought up for trial for an offence under section 3 or section 4 of this Act; or

(b) a protected prisoner of war is brought up for trial for any offence;

shall not proceed with the trial unless—

(i) the accused is represented by counsel; and

(ii) it is proved to the satisfaction of the court that a period of not less than 14 days has elapsed since instructions for the representation of the accused at the trial were first given to the counsel;

and, if the court adjourns the trial for the purpose of enabling the requirements of this subsection to be complied with, then, notwithstanding anything in any other law, the court may remand the accused for the period of the adjournment.

(2) Where the accused is a protected prisoner of war, in the absence of counsel accepted by the accused as representing him or her, counsel instructed for the purpose on behalf of the protecting power shall, without prejudice to the requirements of paragraph (ii) of subsection (1), be regarded for the purposes of that subsection as representing the accused.

(3) If the court adjourns the trial in pursuance of subsection (1) by reason that the accused is not represented by counsel, the court shall direct that a counsel be assigned to watch over the interests of the accused at any further proceedings in connection with the offence, and at any such further proceedings, in the absence of counsel either accepted by the accused as representing him or her or instructed as mentioned in subsection (2), counsel assigned in pursuance of this subsection shall, without prejudice to the requirements of paragraph (ii) of subsection (1), be regarded for the purposes of subsection (1) as representing the accused.

(4) Counsel shall be assigned in pursuance of subsection (3) in such manner as may be prescribed in regulations or, in the absence of provision in the regulations, as the court directs, and counsel so assigned shall be entitled to be paid by [the Minister] such sums in respect of fees and disbursements as may be prescribed by regulations.

Appeals by protected prisoners of war and internees

10. (1) Where a protected prisoner of war or a protected internee has been sentenced to imprisonment for a term of two years or more, the time within which the person must give notice of appeal or notice of application for leave to appeal [to INSERT NAME OF APPEAL COURT] shall, notwithstanding anything in any enactment relating to such appeals, be the period from the date of conviction or, in the case of an appeal against sentence, of sentencing, to the expiration of ten days after the date on which the person receives a notice given—

(a) in the case of a protected prisoner of war, by an officer of [the Armed Forces]; or

(b) in the case of a protected internee, by or on behalf of the governor or other person in charge of the prison or place in which he or she is confined;

that the protecting power has been notified of his or her conviction and sentence.

(2) Where, after an appeal against the conviction or sentence by a court of a protected prisoner of war or a protected internee has been determined, the sentence remains or has become a sentence of imprisonment for a term of two years or more, the time within which the person must apply to the [Attorney General] for a certificate authorizing an appeal [to INSERT NAME OF APPEAL COURT] shall be the period from the date of the previous decision on appeal until seven days after the date on which the person receives a notice given by a person referred to in paragraph (a) or (b), as the case may require, of subsection (1) that the protecting power has been notified of the decision of the court on the previous appeal.

(3) Where subsection (1) or (2) applies in relation to a convicted person, then, unless the court otherwise orders, an order of the court relating to the restitution of property or the payment of compensation to an aggrieved person shall not take effect, and a provision of a law relating to the revesting of property on conviction shall not take effect in relation to the conviction, while an appeal by the convicted person against his or her conviction or sentence is possible.

(4) Subsections (1) and (2) do not apply in relation to an appeal against a conviction or sentence, or against the decision of a court upon a previous appeal, if, at the time of the conviction or sentence, or of the decision of the court upon the previous appeal, as the case may be, there is no protecting power.

Reduction of sentence and custody of protected prisoners of war and internees

11. (1) In any case in which a protected prisoner of war or a protected internee is convicted of an offence and sentenced to a term of imprisonment, it shall be lawful for the [Attorney-General] to direct that there shall be deducted from that term a period, not exceeding the period, if any, during which that person was in custody in connection with that offence, either on remand or after committal for trial (including the period of the trial), before the sentence began, or is deemed to have begun, to run.

(2) In a case where the [Attorney-General] is satisfied that a protected prisoner of war accused of an offence has been in custody in connection with that offence, either on remand or after committal for trial (including the period of the trial), for an aggregate period of not less than three months, it shall be lawful for the [Attorney-General] to direct that the prisoner shall be transferred from that custody to the custody of [an officer of the Armed Forces] and thereafter remain in military custody at a camp or place in which protected prisoners of war are detained, and be brought before the court at the time appointed by the remand or committal order.

PART IV—MISUSE OF THE RED CROSS AND OTHER EMBLEMS, SIGNS, SIGNALS, IDENTITY CARDS, INSIGNIA AND UNIFORMS

Use of red cross, red crescent and other emblems, etc.

12. (1) Subject to the provisions of this section, it shall not be lawful for any person, without the consent in writing of the [Minister of Defence or a person authorized in writing by the Minister to give consent under this section], to use or display for any purpose whatsoever any of the following:

(a) the emblem of a red cross with vertical and horizontal arms of the same length on, and completely surrounded by, a white ground, or the designation 'Red Cross' or 'Geneva Cross';

(b) the emblem of a red crescent moon on, and completely surrounded by, a white ground, or the designation 'Red Crescent';

(c)   the emblem in red on, and completely surrounded by, a white ground, that is to say, a lion passing from right to left of, and with its face turned towards, the observer, holding erect in its raised right forepaw a scimitar, with, appearing above the lion's back, the upper half of the sun shooting forth rays, or the designation 'Red Lion and Sun';

(d)   the emblem in red on, and completely surrounded by, a white ground, that is to say; a red frame in the shape of a square on edge (whether or not incorporating within its centre another emblem or sign or combination thereof in accordance with Article 3, paragraph 1 of Additional Protocol III), or the designation 'Red Crystal', or the designation 'third Protocol emblem';

(e)   the emblem of a white or silver cross with vertical and horizontal arms of the same length on, and completely surrounded by, a red ground, being the heraldic emblem of the Swiss Confederation;

(f)   the sign of an equilateral blue triangle on, and completely surrounded by, an orange ground, being the international distinctive sign of civil defence;

(g)   any of the distinctive signals specified in Chapter III of Annex I to Protocol I, being the signals of identification for medical units and transports;

(h)   the sign consisting of a group of three bright orange circles of equal size, placed on the same axis, the distance between each circle being one radius, being the international special sign for works and installations containing dangerous forces;

(i)   a design, wording or signal so nearly resembling any of the emblems, designations, signs or signals specified in paragraph (a), (b), (c), (d), (e), (f) (g) or (h) as to be capable of being mistaken for, or, as the case may be, understood as referring to, one of those emblems, designations, signs or signals;

(j)   such other flags, emblems, designations, signs, signals, designs, wordings, identity cards, information cards, insignia or uniforms as are prescribed for the purpose of giving effect to the Conventions or Protocols.

(2)   The [Minister of Defence or a person authorized in writing by the Minister to give consent under this section] shall not give such consent except for the purpose of giving effect to the provisions of the Conventions or Protocols and may refuse or withdraw such consent as necessary.

(3)   This section extends to the use in or outside [INSERT COUNTRY NAME] of an emblem, designation, sign, signal, design, wording, identity card, identification cards, insignia or uniform referred to in subsection (1) on any ship or aircraft registered in [INSERT COUNTRY NAME].

Offences and penalties

13. (1)   Any person who contravenes section 12(1) shall be guilty of an offence and shall be liable on conviction to a fine not exceeding [INSERT MAXIMUM FINE] or to imprisonment for a term not exceeding [INSERT MAXIMUM PERIOD OF IMPRISONMENT] or both.

(2) Where a court convicts a person of an offence against section 12(1), the court may order the forfeiture to the State of:

    (a) any goods or other article upon or in connection with which an emblem, designation, sign, signal, design or wording was used by that person; and

    (b) any identity cards, identification cards, insignia or uniforms used in the commission of the offence.

(3) Where an offence against section 12(1) committed by a body corporate is proved to have been committed with the consent or connivance of a director, manager, secretary or other officer of the body corporate, or a person purporting to act in any such capacity, he or she, as well as the body corporate, shall be deemed to be guilty of the offence and shall be liable to be proceeded against and punished accordingly.

(4) Proceedings under section 12(1) shall not be instituted without the consent in writing of the [Attorney-General].

Saving

14.   In the case of a trade mark registered before the passing of this Act, sections 12 and 13 do not apply by reason only of its consisting of or containing an emblem specified in subparagraph 12(1) (b), (c) or (d) or a design resembling such an emblem, and where a person is charged with using such an emblem, sign or design for any purpose and it is proved that the person used it otherwise than as, or as part of, a trade mark so registered, it is a defence for the person to prove:

    (a) that the person lawfully used that emblem, sign or design for that purpose before the passing of this Act; or

    (b) in a case where the person is charged with using the emblem, sign or design upon goods or any other article, that the emblem, sign or design had been applied to the goods or that article before the person acquired them or it by some other person who had manufactured or dealt with them in the course of trade and who lawfully used the emblem, sign or design upon similar goods or articles before the passing of this Act.

PART V—REGULATIONS

Regulations

15.   [INSERT NAME OF REGULATION-MAKING AUTHORITY] may make regulations:

    (a) prescribing the form of flags, emblems, designations, signs, signals, designs, wordings, identity cards, information cards, insignia or uniforms for use for the purposes of giving effect to the Conventions or the Protocols or both, and regulating their use;

(b)   prescribing the penalty that may be imposed in respect of contravention of, or non-compliance with, any regulations made under paragraph (a) of this section, which may be a fine not exceeding [INSERT MAXIMUM FINE] or imprisonment for a term not exceeding [INSERT MAXIMUM PERIOD OF IMPRISONMENT] or both; and

(c)   providing for such other matters as are required or permitted to be prescribed, or that are necessary or convenient to be prescribed, for carrying out or giving effect to this Act.

SCHEDULE

1.   The Geneva Convention for the Amelioration of the Condition of the Wounded and Sick in Armed Forces in the Field, adopted at Geneva on 12 August 1949.

2.   The Geneva Convention for the Amelioration of the Condition of Wounded, Sick and Shipwrecked Members of Armed Forces at Sea, adopted at Geneva on 12 August 1949.

3.   The Geneva Convention relative to the Treatment of Prisoners of War, adopted at Geneva on 12 August 1949.

4.   The Geneva Convention relative to the Protection of Civilian Persons in Time of War, adopted at Geneva on 12 August 1949.

5.   The Protocol Additional to the Geneva Conventions of 12 August 1949, and relating to the Protection of Victims of International Armed Conflicts (Protocol I), done at Geneva on 8 June 1977.

6.   The Protocol Additional to the Geneva Conventions of 12 August 1949, and relating to the Protection of Victims of Non-International Armed Conflicts (Protocol II), done at Geneva on 8 June 1977.

7.   The Protocol Additional to the Geneva Conventions of 12 August 1949, and relating to the Adoption of an Additional Distinctive Emblem (Protocol III), done at Geneva on 8 December 2005.

8.   Resolution 1 of the 29th International Conference of the Red Cross and Red Crescent (Geneva, 20–21 June 2006).

Model Law: To Implement the Rome Statute of the International Criminal Court

An Act to enable ...... (name of country) to implement and give effect to its obligations under the Rome Statute of the International Criminal Court; and for connected matters

Note: This model law should be read with reference to the Report of the Commonwealth Expert Group on Implementing Legislation for the Rome Statute of the International Criminal Court, Marlborough House, London, 7–9 July 2004 (the Report which can be found in Part II of this document). The footnotes to the sections provide cross-references to relevant sections of the report.

PREAMBLE

RECOGNIZING that genocide, crimes against humanity and war crimes, as the most serious crimes of concern to the international community must not go unpunished and effective prosecution must be ensured by taking measures at the national level and enhancing international co-operational;

EMPHASIZING that the International Criminal Court established under the Rome Statute is complementary to national criminal jurisdictions;

MINDFUL of the need for ...... (name of country) as a State Party to implement the obligations under the Rome Statute in 00domestic law;

NOW BE IT ENACTED by (Parliament) of ...... (name of country) as follows:

PART I-PRELIMINARY

1. Short title

This Act may be cited as the International Criminal Court Act ...... (year).

2. Act to bind the (Crown/Republic)[1]

This Act shall bind the (Crown/Republic) and shall apply to persons in the public service of the (Crown/Republic) and to property held for the purposes of the public

---

[1] See discussion under Part XXVI of the Report on Sovereign Immunity and Clause 47 of the drafting instructions.

service of the (Crown/Republic), in all respects, as it applies to other persons and property.

3. Interpretation

(1) In this Act, unless the context otherwise requires—

'the Agreement on the Privileges and Immunities of the ICC' means the agreement set out in Schedule 2 to this Act;

'crime within the jurisdiction of the ICC' means

(a) a crime over which the ICC has jurisdiction under article 5 of the Statute; or

(b) an offence against the administration of justice over which the ICC has jurisdiction under article 70 of the Statute;

'ICC' means the International Criminal Court established under the Statute;

'ICC prisoner' means a person on whom a sentence of imprisonment has been imposed by the ICC and includes a person who is held in custody at the request of the ICC during a sitting of the ICC in ...... (name of country);

'Minister' means the Minister of ......;

'Prescribed' means prescribed by regulations made under this Act;

'Pre-Trial Chamber' means the Pre-Trial Chamber of the ICC;

'Property' means movable or immovable property of every description, whether situated in ...... (name of country) or elsewhere and whether tangible or intangible; and includes an interest in any such movable or immovable property;

'Prosecutor' means the Prosecutor of the ICC;

'Restraining order' means an order prohibiting any person from dealing in the property specified in the order other than in accordance with the conditions and exceptions specified in the order;

'Rules' means the Rules of Procedure and Evidence adopted under article 51 of the Statute;

'Seizing order' means an order authorizing a police officer to search for any property and to seize the property if found or any other property that the police officer believes on reasonable grounds may relate to the request from the ICC;

'Statute' means the Rome Statute of the ICC set out in Schedule 1 to this Act;

'Trial Chamber' means the Trial Chamber of the ICC.

[**Optional Alternative Definition** (to be included if employing optional alternative offence provisions under section 5, 6 or 7)

'conventional international law' means a convention, treaty or other international agreement to which ...... (name of country) is a party and for the time being in force.]

(2) For the purposes of this Act—

(a) a reference in this Act to a request by the ICC for assistance includes a reference to a request by the ICC for co-operation;

(b) a reference in this Act to a request by the ICC for assistance under a specified provision or in relation to a particular matter includes a reference to a request by the ICC for co-operation under that provision or in relation to that matter;

(c) a reference in this Act to a figure in brackets immediately following the number of an article of the Statute is a reference to the paragraph of that article with the number corresponding to the figure in brackets;

(d) a reference in this Act to a sentence of imprisonment imposed by the ICC includes a reference to a sentence of imprisonment extended by the ICC (whether for the non-payment of a fine or otherwise).

4. Obligations imposed by Statute or Rules

Where any provision of the Statute or the Rules confers or imposes a power or duty on, or assigns a function to, a State including but not limited to a power, duty or function relating to the execution of a request for assistance from the ICC, that power, duty, or function may, unless there is provision to the contrary in this Act, be exercised, performed and discharged by the Minister on behalf of the Government of ...... (name of country).

PART II—INTERNATIONAL CRIMES AND OFFENCES AGAINST THE ADMINISTRATION OF JUSTICE

International Crimes[2]

5. Genocide

(1) Every person who, in ...... (name of country) or elsewhere—

(a) commits genocide; or

(b) conspires or agrees with any person to commit genocide, whether that genocide is to be committed in ...... (name of country) or elsewhere,

shall be guilty of an offence and shall be liable, on conviction after trial on indictment, to the penalty specified in subsection (3).

(2) For the purposes of this section, 'genocide' is an act referred to in article 6 of the Statute.[3]

Option 1

(3) The penalty for the offence referred to in subsection (1) shall—

(a) if the offence involves the willful killing of a person, be the same as the penalty for murder prescribed by the law of ...... (name of country); and

(b) in any other case, be imprisonment for a term not exceeding 30 years or a term of life imprisonment when justified by the extreme gravity of the crime and the individual circumstances of the convicted person.

OR

---

2 See discussion in the Report of offences and penalties for core crimes in Part II on Core Crimes—Substance and Part IV on Core Crimes—Penalties and Clauses 1 and 3 of the drafting instructions.

3 The intention of subparagraph 2 of this section and sections 6 and 7 is to incorporate the crime definitions by reference to the Statute. If there are concerns about the sufficiency of incorporation by reference, the text of the Statute definitions can be replicated in the legislation.

Option 2

(3) The penalty for an offence referred to subsection (1) shall be ...... (penalty consistent with domestic law).

[Optional Alternative Offence Provision[4]

(1) Every person who, in ...... (name of country) or elsewhere—

    (a) *commits genocide;*

    (b) *conspires or agrees with any person to commit genocide, whether that genocide is to be committed in ...... (name of country) or elsewhere,*

shall be guilty of an offence and shall be liable, after conviction after trial on indictment, to the penalty specified in subsection (3).

(2) For the purposes of this section, 'genocide' is an act specified in article 6 of the Statute and includes any other act which, at the time and in the place of its commission, constitutes genocide according to customary international law or conventional international law or by virtue of it being criminal according to the general principles of law recognized by the community of nations, whether or not it constitutes a contravention of the law in force at the time and in the place of its commission.]

6. Crimes against humanity

(1) Every person who, in ...... (name of country) or elsewhere, commits a crime against humanity shall be guilty of an offence and shall be liable, on conviction after trial on indictment, to the penalty specified in subsection (3).

(2) For the purposes of this section, a 'crime against humanity' is an act specified in article 7 of the Statute.

Option 1

(1) The penalty for the offence referred to in subsection (1) shall—

    (a) if the offence involves the willful killing of a person, be the same as the penalty for murder prescribed by the law of ...... (name of country); and

    (b) in any other case, be imprisonment for a term not exceeding 30 years or a term of life imprisonment when justified by the extreme gravity of the crime and the individual circumstances of the convicted person.

OR

Option 2

(3) The penalty for an offence referred to in subsection (1) shall be ...... (penalty consistent with domestic law).

---

4   In respect of the optional alternative offence provisions in sections 5, 6 and 7 see discussion in paragraph 7 of the Report on adopting a 'living' definition.

[Optional Alternative Offence Provision

(1) Every person who, in ...... (name of country) or elsewhere, commits a crime against humanity shall be guilty of an offence and shall be liable, on conviction after trial on indictment, to the penalty specified in subsection (3).

(2) For the purposes of this section, 'crime against humanity' is an act specified in article 7 of the Statute and includes any other act which, at the time and in the place of its commission, constitutes a crime against humanity according to customary international law or conventional international law or by virtue of it being criminal according to the general principles of law recognized by the community of nations, whether or not it constitutes a contravention of the law in force at the time and in the place of its commission.]

7. War crimes

(1) Every person who, in ...... (name of country) or elsewhere, commits a war crime shall be guilty of an offence and shall be liable, on conviction after trial on indictment, to the penalty specified in subsection (3).

(2) For the purposes of this section, a 'war crime' is an act specified in—

    (a) article 8(2)(a) of the Statute (which relates to grave breaches of the First, Second, Third, and Fourth Geneva Conventions); or

    (b) article 8(2)(b) of the Statute (which relates to other serious violations of the laws and customs applicable in international armed conflict); or

    (c) article 8(2)(c) of the Statute (which relates to armed conflict not of an international character involving serious violations of article 3 common to the four Geneva Conventions of 12 August 1949); or

    (d) article 8(2)(e) of the Statute (which relates to other serious violations of the laws and customs applicable in armed conflict not of an international character).

Option 1

(3) The penalty for an offence referred to in subsection (1) shall—

    (a) if the offence involves the willful killing of a person, be the same as the penalty for murder prescribed by the law of ...... (name of country); and

    (b) in any other case, be imprisonment for a term not exceeding 30 years or a term of life imprisonment when justified by the extreme gravity of the crime and the individual circumstances of the convicted person.

OR

Option 2

(3) The penalty for an offence referred to in subsection (1) shall be ...... (penalty consistent with domestic law).

[Optional Alternative Offence Provision

(1) Every person who, in ...... (name of country) or elsewhere, commits a war crime shall be guilty of an offence and shall be liable, on conviction after trial on indictment, to the penalty specified in subsection (3).

(2) For the purposes of this section, a 'war crime' means an act specified in article 8(2) of the Statute and any other act committed during an armed conflict which, at the time and in the place of its commission, constitutes a war crime according to customary international law or conventional international law applicable to armed conflicts, whether or not it constitutes a contravention of the law in force at the time and in the place of its commission.]

[Optional Additional Provision

7A Other violations of the Geneva Conventions[5]

(1) Every person who, in the course of an international armed conflict or an armed conflict not of an international character, commits any act in violation of the Geneva Conventions of 1949 or the Additional Protocol of 1977 (not being an act specified in section 7(2)), shall be guilty of an offence and shall be liable, on conviction after trial on indictment, to the penalty specified in subsection (2).

(2) The penalty for an offence referred to in subsection (1) shall—

(a) if the offence involves the willful killing of a person, be the same as the penalty for murder prescribed by the law of ...... (name of country); and

(b) in any other case, be imprisonment for life or a term not exceeding 30 years or a term of life imprisonment when justified by the extreme gravity of the crime and the individual circumstances of the convicted person.]

Interpretation and General Principles

8. Interpretation of articles 6, 7 and 8 of the Statute[6]

In interpreting and applying the provisions of articles 6, 7 and 8 of the Statute, the court shall take into account any elements of crime adopted and amended under article 9 of the Statute.

9. Defences to offences under section 5, 6 or 7[7]

Option 1

A person charged with an offence under section 5, 6 or 7 may rely on any defence, excuse or justification available to him or her under the law of ...... (name of country).

OR

Option 2

(1) A person charged with an offence under section 5, 6 or 7 may rely on any defence, excuse or justification available to him or her under the law of ...... (name of country) or under international law.

---

5   See discussion of implementing other international obligations in paragraph 7 of the Report.
6   See discussion of interpretive provisions under Part XIII of the Report on General Interpretative Provisions.
7   See discussion of applicable law for defences under paragraphs 63–67 of the Report and Clauses 17 and 18 of the drafting instructions.

(2) In the case of an inconsistency between a provision of the law of ...... (name of country) and a principle or provision of international law, the principle or provision of international law shall prevail.

OR

Option 3

(1) Subject to subsection 3, a person charged with an offence under section 5, 6 or 7 may rely on any defence, excuse or justification available to him or her under the law of ...... (name of country) or under international law.

(2) In the case of an inconsistency between the law of ...... (name of country) and a principle or provision of international law, the principle or provision of international law shall prevail.

(3) It shall not be a defence to an offence under section 5 or 6 or 7 for the person charged with the offence to plead that the act constituting the offence was committed in obedience to, or in conformity with, the law in force at the time, and in the place at which, such act was alleged to have been committed.

10. Obedience to superior orders not a defence to offences under sections 5, 6 or 7[8]

Option 1

(1) Notwithstanding section 9, it shall not be a defence to an offence under section 5 or 6 or 7 for the person charged with the offence to plead that he or she committed the act constituting such offence pursuant to an order by a Government or a superior, whether military or civilian unless—

   (a) the person was under a legal obligation to obey the order of the Government or the superior in question;

   (b) the person did not know that the order was unlawful; and

   (c) the order was not manifestly unlawful.

(2) For the purposes of this section, orders to commit genocide or a crime against humanity shall be regarded as being manifestly unlawful.

OR

Option 2

Notwithstanding section 9, it shall not be a defence to an offence under section 5 or 6 or 7 for the person charged with the offence to plead that he or she committed the act constituting the offence pursuant to an order by a Government or a superior, whether military or civilian.

---

8 See discussion of superior orders under paragraphs 69–71 of the Report and Clause 19 of the drafting instructions.

OR

Option 3

(Include no provision on superior orders in which case any existing defence available under domestic law relating to obedience to superior orders will apply and if there is none, no defence will be available. However if Option 2 under section 9 is included and international law defences are incorporated then the defence as set out in Article 33 of the Rome Statute will be incorporated unless specifically excluded.)

11. Responsibility of commanders & other superiors[9]

(1) A military commander or a person effectively acting as a military commander shall be responsible for an offence under section 5 or 6 or 7 committed by forces under his or her effective command and control or as the case may be, under his or her effective authority and control, as a result of his or her failure to exercise control properly over such forces where—

   (a) he or she either knew, or owing to the circumstances at the time, should have known that the forces were committing or about to commit such offence; and

   (b) he or she failed to take all necessary and reasonable measures within his or her power to prevent or repress their commission or to submit the matter to the competent authorities for investigation or prosecution.

(2) With respect to superior and subordinate relationships not described in subsection (1), a superior shall be responsible for an offence under section 5 or 6 or 7 committed by subordinates under his or her effective authority and control, as a result of his or her failure to exercise control over such subordinates where—

   (a) he or she either knew, or consciously disregarded information which clearly indicated, that the subordinates were committing or about to commit such offence;

   (b) the offences concerned activities that were within his or her effective responsibility and control; and

   (c) he or she failed to take necessary and reasonable measures within his or her power to prevent or repress their commission or to submit the matter to the competent authorities for investigation and prosecution.

(3) A person responsible under this section for an offence under section 5 or 6 or 7 hall, for the purposes of this Part of this Act, be regarded as having aided, abetted, counselled or procured the commission of that offence.

Optional Additional Provision

[11A Pleas of Autrofois Acquit & convict[10]

---

9   See discussion of command responsibility under paragraphs 56–58 of the Report and Clause 15 of the drafting instructions.

10 See discussion of *ne bis in idem* in paragraphs 47–49 of the Report and Clause 13 of the drafting instructions.

(1) Where a person is alleged to have committed an act which constitutes an offence under section 5 or 6 or 7 and that person has been tried and dealt with by a court in another state outside ...... (name of country) in respect of that offence in such a manner that, had he or she been tried and dealt with in ...... (name of country) for that offence he or she would have been able to plead autrofois acquit, autrofois convict or pardon, he or she shall be deemed to have been so tried and dealt with.

(3) Notwithstanding anything in subsection (1), a person shall not be deemed to have been dealt with as provided for in that subsection, if he or she had been tried and dealt with in a court outside ...... (name of country) and the proceedings in such court—

(a) were for the purpose of shielding that person from criminal liability; or

(b) were not otherwise conducted independently or impartially in accordance with the norms of due process recognized by international law, and conducted in a manner that, in the circumstances, was inconsistent with an intention to bring the person to justice).]

Optional Additional Provision

[11B Knowledge and intent[11]

(1) Unless otherwise provided in the Statute or the elements of crime, a person shall be regarded as having committed an act which constitutes an offence under section 5, 6 or 7 only if he or she has committed such act with intent and knowledge.

(2) For the purposes of this section—

(a) a person has intent—

(i) in relation to conduct, if he or she means to engage in such conduct;

(ii) in relation to a consequence, if he or she means to cause the consequence or is aware that it will occur in the ordinary course of events; and

(b) 'knowledge' means awareness that a circumstance exists or that a consequence will occur in the ordinary course of events).]

Jurisdiction and Procedure for Offences under Sections 5, 6 and 7

12. Temporal jurisdiction for offences under sections 5, 6 or 7[12]

Option I

Include no provision on temporal jurisdiction in which case by operation of law proceedings will be prospective only, i.e. the Act will apply only to offences alleged to have been committed on or after the date on which this Act comes into force.

OR

---

11 See discussion on mental element in paragraphs 60–62 of the Report and Clause 16 of the drafting instructions.

12 See discussion under Part III of the Report on Core Crimes—Temporal Jurisdiction and Clause 2 of the drafting instructions. In some states treaties are self-implementing and become part of domestic law upon ratification. For those states it may be that no provision on temporal jurisdiction may be needed for the offence provisions if it is considered that the offences under the Rome Statute become offences under domestic law with ratification taking effect at that time. However given that the Rome Statute does not mandate the adoption of the offences under domestic law consideration needs to be given to whether additional legislation may be needed to create offences in those states even though treaties are generally self implementing.

Option 2

> Proceedings for an offence under section 5 or 6 or 7 may be instituted if the act or omission constituting the offence is alleged to have been committed—
>
> (a)   on or after the date on which this Act comes into force; or
>
> (b)   on or after 1 July 2002 and before the date on which this Act comes into force.

13. Jurisdiction to try offences under sections 5, 6 or 7[13]

Option 1

> (1) Where an act constituting an offence under section 5 or 6 or 7 is committed by any person outside the territory of ...... (name of country), proceedings may be instituted against that person for that offence in ...... (name of country), if—
>
> (a)   the person is a citizen or permanent resident of ...... (name of country);
>
> (b)   the person has committed the offence against a citizen or permanent resident of ...... (name of country); or
>
> (c)   the person is, after the commission of the offence, present in ...... (name of country).

OR

Option 2

> Proceedings may be instituted against any person for an offence under section 5 or 6 or 7 in ...... (name of country), whether or not such person is a citizen or permanent resident of ...... (name of country) and whether or not the act constituting such offence was committed within or outside the territory of ...... (name of country).

14.   Attorney General's consent required for prosecutions under sections 5, 6 or 7[14]

> (1) No proceedings for an offence under section 5 or 6 or 7 of this Act shall be instituted in any court in ...... (name of country) except with the consent of [the Attorney General/DPP].
>
> (2) Notwithstanding anything in subsection (1), a person charged with an offence under section 5 or 6 or 7 may be arrested, or a warrant for his or her arrest may be issued and executed, and he or she may be remanded in custody or on bail, even though the consent of the Attorney General for the institution of proceedings against that person for that offence has not been obtained, but no further steps shall be taken in the proceedings until that consent has been obtained.

---

13 See discussion under Part V of the Report on Core Crimes—Jurisdiction to Prosecute and Clause 4 of the drafting instructions.

14 See discussion under Part V of the Report on Consent to Prosecution and Clause 5 of the drafting instructions.

[Optional Additional Provision

(3) *Proceedings for an offence under section 5 or 6 or 7 may be conducted only by the Attorney General or counsel acting on his or her behalf).]*

Offences against Administration of Justice[15]

Option I

Extend existing administration of justice offences relating to domestic courts and proceedings to the ICC and extend jurisdiction to nationals.

OR

Option 2

Create new offences based on the optional administration of justice offence provisions set out in sections 14A–14G.

[Optional Administration of Justice Provisions

14A Corruption of Judge etc.

(1) *A Judge who, in ...... (name of country) or elsewhere, corruptly accepts or obtains, or agrees or offers to accept or attempts to obtain, a bribe for himself or herself or any other person in respect of an act—*

   (a) *done or omitted to be done by that Judge in his or her judicial capacity; or*

   (b) *to be done or to be omitted to be done by that Judge in his or her judicial capacity,*

shall be guilty of an offence and shall be liable, on conviction after trial on indictment, to imprisonment for a term not exceeding ...... years.

(2) *A Judge, Registrar, Deputy Registrar, Prosecutor or Deputy Prosecutor who, in ...... (name of country) or elsewhere, corruptly accepts or obtains, or agrees or offers to accept or attempts to obtain, a bribe for himself or herself or any other person in respect of an act—*

   (a) *done or omitted to be done by that Judge, Registrar, or Deputy Registrar, Prosecutor, or Deputy Prosecutor, in his or her official capacity (other than an act or omission to which subsection (1) applies); or*

   (b) *to be done or to be omitted to be done by that Judge, Registrar, Deputy Registrar, Prosecutor or Deputy Prosecutor in his or her official capacity (other than an act or omission to which subsection (1) applies),*

shall be guilty of an offence and shall be liable, on conviction after trial on indictment, to imprisonment for a term not exceeding ...... years.

(3) *In this section and in sections 14B and 14G—*

   'Deputy Registrar' means a Deputy Registrar of the ICC;

   'Judge' means a Judge of the ICC;

---

15 See discussion under Part VII of the Report on Article 70—Administration of Justice Offences and Clause 6 of the drafting instructions.

'Registrar' means the Registrar of the ICC;

'Prosecutor' means the Prosecutor of the ICC; and

'Deputy Prosecutor' means a Deputy Prosecutor of the ICC.

14B Bribery of Judge & c.

(1) Every person who, in ...... (name of country) or elsewhere, corruptly gives or offers, or agrees to give, a bribe to any person with intent to influence a Judge in respect of any act or omission by that Judge in his or her judicial capacity shall be guilty of an offence and shall be liable, on conviction after trial on indictment, to imprisonment for a term not exceeding ...... years.

(2) Every person who, in ...... (name of country) or elsewhere, corruptly gives or offers, or agrees to give, a bribe to any person with intent to influence a Judge or the Registrar or the Deputy Registrar or the Prosecutor or the Deputy Prosecutor in respect of an act or omission by that Judge, Registrar, Deputy Registrar, Prosecutor or Deputy Prosecutor in his or her official capacity (other than an act or omission to which subsection (1) applies) shall be guilty of an offence and shall be liable, on conviction after trial on indictment, to imprisonment to a term not exceeding ...... years.

14C Corruption and bribery of official of ICC

(1) An official of the ICC who, in ...... (name of country) or elsewhere, corruptly accepts or obtains, or agrees or offers to accept or attempts to obtain, a bribe for himself or herself or any other person in respect of an act—

    (a)   done or omitted to be done by that officer in his or her official capacity; or

    (b)   to be done or to be omitted to be done by that officer in his or her official capacity,

shall be guilty of an offence and shall be liable, on conviction after trial on indictment, to imprisonment for a term not exceeding ...... years.

(2) Every person who, in ...... (name of country) or elsewhere, corruptly gives or offers, or agrees to give, a bribe to any person with intent to influence an official of the ICC in respect of an act or omission by that officer in his or her official capacity shall be guilty of an offence and shall be liable, on conviction after trial on indictment, to imprisonment for a term not exceeding ...... years.

(3) In this section and in section 14G 'official of the ICC' means a person employed under article 44 of the Statute.

14D False evidence

(1) Every person who gives evidence for the purposes of a proceeding before the ICC or in connection with a request made by the ICC that contains an assertion that, if made in a judicial proceeding in ...... (name of country) as evidence on oath, would constitute perjury, shall be deemed to have given false evidence.

(2) Every person, who in ...... (name of country) or elsewhere, gives false evidence shall be guilty of an offence and shall be liable, on conviction after trial on indictment, to imprisonment for a term not exceeding ...... years.

14E Fabricating evidence before ICC

Every person who, in ...... (name of country) or elsewhere, with intent to mislead the ICC, fabricates evidence by any means other than by the giving of false evidence shall be guilty of an offence and shall be liable, on conviction after trial on indictment, to imprisonment for a term not exceeding ...... years.

14F Conspiracy to defeat justice in ICC

Every person who, in ...... (name of country) or elsewhere, in relation to any proceedings, request, or other matter referred to in the Statute, conspires to obstruct, prevent, pervert, or defeat the course of justice, shall be guilty of an offence and shall be liable, on conviction after trial on indictment, to imprisonment for a term not exceeding ...... years.

14G Interference with witnesses or officials

Every person who, in ...... (name of country) or elsewhere—

(a) dissuades or attempts to dissuade any person, by threats, force, bribery or other means, from giving evidence for the purposes of a proceeding before the ICC or in connection with a request made by the ICC; or

(b) makes threats or uses force against any Judge, the Registrar, a Deputy Registrar, the Prosecutor or a Deputy Prosecutor or any official of the ICC with intent to influence or punish that person, in respect of an act—

(i) done or omitted by that person or any Judge, the Registrar, a Deputy Registrar, the Prosecutor or a Deputy Prosecutor or any official of the ICC, in his or her official capacity; or

(ii) to be done or omitted by that person or any Judge, the Registrar, a Deputy Registrar, the Prosecutor or a Deputy Prosecutor or any official of the ICC, in his or her official capacity; or

(c) intentionally attempts in any other way to obstruct, prevent, pervert, or defeat the course of justice, in relation to any proceedings, request, or other matter referred to in the Statute,

shall be guilty of an offence and shall be liable, on conviction after trial on indictment, to imprisonment to a term not exceeding ...... years.]

15. Jurisdiction to try offences under sections 14A–14G[16]
Option 1

(1) Where an act constituting an offence under section 14A–14G is committed by any person outside the territory of ...... (name of country), proceedings may be instituted against that person for that offence in ...... (name of country), if—

(a) the person is a citizen or permanent resident of ...... (name of country);

---

16 See discussion under Part VIII of the Report on Jurisdiction for the Administration of Justice Offences and Clause 7 of the drafting instructions.

(b) the person has committed the offence against a citizen or permanent resident of …… (name of country); or

(c) the person is, after the commission of the offence, present in …… (name of country).

OR

Option 2

Where an act constituting an offence under sections 14A–14G is committed by any person outside the territory of …… (name of country) proceedings may be instituted against that person for that offence in …… (name of country) if that person is a citizen of …… (name of country).

16. Attorney General's consent required for prosecutions under sections 4A–14G[17]

(1) No proceedings for an offence under sections 14A–14G shall be instituted in any court in …… (name of country) except with the consent of the [Attorney General/DPP].

(2) Notwithstanding anything in subsection (1), a person charged with an offence under sections 14A–14G may be arrested, or a warrant for his or her arrest may be issued and executed, and he or she may be remanded in custody or on bail, even though the consent of the Attorney General for the institution of proceedings against that person for that offence has not been obtained, but no further steps shall be taken in the proceedings until that consent has been obtained.

General

Optional Additional Provision
[*16A Conspiracy*[18]

Every person who conspires in …… (name of country) to commit an offence under this Part of this Act in or outside the territory of …… (name of country) or who conspires outside …… (name of country) to commit an offence under this Part of this Act in …… (name of country) shall be guilty of an offence and shall be liable, on conviction after trial on indictment, to the same penalty as the penalty prescribed for the first mentioned offence).]

Optional Additional Provision
[*16B Aiding and abetting &c.*

Every person who—

(a) *attempts to commit,*

(b) *counsels or procures the commission of,*

(c) *orders, incites, solicits or induces the commission of,*

(d) *aids or abets or otherwise assists in the commission or attempted commission of,*

---

17 See discussion under Part X of the Report on Consent to Prosecution of Administration of Justice Offences and Clause 9 of the drafting instructions.

18 With reference to 16A and 16B see discussion under Part XI of the Report on Ancillary Offences for the Administration of Justice Offences and Clause 10 of the drafting instructions.

(e) is an accessory after the fact in relation to,

(f) intentionally contributes in any other way to the commission or attempted commission of,

an offence under this Part of this Act shall be guilty of an offence and shall be liable, on conviction after trial on indictment, to the same penalty as the penalty prescribed for the first mentioned offence.]

17. Offences to be tried on indictment[19]

Every person charged with an offence under this Part of this Act shall be tried on indictment.

18. Trial of offences committed outside ...... (name of country)[20]

Where an act constituting an offence under this Part of this Act is alleged to have been committed by a person outside the territory of ...... (name of country) proceedings may be instituted against such person for that offence in any court in ...... (name of country) having jurisdiction to try offences on indictment, and such court shall have all the powers to try such offence as if the offence had been committed within the territorial limits of the court's jurisdiction.

19. Interpretation

For the avoidance of doubt it is hereby declared that 'an offence under this Part of this Act' means an offence under section 5, 6, 7, (14A, 14B, 14C, 14D, 14E, or 14F, or 14G).

PART III—GENERAL PROVISIONS RELATING TO REQUESTS FOR ASSISTANCE[21]

20. Application[22]

(1) This Part of this Act shall apply to all requests for assistance received under Parts, IV, V and VI.

(2) Parts IV, V and VII shall apply to every request made by the ICC, whether the acts under investigation or subject to prosecution are alleged to have been committed before or after the date on which this Act comes into force.

(3) Part VI shall apply to the enforcement of every sentence, penalty or order of the ICC, whether the offence to which the sentence, penalty or order relates was committed before or after the date on which this Act comes into force.

(4) Part VIII shall apply to every investigation or sitting of the ICC whether the alleged offence or offence to which the investigation or sitting relates was committed before or after the date on which this Act comes into force.

---

19 See discussion in Part XII of the Report on Place of Trial and Relevant Court and Procedure and Clause 11 of the drafting instructions.

20 See discussion in Part XII of the Report on Place of Trial and Relevant Court and Procedure and Clause 11 of the drafting instructions.

21 See discussion in paragraphs 73, 74 and 75 of the Report on general provisions for requests for assistance and Clause 21 of the drafting instructions.

22 See comments on jurisdiction regarding the cooperation regime in paragraph 72 of the Report and Clause 20 of the drafting instructions.

21. Requests for assistance

A request for assistance is a request made by the ICC to the Minister, in respect of an investigation or prosecution that the Prosecutor is conducting or proposing to conduct, in relation to a crime within the jurisdiction of the ICC, for:

(a) assistance in respect of any one or more of the following, namely—

    (i) the provisional arrest, arrest, and surrender to the ICC of a person in relation to whom the ICC has issued an arrest warrant or given a judgment of conviction;

    (ii) the identification and whereabouts of persons or the location of things;

    (iii) the taking of evidence, including testimony under oath, and the production of evidence, including expert opinions and reports necessary to the ICC;

    (iv) the questioning of any person being investigated or prosecuted;

    (v) the service of documents, including judicial documents;

    (vi) facilitating the voluntary appearance of persons (other than prisoners) as witnesses or experts before the ICC;

    (vii) the temporary transfer of prisoners;

    (viii) the examination of places or sites, including the exhumation and examination of gravesites;

    (ix) the execution of searches and seizures;

    (x) the provision of records and documents, including official records and documents;

    (xi) the protection of victims and witnesses and the preservation of evidence;

    (xii) the identification, tracing and restraining, or seizure of proceeds of crimes for the purpose of eventual forfeiture, without prejudice to the rights of bona fide third parties; and

(b) any other type of assistance that is not prohibited by the law of ...... (name of country) with a view to facilitating the investigation and prosecution of crimes within the jurisdiction of the ICC and the enforcement of orders of the ICC made after convictions for such crimes.

22. Making of requests

(1) Subject to subsection (2), a request for assistance shall be made in writing, directly to the Minister.

(2) A request for provisional arrest under article 92 of the Statute or an urgent request for other forms of assistance under article 93 of the Statute may be made using any medium capable of delivering a written record including facsimile or electronic mail.

(3) Where a request is made, or supporting documents transmitted, by the use of facsimile or electronic mail, this Act shall apply as if the documents so sent were the originals and a copy of the facsimile or electronic mail shall be receivable in evidence.

(4) If a request is made by the use of facsimile or electronic mail in accordance with subsection (2), it shall be followed by a written request under subsection (1).

23. Confidentiality of requests

A request for assistance and any document or part of a document supporting the request shall be kept confidential by any person dealing with the request in whole or in part, except to the extent that disclosure is necessary for execution of the request.

24. Execution of requests[23]

A request for assistance shall be executed in the manner specified in the request, including following any procedure outlined therein and permitting the presence and partic-ipation of persons specified in the request in the execution process, unless execution in this manner is prohibited under the law of ...... (name of country).

25. State or diplomatic immunity[24]

(1) Any state or diplomatic immunity attaching to a person or premises by reason of a connection with a State Party to the ICC Statute does not prevent proceedings under Parts III–VIII of this Act, in relation to that person.

(2) If the Minister is of the opinion that a request for provisional arrest, arrest and surrender or other assistance would require ...... (name of country) to act incon-sistently with its obligations under international law with respect to the State or diplomatic immunity of a person or property of another state which is not a party to the Statute, he or she shall consult with the ICC and request a determination as to whether article 98(1) of the Statute applies.

(3) If the Minister is of the opinion that a request for provisional arrest or arrest and surrender would require ...... (name of country) to act inconsistently with its obli-gations under an international agreement with a state which is not a party to the Statute pursuant to which the consent of the sending state is required to surrender a person of that State to the ICC, he or she shall consult with the ICC and request a determination as to whether article 98(2) of the Statute applies.

26. Response to requests

(1) The Minister shall notify the ICC without undue delay, of his or her response to a request for assistance and the outcome of any action that has been taken to execute the request.

(2) Before deciding to postpone or refuse a request the Minister shall consult with the ICC to ascertain whether the assistance sought could be provided subject to conditions or at a later date or in an alternative manner.

(3) If the Minister decides, in accordance with the Statute and this Act, to refuse or postpone the assistance requested, in whole or in part, the notification to the ICC shall set out the reasons for the decision.

(4) If the request for assistance cannot be executed for any other reason, the Minister shall set out in the notification to the ICC, the reasons for the inability to execute the request.

---

23 See discussion on execution of requests in paragraph 106 of the Report and Clause 33 of the drafting instructions.
24 See discussion under Part XXV of the Report on Conflicting Obligations under International Law (Arti-cle 98) and Clause 46 of the drafting instructions.

(5) In the case of an urgent request for assistance, any documents or evidence transmitted in response shall, if the ICC so requests, be sent expeditiously to it.

PART IV—ARREST AND SURRENDER OF PERSON TO ICC[25]

27. Application of this Part

This Part of this Act applies to requests for assistance from the ICC, for the arrest and surrender, or the provisional arrest, of a person.

28. Request for arrest and surrender

(1) Subject to sections 29 and 30, when the Minister receives a request for arrest and surrender of a person alleged to have committed a crime within the jurisdiction of the ICC or on whom a judgment of conviction has been imposed by the ICC the Minister shall, if satisfied that the request is supported by the information and documents required by article 91 of the Statute—

(a) transmit the request and any supporting documents to (a magistrate); and

(b) notify (the Director of Public Prosecutions).

(2) Upon receipt of a request under subsection (1)(a) (the magistrate) shall—

(a) if the request is accompanied by a warrant of arrest issued by the ICC, endorse the warrant for execution by a police officer in any part of ...... (name of country); or

(b) if the request is accompanied by a judgment of conviction of the ICC, issue a warrant for the arrest of the person to whom the judgment relates, for execution by a police officer in any part of ...... (name of country).

29. Refusal of request for arrest and surrender[26]

(1) The Minister shall refuse a request for arrest and surrender, at any time before the surrender of the person, only if—

(a) the ICC has determined that the case to which the request relates is inadmissible on any ground; or

(b) the ICC advises that it does not intend to proceed with the request for any reason, including but not limited to a determination by the ICC that article 98 of the Statute applies to the execution of the request.

(2) The Minister may refuse a request for arrest and surrender of a person, at any time before the surrender of the person only if—

(a) there is a competing request from one or more States not party to the Statute for the extradition of the person for the same conduct as that which constitutes the crime for which the ICC seeks the person's surrender and a decision

---

25 See generally Part XVI of the Report on Arrest and Surrender.

26 See discussion of grounds of refusal in paragraphs 96 and 97 of the Report and Clause 28 of the drafting instructions.

to extradite to a State is made in accordance with article 90 of the Statute and section 31; or

(b) there is a competing request from one or more States not party to the Statute for the extradition of the person for different conduct from that which constitutes the crime for which the ICC requests the person's surrender and a decision to extradite to a State is made in accordance with article 90 of the Statute and section 31.

(3) If the Minister decides to refuse a request for arrest and surrender in accordance with subsection (1) or (2) after he or she has transmitted a request under section 28, he or she shall notify (the magistrate) who shall cancel any warrant or delivery order issued by him or her and ensure the person's release from custody or conditions prescribed in relation to bail arising from that warrant or order.

30. Postponement of execution of request for arrest and surrender[27]

(1) The Minister may postpone the execution of a request for arrest and surrender at any time before the surrender of the person only if—

(a) a determination on admissibility is pending before the ICC;

(b) the request would interfere with an investigation or prosecution in ...... (name of country) involving a different offence from that for which surrender to the ICC is requested;

(c) the Minister is consulting with the ICC under section 25 as to whether or not article 98 of the Statute applies to the execution of the request.

(2) If execution of the request for arrest and surrender is postponed under subsection (1)(a) and the ICC decides that the case is admissible, the Minister shall proceed with the execution of the request as soon as possible after the decision of the ICC.

(3) If the execution of the request for arrest and surrender is postponed under subsection (1)(b), the Minister shall consult with the ICC and agree on a period of time for postponement of the execution of the request in accordance with article 94 of the Statute; and the Minister shall proceed with execution of the request after the lapse of that period, unless otherwise agreed with the ICC.

(4) If execution of the request for arrest and surrender is postponed under subsection (1)(c) and the ICC decides to proceed with the request, the Minister shall proceed with the execution of the request as soon as possible after the decision of the ICC.

(5) If the Minister decides to postpone execution of a request for arrest and surrender in accordance with this section after he or she has transmitted a request under section 28, he or she shall—

(a) notify (the magistrate) of the postponement and the magistrate shall adjourn any pending proceedings until further notice from the Minister; and

---

27 See discussion on postponement of execution of requests in paragraph 95 of the Report and Clause 27 of the drafting instructions.

(b) notify (the magistrate) at the relevant time whether the execution of the request is to proceed or not, and (the magistrate) shall proceed accordingly with the execution of the request or the discharge of the person.

(6) A decision by the Minister to postpone the execution of a request shall not affect the validity of any act that has been done or any warrant or order made under this Part of this Act prior to the decision, and any such warrant or order shall remain in force unless cancelled by (the magistrate) in accordance with subsection (5)(b).

31. Competing requests[28]

(1) Where a request for arrest and surrender of a person is received from the ICC and one or more states also request the extradition of the person for the same conduct as that which constitutes the crime for which ICC seeks the person's surrender, the Minister—

   (a) shall notify ICC and the requesting state of that fact; and

   (b) shall determine whether the person is to be surrendered to the ICC or to the requesting state.

(2) Where the request for extradition of a person for the same conduct as that which constitutes the crime for which the ICC seeks the person's surrender is made by a state which is a party to the Statute, priority shall be given to the request from the ICC if the ICC has determined under articles 18 or 19 of the Statute that the case is admissible; and where an admissibility decision is pending before the ICC, no person shall be extradited under the laws relating to extradition until the ICC makes a decision on admissibility and determines that the case is inadmissible.

(3) Where the request for extradition of a person for the same conduct as that which constitutes the crime for which the ICC seeks the person's surrender is made by a state which is not a party to the Statute, priority shall be given to the request for arrest and surrender from the ICC, if ...... (name of country) is not under an international obligation to extradite the person to the requesting state and the ICC has determined under article 18 or 19 of the Statute that the case is admissible.

(4) Where the request for extradition of a person for the same conduct as that which constitutes the crime for which the ICC seeks the person's surrender is made by a state which is not a party to the Statute and ...... (name of country) is under an international obligation to extradite the person to the requesting state and the ICC has determined under article 18 or 19 of the Statute that the case is admissible, the Minister shall determine whether the person is to be surrendered to the ICC or extradited taking into consideration all the relevant factors including but not limited to, the respective dates of the requests, the interests of the requesting state including, where relevant, whether the crime was committed in its territory, the nationality of the victims and the person sought to be extradited, and the possibility of subsequent surrender between the ICC and the requesting state.

(5) Where a request for arrest and surrender is received from the ICC and one or more states also request the extradition of the person for conduct other than that which constitutes the crime for which ICC seeks the person's surrender, priority

---

28 See discussion of competing requests in paragraphs 91 and 92 of the Report and Clause 24 of the drafting instructions.

shall be given to the request from the ICC if ...... (name of country) is not under an international obligation to extradite the person to any requesting state.

(6) Where a request for surrender is received from the ICC and one or more states also request the extradition of the person for conduct other than that which constitutes the crime for which ICC seeks the person's surrender, and ...... (name of country) is under an international obligation to extradite to one or more of the requesting states, the Minister shall determine whether the person is to be surrendered to the ICC or extradited to a requesting state taking into consideration all the relevant factors referred to in subsection (4) as well as the relative nature and gravity of the conduct in question.

32. Official capacity not a bar to arrest and surrender[29]

Subject to section 25, the existence of any immunity or special procedural rule attaching, under domestic or international law, to a person shall not be a ground for—

(a) refusing or postponing a request by the ICC for the arrest and surrender of that person;

(b) holding that that person is ineligible for arrest and surrender to the ICC.

Provisional Arrest in Urgent Cases

33. Provisional arrest[30]

(1) Where the Minister receives a request from the ICC for provisional arrest of a person under article 92 of the Statute, he or she shall, if satisfied that the request is supported by the information required by paragraph (2) of article 92 of the Statute, transmit the request and any supporting documents to the (Inspector General of Police) with a direction for the arrest of the person.

(2) The Minister shall transmit a copy of the direction to (the Director of Public Prosecutions).

(3) Where (the Inspector General of Police) receives a direction from the Minister under subsection (1) he or she shall instruct the police to carry out the direction.

(4) (The Inspector General of Police) shall, after carrying out the direction, notify the Minister and (the Director of Public Prosecutions) that he or she has done so.

(5) Where a person has been provisionally arrested under this section, and the Minister receives the formal request for arrest and surrender as provided for in article 91 of the Statute, the Minister shall immediately send a notice to (the magistrate) and proceed with the transmission of the request in accordance with section 28.

34. Rights of arrested person[31]

(1) A person arrested under a warrant obtained in accordance with section 28 or pursuant to a direction under section 33 shall be brought before (a magistrate) within 48 hours.

---

29 See discussion under Part XXVI of the Report on Sovereign Immunity and Clause 47 of the drafting instructions.

30 See general discussion of provisional arrest in paragraphs 78 and 79 of the Report.

31 See discussion of rights upon arrest in paragraphs 78 and 79 of the Report.

(2) (The magistrate) may, of his or her own motion or at the request of the person, determine—

  (a) whether the person was lawfully arrested in accordance with the warrant or the direction; and

  (b) whether the person's rights have been respected in the course of the arrest.

(3) In making a determination under subsection (2) (the magistrate) shall apply the principles applicable to judicial review.

(4) If (the magistrate) determines that—

  (a) the person was not lawfully arrested; or

  (b) the person's rights were not respected,

(the magistrate) shall make a declaration to that effect with any explanation required but may not grant any other form of relief.

(5) (The magistrate) shall send any declaration made under subsection (4) to the Minister, and the Minister shall transmit it to the ICC.

35. Person arrested on a provisional warrant

(1) Where a person has been provisionally arrested under section 33, (the magistrate) shall not proceed under section 37 until—

  (a) (the magistrate) has received a notice from the Minister that the request for surrender and supporting documents required under article 91 of the Statute have been received by the Minister; and

  (b) the relevant documents have been transmitted to (the magistrate) by the Minister under section 33(5).

(2) Pending the receipt of the notice and documents under subsection (1), (the magistrate) may adjourn the proceedings from time to time.

(3) If (the magistrate) has not received the notice specified in subsection (1)(a) within 60 days of the date of the provisional arrest of the person, he or she shall release the person from custody or on bail unless satisfied that the period for submission of the notice should be extended in the interests of justice.

(4) The release of a person under subsection (3) shall be without prejudice to any subsequent proceedings that may be brought for the arrest and surrender of the person to the ICC whether for the same facts and offence or not.

Bail[32]

36. Application for bail

(1) A person brought before (a magistrate) under section 34 may make an application for bail.

---

32 See discussion on interim release in paragraphs 80 and 81 of the Report.

(2) Where an application for bail is made under subsection (1), (the magistrate) shall adjourn the hearing of the application and notify the Minister.

(3) The Minister shall, on receipt of a notification under subsection (2), consult immediately with the ICC to obtain any recommendations from the Pre-Trial Chamber under article 59(5) of the Statute, and shall convey those recommendations to (the magistrate).

(4) (The magistrate) shall give full consideration to any recommendations conveyed to him or her under subsection (3) before making a decision on the application for bail.

(5) Where no recommendations are received from the ICC within seven days of the Minister being notified of the application for bail, (the magistrate) may proceed to hear the application.

(6) (A magistrate) shall not release a person brought before him or her under section 34 on bail, unless (the magistrate) is satisfied that, having regard to the crimes alleged to have been committed by that person, there are urgent and exceptional circumstances that justify the person's release on bail and that there are sufficient safeguards to ensure that ...... (name of country) will be able to fulfil its obligations under the Statute to surrender such person to the ICC.

Surrender[33]

37. Surrender hearing

(1) (The magistrate) before whom a person arrested under section 28 or 33 is brought shall satisfy himself or herself that—

(a) there is a warrant of arrest issued by the ICC or a judgment of conviction by the ICC, in respect of that person; and

(b) the warrant or judgment relates to the person before (the magistrate).

(2) Upon the magistrate being satisfied of the matters referred to in paragraphs (a) and (b) of subsection (1) with respect to the arrested person, (the magistrate) shall, subject to section 35, issue a delivery order in respect of that person in accordance with article 59(7) of the Statute.

(3) Where (the magistrate) issues a delivery order under subsection (2) he or she shall—

(a) transmit the delivery order to (the Inspector General of Police) for execution;

(b) commit the person to custody pending the execution of the delivery order by (the Inspector General of Police);

(c) send a copy of the delivery order to the Minister; and

(b) inform the person in ordinary language of his or her right to make an application to the appropriate court for a mandate in the nature of a writ of habeas corpus.

(4) If the person who is the subject of a delivery order—

---

33 See discussion of evidence and structure for surrender procedure in paragraphs 83–86 of the Report.

(a) is in custody, (the magistrate) shall order the continued detention of the person under the delivery order and notify (the Commissioner of Prisons) and (the Superintendent of the prison), of the delivery order; or

(b) is not in custody, the magistrate shall, subject to any order with regard to bail, commit him or her to custody and shall notify (the Commissioner of Prisons) and (the Superintendent of the prison).

(5) Subject to subsection (6), (the Inspector General of Police) shall make arrangements with the ICC for the execution of the delivery order as soon as possible, and shall notify the Minister when the person has been surrendered to the ICC or the state of enforcement, in execution of the delivery order.

(6) Subject to section 39, (the Inspector General of Police) shall not make arrangements with the ICC for the execution of the delivery order—

(a) until after the expiration of the period prescribed by law for making an application for habeas corpus by the person to whom the order relates; or

(b) if an application for habeas corpus is made by such person within such period, until after the final determination of the application.[34]

(7) A delivery order issued under this section is sufficient authority for holding the person specified in the order in custody until his or her delivery to the ICC.

(8) In deciding whether to make a delivery order under this section[35]—

(a) (the magistrate) shall not require evidence to establish that the trial of the person for the crime that he or she is alleged to have committed is justified before the ICC or would be justified under the law of ...... (name of country) if the act constituting such crime had been committed in ...... (name of country); and

(b) (the magistrate) shall not receive evidence with respect to, nor adjudicate on, any claim by the person that he or she has been previously tried or convicted for the conduct for which the ICC seeks surrender of the person.

(9) If the person makes a claim, under subsection (8)(b), (the magistrate) shall advise the Minister of this claim and the Minister shall transmit that information to the ICC.

38. Magistrate not to inquire into validity of warrant[36]

In proceedings under this Part of this Act (the magistrate) shall not inquire into, receive any evidence regarding, or make any decisions as to, the validity of any warrant or order issued or made by the ICC.

---

34 If the general law of the country does not provide for habeas corpus as an automatic right, a statutory provision giving the person a right to make such an application should be included. (See paragraph 88 of the Report.)

35 See discussion on guidance on the role of the judge in the surrender proceedings in paragraph 90 of the Report and Clause 23 of the drafting instructions.

36 See discussion of Guidance on the Role of the Judge in Surrender Proceedings in paragraph 90 of the Report and Clause 23 of the drafting instructions.

39. Surrender by consent

(1) A person may at any time notify (a magistrate) that he or she consents to being surrendered to the ICC for the crime or crimes for which the ICC seeks the surrender of the person.

(2) (The magistrate) may accept the notification of consent under subsection (1) if—

(a) the person is before (the magistrate) when notification of the consent to surrender is given; and

(b) (the magistrate) is satisfied that the person has freely consented to the surrender in full knowledge of its consequences.

(3) Nothing in this section shall be construed as preventing a person, in respect of whom (the magistrate) has made a delivery order, from subsequently notifying the Minister that he or she consents to surrender.

(4) For the avoidance of doubt a person arrested under a provisional warrant may consent to surrender before a request for surrender is received, in which case (the magistrate) may make an order under subsection (5).

(5) Where the consent to surrender has been given, (the magistrate) shall immediately make a delivery order in the same terms as section 37(2) and such of the provisions of sections 37 and 38 as are applicable shall thereupon apply.

40. Effect of delivery order

(1) A delivery order is sufficient authority for any person to receive the person to whom the order relates, keep him or her in custody and convey him or her to the place where he or she is to be delivered up into the custody of the ICC or of the state of enforcement, in accordance with arrangements made by (the Inspector General of Police).

(2) A person in respect of whom a delivery order is in force shall be deemed to be in legal custody pending delivery up under the order.

(3) If a person in respect of whom a delivery order is in force escapes or is unlawfully at large, he or she may be arrested without warrant and taken to the place where he or she is required to be or to be taken.

41. Procedure where magistrate refuses order[37]

(1) Where (the magistrate) refuses to make a delivery order under section 37, he or she shall make an order remanding the person arrested in custody for 14 days, and shall notify the Minister of his or her decision and of the grounds for it.

(2) The Minister may appeal to the (High Court) (highest appeal court) against the decision by (the magistrate) refusing to make a delivery order.

(3) Where (the magistrate) is informed that an appeal is to be taken against the decision, the order remanding the person arrested shall continue to have effect until the appeal is determined and the person is either discharged or the delivery order is executed.

---

37 See discussion on appeals in paragraphs 87–89 of the Report and Clause 22 of the drafting instructions.

(4) Where (the High Court) allows the appeal, it may make a delivery order or remit the case to the magistrate to make a delivery order in accordance with the decision of (the High Court).

(5) Where (the High Court) dismisses the appeal, the person shall be discharged in accordance with the decision of (the High Court).

42. Discharge of person not delivered up

(1) If the person in respect of whom a delivery order has been made is not delivered up under the order within 60 days after the expiration of the period prescribed by law for making an application for habeas corpus or, if such an application is made within 60 days, after the final determination of the application, that person or someone duly authorized by him or her may make an application to (the magistrate) who made the delivery order, for the person's discharge.

(2) On an application made under this section, (the magistrate) shall order the person's discharge unless reasonable cause is shown for the delay.

(3) The discharge of a person under subsection (2) shall be without prejudice to any subsequent proceedings that may be brought for the arrest and surrender of the person to the ICC whether for the same facts and offence or not.

43. Discharge of person no longer required to be surrendered

(1) Where the ICC informs the Minister that the person arrested upon the request of the ICC is no longer required to be surrendered, the Minister shall notify (the magistrate) of that fact and (the magistrate) shall on receipt of the notification make an order for the discharge of the person.

(2) The discharge of a person under subsection (1) shall be without prejudice to any subsequent proceedings that may be brought for the arrest and surrender of the person to the ICC whether for the same facts and offence or not.

44. Request for temporary surrender[38]

(1) Where a request for arrest and surrender by the ICC relates to a crime within the jurisdiction of the ICC but the person is subject to proceedings for a different offence in ...... (name of country) which have not been finally disposed of or is liable to serve a sentence of imprisonment imposed by a court in ...... (name of country) for a different offence, the Minister may authorize the temporary transfer of that person to the ICC.

(2) The Minister may, before making an authorization under subsection (1), seek an undertaking from the ICC that the person shall be returned on completion of proceedings before the ICC or service of sentence imposed by the ICC, as the case may be.

(3) Subsections (2), (3), (4) and (5) of section 59 shall apply to an authorization under subsection (1) with any necessary modifications.

---

38 See discussion on temporary surrender in paragraph 93 of the Report and Clause 25 of the drafting instructions.

45. Request for transit of a person to ICC[39]

(1) Subject to subsection (4), where the Minister receives a request from the ICC for transit through the territory ...... (name of country) of a person—

   (a) being surrendered or transferred by another state to the ICC;

   (b) being transferred from the ICC to a State of enforcement;

   (b) being transferred to or from the State of enforcement as a result of a review hearing or other appearance by the person before the ICC,

the Minister shall accede to the request for transit and the person shall be deemed, during transit, to be in lawful custody and may be held in any police station, prison or any other place of detention which may be designated by the Minister in consultation with the other relevant Ministers.

(2) If a person referred to in subsection (1) arrives in ...... (name of country) without prior consent to transit, a police officer may at the request of the officer who has custody of the person being transported, hold the person in custody for a maximum period of 96 hours pending receipt by the Minister of a request under subsection (1).

(3) No authorization for transit is required if the person being transported is transported by air and no landing is scheduled on the territory of ...... (name of country).

(4) Notwithstanding subsection (1), the Minister may refuse a request for transit if the Minister considers that transit through ...... (name of country) would impede or delay the surrender or transfer of the person being transported.

(5) If an unscheduled landing occurs on the territory of ...... (name of country), the Minister may require the ICC to submit a request under subsection (1), for transit of the person being transported as soon as is reasonably practicable.

46. Waiver of requirements of article 101 of the Statute[40]

Where a person is surrendered to the ICC under this Part of this Act and the ICC requests the waiver of the requirements of paragraph (1) of article 101 of the Statute with respect to that person, the Minister, having regard to the information provided by the ICC with respect to that person, shall endeavour to consent to the person being proceeded against, punished or detained for conduct committed prior to surrender, not being conduct constituting crimes for which he or she has been surrendered to the ICC.

PART V—REQUESTS FOR OTHER TYPES OF ASSISTANCE[41]

47. Application of this Part

This Part of this Act applies to requests for assistance by the ICC, other than requests for arrest and surrender, or the provisional arrest, of a person.

---

39 See discussion on transit in paragraph 94 of the Report and Clause 26 of the drafting instructions.

40 See discussion of the rule of specialty and Article 101 of the Statute in paragraph 98 of the Report and Clause 29 of the drafting instructions.

41 See general discussion of other forms of cooperation in paragraphs 99–101 of the Report and Clause 30 of the drafting instructions.

48. Assistance in locating or identifying persons or things

(1) Where the ICC requests assistance in locating, or identifying and locating, a person or a thing believed to be in ...... (name of country), the Minister shall give authority for the request to proceed and transmit the request to (the appropriate agency in) ...... (name of country), if he or she has reasonable grounds to believe the person to whom or the thing to which the request relates is, or may be in ...... (name of country).

(2) Where the Minister authorizes and transmits the request under subsection (1), (the appropriate agency in) ...... (name of country) shall, without delay—

(a) use its best endeavours to locate or, as the case may be, identify and locate, the person to whom or thing to which the request relates; and

(b) advise the Minister of the outcome of those endeavours.

(3) This section shall not be construed as giving any person a power to enter property in order to locate a person or thing.

49. Assistance in taking evidence

(1) Where the ICC requests assistance in the taking of evidence, the Minister shall give authority for the request to proceed and transmit the request to (a magistrate), if the Minister has reasonable grounds to believe that the evidence can be taken in ...... (name of country).

(2) Where the Minister authorizes and transmits the request under subsection (1), (the magistrate) shall issue an order compelling the witness to appear at a specified time and place for his or her evidence to be taken.

(3) (The magistrate) shall, if the ICC so requests, permit a representative of the ICC or a representative of the person to whom the request relates to be present at the taking of the evidence and to put questions to the witness.

(4) In taking evidence under this section, (the magistrate) shall do so in the manner specified in the request for assistance made by the ICC, including complying with any procedure outlined therein unless the manner of execution or the procedure is prohibited under the law of ...... (name of country).

(5) (The magistrate) taking evidence under this section shall—

(a) certify that the evidence was taken before him or her and that the persons named in the certificate were present when the evidence was taken; and

(b) cause the evidence together with the certificate to be transmitted to the Minister.

[*Optional Additional Provision*

49A (1) The magistrate may order evidence to be given to the ICC by means of video or satellite link or through any other technology.

(2) To facilitate the taking of such evidence, the magistrate may order the person to appear at any facility where the relevant technology is available.]

50. Assistance in production of documents and articles

(1) Where the ICC requests assistance in the production of documents or articles the Minister shall give authority for the request to proceed and transmit the request

to (a magistrate), if the Minister has reasonable grounds to believe that the documents or articles can be produced in ...... (name of country).

(2) Where the Minister authorizes and transmits the request under subsection (1), (the magistrate) shall issue an order for the production of the documents or articles.

(3) The order may provide for any form of certification or authentication of the document or article as may be required by the ICC and may specify any other terms and conditions that may be appropriate in the circumstances.

(4) Where the documents and articles are produced duly authenticated or certified as required by the order made under subsection (3), (the magistrate) shall cause them to be sent to the Minister, with a written statement signed by (the magistrate) that they were produced to him or her.

51. Applicable law

(1) The applicable law for the taking of evidence under section 49 or the production of documents or articles under section 50 shall be the Statute and Rules unless the magistrate orders that the evidence shall be taken in accordance with the laws of ...... (name of country).

(2) Notwithstanding subsection (1), a person compelled to give evidence or produce documents shall have the same privileges as if the investigation or proceeding was conducted under the laws of ...... (name of country) and the laws of ...... (name of country) relating to the non-disclosure of information, including national security information, shall apply.

(3) Nothing in subsection (1) shall be construed as requiring a person to give evidence or answer any question or produce any document or article that the person could not be compelled to give or answer or produce in an investigation being conducted by the Prosecutor or in any proceedings before the ICC.

52. Assistance in questioning persons

(1) Where the ICC requests assistance in questioning a person who is being investigated or prosecuted by the ICC, the Minister shall give authority for the request to proceed and transmit the request to (the appropriate agency) in ...... (name of country) if the Minister has reasonable grounds to believe that the person is or may be in ...... (name of country).

(2) Where the Minister authorizes and transmits the request under subsection (1), (the appropriate agency) in ...... (name of country) shall, without delay—

(a) use its best endeavours to undertake the questioning that the ICC has requested;

(b) ensure that the answers to the questions put are recorded in writing and make any other report on the questioning as it considers to be appropriate in the circumstances; and

(c) advise the Minister of the outcome of those endeavours and, if relevant, deliver the record and any report of the questioning to the Minister.

(3) A person questioned under this section shall notwithstanding anything to the contrary in any other law, be entitled to all the rights referred to in article 55(2) of the Statute.

53. Assistance in arranging service of documents

(1) Where the ICC requests assistance in arranging for the service of a document in ...... (name of country), the Minister shall give authority for the request to proceed and transmit the request to (the appropriate agency) in ...... (name of country), if the Minister has reasonable grounds to believe that the person or body to be served is or may be in ...... (name of country).

(2) Where the Minister authorizes and transmits the request under subsection (1), (the appropriate agency) in ...... (name of country) shall, without delay—

   (a) use its best endeavours to have the document served—

      (i) in accordance with any procedure specified in the request; or

      (ii) if that procedure would be unlawful or inappropriate in ...... (name of country), or if no procedure is specified, in accordance with the law of ...... (name of country); and

   (b) transmit to the Minister—

      (i) a certificate as to service, if the document is served; or

      (ii) a statement of the reasons that prevented service, if the document is not served.

(3) In this section, document includes—

   (a) a summons requiring a person to appear as a witness; and

   (b) a summons to an accused that has been issued under article 58(7) of the Statute.

54. Assistance in facilitating the voluntary appearance of witness

(1) Where the ICC requests assistance in facilitating the voluntary appearance of a witness before the ICC the Minister shall give authority for the request to proceed and transmit the request to (the appropriate agency) in ...... (name of country) if the Minister is satisfied that there are reasonable grounds to believe that the witness is or may be in ...... (name of country).

(2) In this section and in section 55 and 56, 'witness' includes a person who may give expert evidence; but does not include—

   (a) a person who has been accused of a crime in the proceedings to which the request relates; or

   (b) a prisoner who is detained in relation to an offence against the law of ...... (name of country).

55. Consent required

(The appropriate agency) to which a request is transmitted under section 54 shall make such inquiries as may be necessary to ascertain whether the prospective witness consents to giving evidence or assisting the ICC.

56. Minister may facilitate appearance

(1) The Minister may assist in the making of arrangements to facilitate a witness's attendance before the ICC if the Minister is satisfied that—

(a) the prospective witness has consented to giving the evidence or assistance requested; and

(b) the ICC has given any assurance requested by the Minister in respect of the witness including but not limited to an assurance that the witness will not be prosecuted or detained by the ICC in respect of any specified act or omission that occurred before the witness's departure from ...... (name of country).

(2) The Minister may—

(a) approve and make arrangements for the travel of the witness to the ICC at the cost of the ICC; including but not limited to, the obtaining of such approvals, authorities, and permissions as are required for that purpose, including, in the case of a person who although not liable to be detained in a prison is subject to a sentence—

(i) the variation, discharge, or suspension of the conditions of the person's release from prison; or

(ii) the variation, cancellation, or suspension of the person's sentence, or of the conditions of the person's sentence; and

(b) take such other action for the purposes of subsection (1) as the Minister thinks appropriate.

57. Assistance in facilitating temporary transfer of prisoner[42]

Where the ICC requests assistance in facilitating the temporary transfer to the ICC of a prisoner serving a sentence in ...... (name of country) for an offence against the law of that country, the Minister shall give authority for the request to proceed and transmit the request to (the appropriate agency) in ...... (name of country), if the Minister has reasonable grounds to believe that the prisoner's assistance is sought for the purpose of identification or obtaining evidence or other assistance.

58. Consent required and assurances may be sought

Where the Minister authorizes and transmits a request under section 57, (the appropriate agency) in ...... (name of country) shall make such inquiries as may be necessary to ascertain whether the prisoner will consent to the transfer.

59. Minister may arrange for transfer

(1) The Minister may authorize the temporary transfer of a prisoner serving a sentence in ...... (name of country) to the ICC if the Minister is satisfied that—

(a) the prisoner has consented to giving the evidence or other assistance requested; and

(b) the ICC has given any assurances requested by the Minister including but not limited to an assurance that the prisoner will not be released without prior approval of the Minister.

---

42 For sections 57–60 see discussion on temporary transfer of witnesses in paragraph 105 of the Report and Clause 32 of the drafting instructions.

(2) Where the Minister authorizes the temporary transfer of the prisoner serving a sentence in …… (name of country) to the ICC, the Minister may—

   (a)   direct that the prisoner be released from the prison in which that prisoner is detained, for the purpose of the transfer to the ICC; and

   (b)   make arrangements for the prisoner to travel to the ICC in the custody of a person authorized for the purpose by the ICC.

(3) A direction given by the Minister under subsection (2) in respect of a prisoner is sufficient authority for the release of the prisoner from the prison in which the prisoner is detained, for the purposes of the transfer.

(4) Every person released under a direction given under subsection (2) shall be treated, for the purposes of the law in force relating to escape from lawful custody and for that purpose only, as continuing to be in the legal custody of the officer in charge of a prison from which he or she is so released, while in …… (name of country) during the period of that release.

(5) Where there is any inconsistency between subsection (4) and any other law, subsection (4) shall prevail.

60.   Effect of transfer on prisoner's sentence

Where a prisoner who is serving a sentence for an offence committed in …… (name of country) is transferred to the ICC—

   (a)   the prisoner shall be treated, while in custody outside …… (name of country) in connection with the request, as being in custody for the purposes of the sentence imposed for the offence committed in …… (name of country) which shall continue to run; and

   (b)   the Minister—

        (i) may at any time notify the ICC that the prisoner is no longer required to be kept in custody; and

        (ii) shall notify the ICC if the prisoner is no longer liable to be detained in a prison in …… (name of country).

61.   Assistance in examining places or sites

(1) Where the ICC requests assistance in examining places or sites in …… (name of country) the Minister shall give authority for the request to proceed and transmit the request to (the appropriate agency) in …… (name of country) if the Minister has reasonable grounds to believe that the place or site is located in …… (name of country).

(2) Where the Minister authorizes and transmits the request under subsection (1), (the appropriate agency) in …… (name of country)—

   (a)   shall without delay use its best endeavours to undertake the examination of the place or site in the manner that the ICC has requested;

   (b)   shall make such report on the examination as it considers to be appropriate in the circumstances; and

   (c)   shall deliver the report of the examination to the Minister; and

   (d)   may, where appropriate, apply to (a magistrate) for an exhumation order for the exhumation and examination of the remains at a grave site.

(3) An authorization under this section shall be deemed to authorize (the appropriate agency) to enter a place or site for the purpose of examining it.

62. Assistance involving search and seizure

(1) Where the ICC makes a request for search and seizure, the Minister shall give authority for the request to proceed and authorize in writing, a police officer to apply to (a magistrate) for a search warrant if the Minister has reasonable grounds to believe that anything relevant to an investigation being conducted by the Prosecutor or proceeding before the ICC is or may be located in ...... (name of country).

(2) Upon an application made to a magistrate under subsection (1) by a police officer authorized under that subsection, (the magistrate) may, if satisfied that the thing specified in the request made by the ICC is located in ...... (name of country) issue a warrant authorizing that police officer or any other police officer specified in the warrant to search for and seize that thing.

(3) (The magistrate) may issue a warrant under subsection (2) subject to such conditions as he or she may think fit to impose.

(4) Subject to any condition specified in the warrant, a warrant issued under subsection (2) shall authorize the police officer executing the warrant—

   (a) to enter and search any place or to stop and search any vehicle in which the thing specified in the warrant is located or held, at any time by day or night;

   (b) to use such assistants as may be reasonable in the circumstances for the purpose of such entry and search;

   (c) to use such force as is reasonable in the circumstances to effect entry to such place or to stop or board such vehicle, and to break any receptacle in which the thing specified in the warrant is placed; and

   (d) to search for and seize the thing.

(5) A person called on to assist a police officer executing a warrant issued under subsection (2) may exercise the powers referred to in paragraph (c) and (d) of subsection (4).

(6) A police officer executing a warrant issued under subsection (2) shall—

   (a) produce such warrant on initial entry, and if required to do so, at any time there after;

   (b) give to the owner of the thing seized or any other person whom he or she has reason to believe has an interest in such thing, a notice specifying—

      (i) the date and time of execution of the warrant;

      (ii) the name and position of the person executing the warrant;

      (iii) the thing seized under the warrant.

(7) A police officer seizing a thing under the authority of a warrant issued under subsection (2) shall deliver it into the custody and control of (the Inspector General of Police).

(8) (The Inspector General of Police) shall inform the Minister that the thing has been delivered to him or her and await the Minister's directions as to how the thing is to be dealt with.

(9) Except as otherwise provided in this section, the law relating to search and seizure generally, shall apply to a search and seizure under this section.

63. Assistance involving the use of other domestic investigative procedures[43]

(1) Where the ICC requests assistance in the gathering of evidence for an investigation, the Minister shall give authority for the request to proceed and transmit the request to (the appropriate agency) in …… (name of country) if the Minister has reasonable grounds to believe that the assistance requested is not prohibited by the law of …… (name of country).

(2) Where the Minister authorizes and transmits the request under subsection (1), (the appropriate agency) may

(a) make use of any domestic powers as would be available in a domestic investigation of a similar matter to gather such evidence and any such powers under domestic law shall apply with the necessary modifications;

(b) make such report as it considers to be appropriate in the circumstances; and

(c) deliver the report to the Minister.

64. Assistance in protecting victims and witnesses and preserving evidence[44]

(1) Where the ICC requests—

(a) assistance under article 93(1)(j) of the Statute in protecting victims and witnesses or preserving evidence;

(b) assistance under article 19(8), or article 56(2) or (3), in preserving evidence,

in relation to an investigation by, or a proceeding before, the ICC, the Minister shall give authority for the request to proceed and transmit the request to (the appropriate agency) in …… (name of country) if the Minister has reasonable grounds to believe that the assistance requested is not prohibited by the law of …… (name of country).

(2) Where the Minister authorizes and transmits the request under subsection (1), (the appropriate agency) in …… (name of country) shall without delay—

(a) use its best endeavours to give effect to the request;

(b) make such report on the outcome of its endeavours as it considers to be appropriate in the circumstances; and

(c) deliver the report to the Minister.

65. Request for assistance in the restraining and seizure of property associated to crime

(1) Where the ICC requests assistance in identifying, tracing and restraining or seizing property for the purpose of eventual forfeiture, the Minister shall give authority for the request to proceed and transmit the request to (the appropriate agency) in …… (name of country) if the Minister has reasonable grounds to believe that the property is or may be located in …… (name of country).

2. Where the Minister authorizes and transmits the request under subsection (1), (the appropriate agency) in …… (name of country)—

(a) shall use its best endeavours to give effect to the request; or

---

43 See discussion in paragraph 101 of the Report on use of domestic powers and Clause 30 of the drafting instructions.

44 See discussion on protection of victims and witnesses in paragraphs 102–104 of the Report and Clause 31 of the drafting instructions.

(b) may, where appropriate, apply to (a magistrate) for a restraining or seizing order with respect to the property.

(3) An application under subsection 2(b) may be made *ex parte* and may be granted without a hearing.

(4) (The magistrate) considering an application under subsection 2(b) may make a restraining or seizing order, as appropriate, if satisfied—

(a) that a forfeiture order has been made in proceedings before the ICC; or

(b) that there are reasonable grounds to believe that a forfeiture order may be made in such proceedings,

and that the property to which the application for the restraining or seizing order relates consists of or includes property that is or may be affected by such a forfeiture order.

(5) A restraining or seizing order shall provide for notice to be given to any persons with an interest in the property or otherwise affected by the order.

(6) A person affected by the order may apply to a magistrate for an order to vary or discharge the restraining or seizing order in relation to his or her interest.

(7) (The magistrate) may vary or discharge the restraining or seizure order in relation to the interest of a person making an application under subsection (6) only if (the magistrate) is satisfied that the applicant has an interest in the property, was not in any way involved in the commission of the crime to which the property relates, and had no basis to believe that the property was the proceeds of, or associated with, the crime.

(8) Subject to subsection (7), the property shall remain subject to the restraining or seizing order until the ICC issues a relevant forfeiture order in respect of the property and that order has been registered for enforcement under section 85 or the ICC advises that no such order will be issued, in which case the property shall be discharged from the restraining or seizing order.

(Note: It may be necessary to place a time limitation on restraint orders or alternatively provide for a periodic review by a magistrate.)

66. Refusal of request[45]

(1) The Minister shall refuse a request for assistance under this Part only if—

(a) the ICC has determined that the case to which the request relates is inadmissible on any ground;

(b) the ICC advises that it does not intend to proceed with the request for any reason, including but not limited to a determination of the ICC that article 98(1) of the Statute applies to the execution of the request;

(c) the assistance sought is outside the listed types of assistance set out in article 93(1) and the provision of the assistance is prohibited by the law of ...... (name of country) and the ICC does not accept the conditions, as contemplated by article 93(5) of the Statute, subject to which the Minister was willing to provide the assistance; or

---

45 See discussion of grounds of refusal in paragraphs 110 and 111 of the Report and Clause 36 of the drafting instructions.

(d) the execution of a particular measure of assistance is prohibited in ......
(name of country) on the basis of an existing fundamental legal principle of
general application and the ICC does not accept the conditions, as contemplated by article 93(5) of the Statute, subject to which the Minister was willing
to provide the assistance.

(2) The Minister may refuse a request for assistance under this Part of this Act only
if—

  (a) there are competing requests for assistance from the ICC and a state and the
  Minister has decided, in consultation with the ICC and the state, that it is not
  possible to execute both requests and has decided further to proceed with
  the execution of the request of the state, in accordance with the principles
  established by article 90 of the Statute and section 31; or

  (b) the refusal is authorized under Part VII.

(3) If the Minister decides to refuse a request for assistance in accordance with
subsection (1) or (2) after he or she has transmitted the request to (the appropriate agency) in ...... (name of country), he or she shall inform that agency not to
take any further steps to execute the request.

67. Postponement of execution of request for assistance[46]

(1) The Minister may postpone the execution of a request for assistance under this
Part only if—

  (a) a determination on admissibility is pending before the ICC;

  (b) the execution of the request would interfere with an investigation or prosecution in ...... (name of country) involving a different offence from that to
  which the request relates;

  (c) the Minister is consulting with the ICC under section 25(2) as to whether or
  not article 98(1) of the Statue applies to execution of the request; or

  (d) there are competing requests for assistance from ICC and a state, and the
  Minister in consultation with ICC and the state decides to postpone the
  execution of the ICC's request.

(2) If execution of the request for assistance is postponed under subsection (1)(a) and
the ICC decides that the case is admissible, the Minister shall proceed with the
execution of the request as soon as possible after the decision of the ICC.

(3) If the execution of the request for assistance is postponed under subsection (1)(b),
the Minister shall consult with the ICC and agree on a period of time for postponement of the execution of the request in accordance with article 94 of the Statute;
and the Minister shall proceed with execution of the request after the lapse of the
period, unless otherwise agreed with the ICC.

(4) If execution of the request for assistance is postponed under subsection (1)(c) and
the ICC decides to proceed with the request, the Minister shall proceed with the
execution of the request as soon as possible after the decision of the ICC.

---

46 See discussion of postponement of execution of requests in paragraph 109 of the Report and Clause 35
of the drafting instructions.

(5) If the execution of the request for assistance is postponed under subsection (1)(d), the Minister shall proceed with the execution of the ICC's request as soon as practicable.

(6) If the Minister decides to postpone execution of a request for assistance in accordance with this section after he or she has transmitted the request for execution to the appropriate agency in ...... (name of country), he or she shall direct that agency to postpone the execution of the request for such period as is specified in the direction.

(7) A decision by the Minister to postpone the execution of a request shall not affect the validity of any act that has been done or any warrant or order made under this Part of this Act prior to the decision, and any such warrant or order shall remain in force unless cancelled.

Supplementary Provisions

68. Verification or authentication of material[47]

Where, in order to comply with a request of the ICC for assistance it is necessary for any evidence or other material obtained under this Part to be verified or authenticated in any manner the Minister may give directions as to the manner in which such evidence or material shall be verified.

69. Transmission of material to ICC

(1) Any evidence or other material obtained under this Part by a person other than the Minister together with any requisite verification shall be sent to the Minister for transmission to the ICC unless the Minister authorizes otherwise.

(2) Where any evidence or other material is to be transmitted to the ICC there shall be transmitted—

(a) where the material consists of a document, the original or a copy; and

(b) where the material consists of any other article, the article itself or a photograph or other description of it as may be necessary to comply with the request of the ICC.

70. Certificates issued by Minister[48]

(1) If the Minister receives a request for assistance from the ICC to which this Part of this Act applies, the Minister may issue a certificate certifying all or any of the following facts—

(a) that a request for assistance has been made by the ICC;

(b) that the request meets with the requirements of this Act; and

(c) that the request has been duly accepted under and in accordance with the provisions of this Act.

---

47 See discussion of authentication of documents in paragraphs 162 and 163 of the Report and Clause 48 of the drafting instructions.

48 See discussion of certificates in paragraphs 162 and 163 of the Report and Clause 48 of the drafting instructions.

(2) In any proceeding under this Act, a certificate purporting to have been issued under subsection (1) shall, in the absence of proof to the contrary, be sufficient evidence of the facts certified therein.

71. Minister may request assistance from ICC[49]

The Minister may make a request to the ICC for assistance in accordance with this Part of this Act in an investigation into, or trial in respect of, conduct that may constitute a crime within the jurisdiction of the ICC or that constitutes a crime for which the maximum penalty under the law of ...... (name of country) is a term of imprisonment of not less than five years.

PART VI—ENFORCEMENT OF SENTENCES AND ORDERS OF THE ICC IN ...... (NAME OF COUNTRY)[50]

72. Application of this Part

This Part of this Act applies to the enforcement of sentences imposed by the ICC and of orders for the payment of fines, restraining orders, forfeiture orders and orders for reparation, made by the ICC.

73. ...... (name of country) may act as State of enforcement[51]

(1) The Minister may notify the ICC that ...... (name of country) is willing to allow persons who are ICC prisoners as a result of being sentenced to imprisonment by the ICC to serve those sentences in ...... (name of country), subject to any conditions specified in the notification.

(2) The Minister shall, before issuing a notification under subsection (1), consult with any other relevant Minister.

74. Request for sentence to be served in ...... (name of country)

(1) Where—

    (a) the Minister has issued a notification under section 73 and has not withdrawn that notification and the ICC imposes a sentence of imprisonment under the Statute on a person convicted of a crime within the jurisdiction of the ICC; and

    (b) the ICC designates ...... (name of country) under article 103 of the Statute, as the State in which the sentence is to be served, the Minister shall consider whether to accept the designation.

(2) The Minister may accept the designation of ...... (name of country) as the State in which the sentence is to be served if the Minister is satisfied that ICC has

---

49 See discussion under Part XIX of the Report on Assistance by the Court and Clause 37 of the drafting instructions.

50 See general discussion under Part XX of the Report on the Enforcement of Sentences and Clause 38 of the drafting instructions.

51 See discussion of general powers in enforcement in paragraph 120 of the Report.

agreed to the conditions specified in the notification made under section 73, and in the case of a prisoner who is not a citizen of ...... (name of country), the (relevant Minister) has consented to the sentence being served in ...... (name of country).

75. Prisoner to be held in custody

(1) Where the Minister accepts the designation of ...... (name of country) as the State in which a sentence of imprisonment imposed by the ICC is to be served, the ICC prisoner may be transported to ...... (name of country) in the custody of a person authorized for the purpose by the ICC.

(2) On arrival in ...... (name of country) or, if the person is already in ...... (name of country) when the sentence is imposed, on the imposition of the sentence, the Minister shall issue an order of detention in respect of the ICC prisoner and shall cause a copy of the order to be sent to (the Commissioner of Prisons).

(3) The order of detention issued under subsection (2) shall be sufficient authority for the detention of the ICC prisoner until he or she completes, or is released from, the sentence or is transferred to another country.

(4) Subject to subsection (7), the ICC prisoner shall be detained in accordance with the laws of ...... (name of country) as if he or she had been sentenced to imprisonment under the law of ...... (name of country).

(5) Notwithstanding anything in subsection (4) or in any other law—

(a) the ICC prisoner shall have the right to communicate on a confidential basis with the ICC, without impediment from any person;

(b) a Judge of the ICC or a member of the staff of the ICC may visit the ICC prisoner for the purpose of hearing any representations by the prisoner without the presence of any other person, except any representative of the prisoner.

(6) The enforcement of a sentence of imprisonment, including any decision to release or transfer the ICC prisoner shall be in accordance with Part 10 of the Statute and the Rules.

(7) The laws of ...... (name of country) relating to parole, remission, reduction or variation of sentence and pardon shall not apply to a sentence imposed by the ICC.[52]

76. Transfer of prisoner to ICC for review of sentence[53]

(1) Where the ICC, under article 110 of the Statute, decides to review the sentence of an ICC prisoner who is serving that sentence in ...... (name of country), the Minister shall direct that the prisoner be transferred to the ICC, at the expense of the ICC, for the purposes of enabling the ICC to review the prisoner's sentence.

(2) The ICC prisoner shall be transferred to and from the ICC in the custody of a person authorized for the purpose by the ICC, at the expense of the ICC.

---

52 See discussion on non-modification of sentence in paragraph 121 of the Report.
53 See discussion of transfers in paragraph 124 of the Report.

77. Transfer of prisoner to another State to complete sentence[54]

(1) An ICC prisoner serving a sentence in ...... (name of country) may, at any time apply to the ICC to be transferred from ...... (name of country) to complete service of sentence in another state.

(2) Where an ICC prisoner of any nationality is to be transferred from ...... (name of country) to another State to complete that sentence, the prisoner may be transported from ...... (name of country) to that State in the custody of a person authorized for the purpose by the ICC at the expense of ICC.

Certificates and Removal Orders[55]

Option 1

[Apply general immigration law provisions to the ICC prisoner]

Option 2

78. Procedure on completion of sentence

Upon—

(a) the completion of sentence in ...... (name of county) by an ICC prisoner who is not a citizen of ...... (name of country);

(b) the release, on the direction of the ICC, of an ICC prisoner who is not a citizen of ...... (name of country),

the Minister may issue a removal order for that ICC prisoner under section 79.

79. Removal order

(1) A removal order made by the Minister under this section—

(a) may either—

(i) require the person who is the subject of the order to be released into or taken into the custody of a police officer; or

(ii) if the person is not in custody, authorize any police officer to take the person into custody; and

(b) shall specify that the person is to be taken by a police officer and placed on board any aircraft or vessel for the purpose of effecting the person's removal from ...... (name of country) to ......; and

(c) may authorize the detention in custody of the person while awaiting removal from ...... (name of country).

(4) A removal order made under this section shall continue in force until it is executed or cancelled.

80. Delay in removal

(1) If a person in respect of whom a removal order has been made is not conveyed out of ...... (name of country) within (...... hours/days) after the order has issued,

---

54 See discussion of transfers in paragraph 124 of the Report.
55 See discussion on situation after service of sentence in paragraph 123 of the Report.

the person shall be brought before (a magistrate) to determine, in accordance with subsection (2), whether the person should be detained in custody or released pending removal from ...... (name of country).

(2) If a person is brought before (a magistrate) under subsection (1), (the magistrate) may, if she or he is satisfied that the person is the person named in the order—

    (a) issue a warrant for the detention of the person in custody if (the magistrate) is satisfied that, if not detained, the person is likely to abscond; or

    (b) order the release of the person subject to such conditions, if any, that (the magistrate) thinks fit to impose.

81. Special rules in certain cases[56]

(1) An ICC prisoner serving a sentence in ...... (name of country) shall not—

    (a) be extradited to another country on completion of his or her sentence; or

    (b) be required to undergo trial for an offence under the law of ...... (name of country) that relates to an act or omission alleged to have been committed prior to his or her arrival in ...... (name of country) to serve such sentence,

without agreement of the ICC.

(2) Nothing in subsection (1) shall apply to an ICC prisoner who remains voluntarily in ...... (name of country) for more than 30 days after the date of completion of, or release from, the sentence imposed on him or her by the ICC or who voluntarily returns to ...... (name of country) after having left ...... (name of country).

82. Immigration permit not required

A person to whom this Part of this Act applies shall not be required to hold a permit or other authorization under the law of ...... (name of country) relating to citizenship and immigration control if, and for so long as, he or she is in ...... (name of country) in accordance with this Part, whether or not he or she is in custody.

83. Application to citizens of ...... (name of country)

Nothing in this Part of this Act shall be deemed to authorize the making of a removal order under section 79 in respect of a citizen of ...... (name of country).

84. Enforcement of fines[57]

(1) Where the ICC requests enforcement in accordance with article 109 of the Statute of an order for the payment of a fine made under article 77(2)(a) of the Statute, the Minister shall give authority for the request to proceed, if he or she has reasonable grounds to believe that—

    (a) neither the conviction in respect of which the order was imposed, nor the order for the payment of the fine is subject to further appeal; and

    (b) the order can be enforced in the manner provided in this section,

and shall refer the request to (the appropriate agency) in ...... (name of country).

---

56 See discussion on protections from other proceedings in paragraph 125 of the Report.
57 See discussion on enforcement of fines in paragraph 127 of the Report and Clause 39 of the drafting instructions.

(2) (The appropriate agency) in ...... (name of country) shall, without delay, cause such order to be filed in (the appropriate court).

(3) An order filed in (the appropriate court) under subsection (2) shall have the same force and effect as if it were an order for the payment of a fine imposed by that court and shall be enforced accordingly.

(4) (The appropriate agency) shall make such report to the Minister on the outcome of any action taken by it to enforce the order as it considers to be appropriate in the circumstances.

(5) Nothing in this section shall be construed as limiting or affecting the provision of other types of assistance to the ICC in relation to a penalty imposed under article 77 of the Statute or as empowering the court to modify or vary the order of the ICC.

85. Enforcement of forfeiture orders[58]

(1) Where the ICC requests enforcement in accordance with article 109 of the Statute, of an order for forfeiture of property made under article 77(2)(b) of the Statute, the Minister shall give authority for the request to proceed if he or she has reasonable grounds to believe that—

(a) neither the conviction in respect of which the order was imposed, nor the forfeiture order, is subject to further appeal; and

(b) the property identified by the ICC is located in ...... (name of country) or that the person concerned, directly or indirectly, holds property in ...... (name of country) that may be the subject of the forfeiture order,

and shall refer the request to (the Director of Public Prosecutions) for enforcement in accordance with this section.

(2) Upon receipt of a referral under subsection (1), (the Director of Public Prosecutions) shall file the original or a certified copy of the forfeiture order of the ICC with (the appropriate court).

(3) Upon the filing of the order in (the appropriate court) under subsection (2), the court may direct (the Director of Public Prosecutions) to do either or both of the following—

(a) give notice of the filing, in the manner and within the time the court considers appropriate to such persons, other than a person convicted of a crime in respect of which the order was made, as the court has reason to believe may have an interest in the property;

(b) publish notice of the filing in the manner and within the time the court considers appropriate.

(4) A forfeiture order filed in (the appropriate court) under subsection (2) shall have, from the date it is filed, the same force and effect as if it were an order for the forfeiture of property issued by that court and shall be enforced accordingly.

(5) A forfeiture order filed under subsection (2) shall not be enforced until after the expiry of any period specified by the court in any notice given or published under

---

58 See discussion of forfeiture orders in paragraph 131 of the Report and Clause 41 of the drafting instructions.

subsection (3), or two months from the filing of the order, whichever is the longer period.

(6) Where a forfeiture order is filed in (the appropriate court) under subsection (2), a person, other than a person convicted of a crime in respect of which the order was made, who claims an interest in the property, may apply to the court, with notice to (the Director of Public Prosecutions).

(7) A person on whom notice of the hearing of the ICC held in connection with the making of the forfeiture order was served or who appeared at the hearing shall not make an application under subsection (6) without leave of the court.

(8) (The appropriate court) shall grant leave under subsection (7) only where it determines that it would be contrary to the interests of justice not to do so.

(9) An application under subsection (6) shall be made before the expiry of any period specified in a notice made or published under subsection (3) or within two months of the filing of the order, whichever is the longer period, unless the court grants leave.

(10) On an application under subsection (6), the court may make an order for the enforcement of the forfeiture order subject to the interest of the applicant if satisfied that—

   (a) the applicant has an interest in the property;

   (b) the applicant did not receive notice of the hearing before the ICC or through no fault of his or her own, did not appear at the hearing;

   (c) the applicant was not in any way involved in the commission of the crime in respect of which the order was made; and

   (d) the applicant had no knowledge that the property constituted the proceeds of, or was associated with, the crime.

(11) Where the court makes an order under subsection (10), the Court may—

   (a) declare the nature, extent and value of the applicant's interest in the property; and

   (b) either direct that the interest be transferred to the applicant or that payment be made to the applicant of an amount equivalent to the value of the interest.

86. Transfer of funds realized to ICC

The Minister shall arrange for the transfer of funds realized through the enforcement of a fine under section 84 or a forfeiture order under section 85 to the ICC (subject to the deduction of reasonable costs related to the enforcement procedure).

87. Orders fomr forfeiture of property on conviction by ICC

(1) Where any person is convicted by the ICC of a crime within the jurisdiction of the ICC, (the High Court) may, on an application made by (the Attorney General), order that any property situated in ...... (name of country)—

   (a) used for, or in connection with; or

   (b) derived directly or indirectly from,

the commission of that crime, be forfeited to the State, if satisfied that no order of forfeiture has been or will be made by the ICC under article 77(2)(b) of the Statute in respect of that property.

(2) Before making an order under subsection (1), the court shall give every person appearing to have an interest in the property in respect of which the order is proposed to be made, an opportunity of being heard, and subsections (3), (4), (5), (6), (7), (8), (9), (10) and (11) of section 85 shall, mutates mutandis, apply to an order made under this section.

(3) Property forfeited to the State under subsection (1) shall vest in the State—

    (a) if no appeal has been made against the order, at the end of the period within which an appeal may be made against the order; and

    (b) if an appeal has been made against the order, on the final determination of the appeal.

88. Enforcement of orders for victim reparation[59]

(1) Where the ICC requests enforcement in accordance with article 109 of the Statute of an order requiring reparation made under article 75 of the Statute, the Minister shall give authority for the request to proceed, if he or she has reasonable grounds to believe that—

    (a) neither the conviction in respect of which the order was imposed nor the order requiring reparation is subject to further appeal; and

    (b) the order can be enforced in the manner provided in this section, and shall refer the request to (the appropriate agency) in ...... (name of country).

(2) (The appropriate agency) in ...... (name of country) shall, without delay file such order in (the appropriate court).

(3) Every order filed in (the appropriate court) under subsection (2) shall—

    (a) if the order requires a monetary payment, have force and effect as if it were an order for the payment of compensation imposed by that court; or

    (b) if the order requires the restitution of assets, property or other tangible items, have force and effect as if it were an order for the restitution of property made by that court; or

    (c) if the order requires the granting of any other relief, have force and effect as if it were an order for the granting of such relief made by that court and every such order shall be enforced accordingly.

(4) (The appropriate agency) in ...... (name of country) shall, without delay, make such report to the Minister on the outcome of any action taken by it to enforce the order as it considers to be appropriate in the circumstances.

(5) Nothing in this section shall be construed as limiting or affecting the provision of other types of assistance to the ICC in relation to an order made under article 75 of the Statute or as empowering the court to modify the order of the ICC.

(6) The Minister shall consult with the ICC as to whether the funds realized through the enforcement of an order under this section should be transferred directly to specified victims or through the Victims Fund of the ICC.

---

59 See discussion of reparations in paragraphs 132–134 of the Report and Clause 42 of the drafting instructions.

(7) The Minister shall make arrangements for the transfer of the funds realized through the enforcement of an order under this section as determined through the consultations under subsection (6).

89. Assistance in enforcement of restraining order[60]

(1) Where the ICC requests assistance in the enforcement of a restraining order issued by the ICC in respect of property in ...... (name of country), the Minister shall give authority for the request to proceed if he or she has reasonable grounds to believe that—

   (a) the restraining order is not subject to further appeal; and

   (b) the property is located in ...... (name of country),

and shall refer the request to (the appropriate agency) in ...... (name of country).

(2) (The appropriate agency) in ...... (name of country) shall file such order in (the appropriate court).

(3) Every order filed in (the appropriate court) under subsection (2) shall have force and effect as if it were a restraining order made by that court and shall be enforced accordingly.

(4) Nothing in this section shall be construed as limiting or affecting the provision of other types of assistance to the ICC in relation to the enforcement of a restraining order made by it or as empowering the court to modify the order of the ICC.

PART VII—NATIONAL SECURITY[61]

(Note: It will depend on domestic context as to whether any provisions on national security need to be included in the legislation.)

90. National security

(1) Where—

   (a) the ICC requests assistance under Part V for the production of documents or the taking of evidence and the Minister is of the opinion that the production of such documents or the disclosure of such evidence would be prejudicial to the national security of ...... (name of country);or

   (b) a person is required to disclose information to, or give evidence before, the ICC and the person refuses to do so on the ground that the disclosure of such information or the giving of such evidence would be prejudicial to the national security of ...... (name of country) and the Minister confirms that in his or her opinion the disclosure of such information or the giving of such evidence would be prejudicial to the national security of ...... (name of country); or

---

60 See discussion on freezing/restraint of assets in paragraphs 128–130 of the Report and Clause 40 of the drafting instructions.

61 See discussion under Part XXIV on National Security and Clause 45 of the drafting instructions.

(c)   the Minister is of the opinion that the disclosure of information to, or giving of evidence before, the ICC in circumstances other than the circumstances referred to in paragraphs (a) and (b) would be prejudicial to the national security of ...... (name of country),

the Minister shall consult with the ICC and take reasonable steps to resolve the matter in accordance with article 72(5) of the Statute.

(2)   If, after consultation with the ICC, the Minister considers that there are no means or conditions under which the information, documents or evidence requested could be provided, disclosed or given without prejudice to the national security of ...... (name of country), the Minister may refuse the request for the production of such document or the disclosure of such evidence or refuse the authorization of the production of such document or the disclosure of such information and shall specify to the ICC, his or her reasons for doing so, unless the specification of those reasons would itself be, in his or her opinion, prejudicial to the national security of ...... (name of country).

PART VIII—SITTINGS OF THE ICC IN ...... (NAME OF COUNTRY)[62]

91.   Prosecutor may conduct investigations in ...... (name of country)[63]

The Prosecutor may conduct investigations in the territory of ...... (name of country)—

(a)   in accordance with the provisions of Part 9 of the Statute;

(b)   as authorized by the Pre-Trial Chamber under article 57(3)(d) of the Statute; or

(c)   as authorized by national authorities.

92.   ICC sittings in ...... (name of country)

The ICC may sit in ...... (name of country) for the purpose of discharging its functions under the Statute and under the Rules, including but not limited to—

(a)   the taking of evidence;

(b)   the conduct or continuation of a proceeding;

(c)   the giving of a judgment in a proceeding; or

(d)   the review of a sentence imposed by the ICC.

93.   ICC powers while sitting in ...... (name of country)

Option I

(1)   When the ICC is sitting in ...... (name of country) it may discharge and exercise any or all of its functions and powers as provided for under the Statute and under the Rules.

---

62 See discussion under Part XXIII on ICC Sittings and Clause 43 of the drafting instructions.

63 See discussion on direct execution by the Prosecutor in paragraphs 107 and 108 of the Report and Clause 34 of the drafting instructions.

(2) Without prejudice to the generality of subsection (1), the ICC shall have the power to—

    (a) commit persons for contempt of its orders; or

    (b) issue summons or other orders requiring the attendance of any person before the ICC or the production of any document or record for examination by the ICC.

(3) Orders or summons issued by the ICC under this section, including committal orders for contempt, shall be enforced by the domestic authorities of ...... (name of country) as if the order had been issued by a domestic court in ...... (name of country).

Option 2

Include no specific provisions like section 96 and require the ICC to seek assistance under the cooperation sections to compel witnesses etc. as per the normal practice.

94. ICC may administer oaths in ...... (name of country)

The ICC may, at any sitting of the ICC in ...... (name of country), administer an oath or affirmation requiring a witness to give an undertaking as to truthfulness of the evidence given by the witness, in accordance with the Rules.

95. Orders made by ICC not subject to review

(1) The conduct of a trial or other proceeding by the ICC sitting in ...... (name of country) is not subject to judicial or other challenge in a court in ...... (name of country).

(2) In particular, none of the following may be brought or made in a court in ...... (name of country) in respect of a judgment, order, determination, or step of the ICC given, made or taken at a sitting of the ICC in ...... (name of country):

    (a) any judicial review;

    (b) an application for, or for relief in the nature of, a declaration, declaratory judgment or injunction;

    (c) an application for, or for relief in the nature of an order of mandamus or prohibition or certiorari;

    (d) an application for, or for relief in the nature of, a writ of habeas corpus;

    (e) an appeal.

96. Power to detain ICC prisoners in prison in ...... (name of country)

(1) Where the ICC holds a sitting in ...... (name of country) and requests that a person whose presence is required at that sitting be held in custody as an ICC prisoner while the sitting continues in ...... (name of country), the Minister shall direct in writing that such person be held in custody at such location as is specified in the direction.

(2) A direction given under subsection (1) in respect of an ICC prisoner is sufficient authority for the detention of that prisoner in accordance with the terms of the direction.

(3) The law relating to prisons so far as is applicable with any necessary modifications shall apply to an ICC prisoner required to be detained in a prison by a direction under subsection (1) as if the prisoner had been remanded in custody or sentenced to imprisonment for an offence under the law of ...... (name of country), as the case may require, and is liable to be detained in a prison under such an order or sentence.

(4) For the purposes of the application of the law relating to escape from lawful custody and aiding prisoners to escape, an ICC prisoner who is in custody in a prison or other detention facility in ...... (name of country) shall be deemed to be in lawful custody while in ...... (name of country).

97. Removal of ICC prisoner

If the Minister is satisfied that the presence in ...... (name of country) of an ICC prisoner who was the subject of a direction under section 96 is no longer necessary, sections 78–83 shall apply to and in relation to that person with any necessary modifications.

PART IX—LEGAL STATUS OF THE ICC AND PRIVILEGES AND IMMUNITIES OF OFFICIALS OF THE ICC[64]

98. Legal personality and privileges and immunities

(1) The ICC shall have legal personality in ...... (name of country) with such legal capacity as may be necessary for the performance of its functions and the fulfilment of its purposes.

(2) Without prejudice to the generality of subsection (1), the ICC shall have the capacity to contract, to acquire and dispose of immovable and movable property and to institute in legal proceedings, in ...... (name of country).

(3) The Judges, the Prosecutor, the Deputy Prosecutors, the Registrar, the Deputy Registrar, staff of the Office of the Prosecutor and of the Registry, counsel, experts, witnesses, and other persons required to be in ...... (name of country) for the performance of official functions or for participation in proceedings before the ICC shall have the privileges and immunities set out in article 48 of the Statute and the Agreement on the Privileges and Immunities of the ICC.

(4) Article 48 of the Statute and articles 2–11, 13–22, 25–27, 29 and 30 of the Agreement on the Privileges and Immunities of the ICC shall have the force of law in ...... (name of country), and references in those articles to the State Party shall, for this purpose, be construed as references to ...... (name of country).

Optional Additional Provision

[(5) Notwithstanding anything in subsections (3) and (4), a national of a State which has made an election under article 23 of the Agreement on Privileges and Immunities of the ICC shall be

---

64 See discussion under Part XXIII on Privileges and Immunities for Court Officials and Other Relevant Persons and Clause 44 of the drafting instructions.

entitled only to the privileges and immunities referred to in article 23 of the Agreement on Privileges and Immunities.][65]

PART X—MISCELLANEOUS

99. Regulations[66]

(1) The Minister may make regulations for the purpose of giving effect to the principles and provisions of this Act.

(2) Without prejudice to the generality of subsection (1), the Minister may make regulations in respect of all or any of the following matters:—

(a) prescribing the procedure to be followed in dealing with requests made by the ICC, and providing for notification of the outcome of action taken to give effect to such requests;

(b) providing for temporary surrender of a person;

(c) prescribing the procedures for obtaining evidence or producing documents or other articles in accordance with a request made by the ICC;

(d) providing for the payment of fees, travelling allowances, and expenses to any person in ...... (name of country) who gives or provides evidence or assistance pursuant to a request made by the ICC;

(e) prescribing conditions for the protection of any property sent to the ICC pursuant to a request made under this Act, and making provision for the return of property to ...... (name of country);

(f) providing for the enforcement of any ICC sentence of imprisonment;

(g) providing for management and disposal of property under a restraining, seizing or forfeiture order;

(h) prescribing the forms of applications, notices, certificates, warrants and other documents for the purposes of this Act, and requiring the use of such forms; and

(i) implementation of any obligation that is placed on States Parties by the Rules in so far as such obligation is not inconsistent with the provisions of this Act.

(3) Every regulation made by the Minister under subsection(1) shall be published in the Gazette and shall come into force on the date of its publication or on such later date as may be specified therein.

(4) Every regulation made by the Minister shall, as soon as convenient after its publication in the Gazette, be placed before (Parliament) for its approval. Every regulation which is not so approved shall be deemed to be rescinded as from the date of disapproval, but without prejudice to anything previously done thereunder.

---

65 See discussion on option of restricting application of certain immunities in paragraph 142 of the Report and Clause 44 of the drafting instructions.

66 See discussion of regulatory power in paragraphs 162 and 163 of the Report and Clause 48 of the drafting instructions.

(5) Notification of the date on which any regulation is deemed to be so rescinded shall be published in the Gazette.

SCHEDULE I

The Rome Statute of the International Criminal Court

SCHEDULE 2

Agreement on the Privileges and Immunities of the International Criminal Court

Index

Page numbers in *Italics* represent tables.
Page numbers in Bold represent figures.

For Product Safety Concerns and Information please contact our EU
representative GPSR@taylorandfrancis.com
Taylor & Francis Verlag GmbH, Kaufingerstraße 24, 80331 München, Germany

41599CB00025B/4575

* 9 7 8 0 4 1 5 8 1 4 8 6 7 *